Copyright ©2017 by David L. Jones
All Rights Reserved

Written by: David L. Jones
www.voiceteacher.com

Cover art and book layout designed by: Samantha McNulty Design
www.samanthamcnulty.com

Head shot by: Samantha McNulty Photography
www.samanthamcnultyphotography.com

A Modern Guide to Old World Singing

Concepts of the Swedish-Italian
and Italian Singing Schools

David L. Jones

PREFACE

Exploring the Swedish-Italian School

Much has been written about the Italian School of singing, but very little information has been made available about the Swedish-Italian School of vocal training and its history. It is a school of singing that combines the brilliance of tone of the Italian tradition with the warmth of deeper pharyngeal vowel forms found in the Swedish, French, and German languages. I learned many of the principles of the Swedish-Italian School from Allan Rogers Lindquest in 1979. As taught by Lindquest, the Swedish-Italian School also included working with reflexive emotional triggers that inspired a more holistic approach to singing. Chapter 1 describes Lindquest's life and work in greater detail.

This book represents the core concepts of both the Italian and the Swedish-Italian Schools—as taught to me by Allan Lindquest—which have formed the foundation of my teaching over the past 40-plus years. It has evolved from articles that appeared originally on my website[1] and it

---
[1] www.VoiceTeacher.com

responds to and elaborates on concepts for which I receive the most inquiries. This book is not intended to be a scientific work, nor does it involve or apply voice science. It has been called "vocal wisdom for contemporary times"; its primary purpose is to establish a modern account of Old World training as taught in the Swedish-Italian and Italian Schools, and to offer concepts that can speak to vocal musicians of many levels.

Note: The same or similar concepts and exercises may occur throughout the book, applied in different ways to address different vocal challenges. Each chapter has been designed to function independently without a great deal of cross-referencing.

Journey

My journey began as a personal search to find my own healthy and complete voice; it evolved over time as an apprenticeship with several additional teachers, with whom I explored and gained a wealth of information about vocal technique; a singing technique that reflects the concepts and teaching of world-renowned vocal pedagogues such as Garcia II and Lamperti.

In addition to the pedagogy of Allan Lindquest, this book also reflects my research and study with several other exceptional vocal pedagogues, including (in chronological order) Virginia Botkin, Barbara Mathis, Dixie Neill, Suzanne Hickman, and Evelyn Reynolds. From Virginia Botkin, student of Allan Lindquest, I learned a great deal about the effects of facial posture on vocal acoustics. Dr. Barbara Mathis is also on my list, an excellent voice researcher, teacher, and student of both Allan Lindquest and Virginia Botkin. (It was Dr. Mathis who proved the therapeutic results of using the Lindquest exercises on damaged voices over a 5-year period, researching in the laryngology office of Dr. Van Lawrence, then laryngologist for the Houston Grand Opera.[2])

---

[2] Barbara Mathis, "Selected Vocal Exercises and Their Relationship to Specific Laryngeal Conditions: a Description of Seven Case Studies" (PhD diss., University of North Texas, Denton, 1990).

In the early 1980's I studied with Dixie Neill, instructor of Ben Heppner. It was through my work with her that I learned a great deal about the concept of laryngeal tilt and its influence on the open throat. It was Ms. Neill who discovered that I was truly a baritone, not a tenor, even though I had been trained as a tenor from an early age. Dr. Suzanne L. Hickman, Professor at The College of New Jersey and former student of Virginia Botkin, was a great influence on releasing jaw/neck tension and use of the French nasals to release tongue tension, which has proven to be critically important work.

Evelyn Reynolds, a master teacher of the Old Italian School, studied with Hollis Arment, a fine Italian-trained tenor; Ralph Errolle, teacher of Arleen Auger; and Lola Fletcher, student of Herbert Witherspoon. Ms. Reynolds helped me to find full balance in registration and expand the lower overtones in my voice without the use of muscular vocal weight. We met weekly for over a decade, having an early meal and then vocalizing each other using Old World concepts. Through this professional and personal collaboration, we allowed ourselves the freedom to learn from each other. It was like having a small vocal seminar every week, an opportunity that has been invaluable in expanding my vocal knowledge.

My study with each of these instructors assisted in building my understanding of the voice, but even more critically important is the fact that it has helped me to instruct others with more efficiency. It is with deep gratitude that I express appreciation to all these dedicated teachers for offering so many concepts that have shaped and enhanced my own teaching knowledge and career.

ACKNOWLEDGEMENTS

A heartfelt thank-you to Janet Steele for final layout design and final edits, and Samantha McNulty for final cover design and layout book design, and to Elaine Bernstein for assisting in early editing. I would also like to thank Ann De Renais, Dr. Julia Hunt-Nielsen, Janet Williams, and Vera Wenkert for their supportive review and feedback on this book.

My career as a vocal pedagogue is based on information learned from my teachers. They include the well-known vocal pedagogue Allan R. Lindquest, his student Virginia Botkin, Dr. Suzanne Hickman, Dixie Neill, and Evelyn Reynolds. Also thank you to Margaretta Sunnegardh, who shared her special vocal information in my New York studio. Thank you to Dr. Barbara Mathis for her scientific research on these vocal principles and their therapeutic properties.

Special thanks go to Leif Lundberg, Director of the University Opera School in Stockholm, for generously sharing his deep knowledge of the historical background of the Swedish-Italian school.

Thank you to those who have hosted me on teaching tours and/or organized master classes including: Samira Baroody, Deborah Carbaugh, Ann De Renais, Helena Döse, Dr. Elizabeth Fresnel, Marja Gamal, Deborah Gilroy, Isabelle Henriquez and Beatrice Hernandez, Dr. Julia Hunt Nielsen, Dina Insley, Maria Knapik, Maria Kransmo, Clay Johnston and family, Katherine Lakoski, Jennifer Lane, Leif Lundberg, Dr. Barbara Mathis, Edwin Metzler, Korby Myrick, Egill Palsson and family, Cathy Pope and Martin Burrel, Daniel Shroyens, Raphael Sikorski, Emma Small, Teodora Spiess, Karen and Nigel Springthorpe, Marjorie Stephens, Shirley Verrett, Vera Wenkert, and Janet Williams and Fred Berndt.

A special thank-you to my sound engineer Patrick Lo Re, who was the sound engineer and editor for my instructional CD; and to Nathan Hull, who helped me to establish my website. I would also like to thank Christian Halseband for German translations of articles from my website, which are located at www.gesanglehrer.de.

I also must express my appreciation to the New York medical professionals whose expertise and caring have helped me and my students: Dr. Benjamin Asher, laryngologist; and voice therapists Sophie Lair-Berreby and Dr. Chandler Thompson.

Thanks and appreciation to all those who have given presentations in my New York Teacher Trainings, including Dr. Benjamin Asher, Gudrun Ayasse, Sophie Lair-Berreby, Lynn Martin, Janet Steele, and Wilma Wever.

Thank you to my long-term New York Alexander Teacher John Nicholls, and to Lynn Martin for assisting me in the study of the Carl Stough Breathing Coordination.

I would like to express special appreciation to Lucia Maya (www.luminousadventures.com) for her healing work.

I must also thank Tamara Haskin for assisting with the David Jones Teacher Mentoring Program.

A special thank you to my family: my parents Gus and Hazel Jones, who provided me with a musical background at an early age, my sisters Sarah Sulka and Judy Pool, and my partner Mark Proctor.

Finally, I extend a big thank you to all of the friends, students, and teachers too numerous to mention, who have shared this school of training with others.

TABLE OF CONTENTS

PREFACE   5

ACKNOWLEDGEMENTS   8

DEDICATION   15

CHAPTER 1   17
    Allan Lindquest and the Swedish-Italian School of Singing

CHAPTER 2   26
    Posture, Breath, and Breath Management

CHAPTER 3   43
    Defining Factors of the Open Throat

CHAPTER 4 — 80
Lindquest's Perfect Attack—Defining Garcia's Coup de Glotte

CHAPTER 5 — 97
Vocal Protection: Its Role in Acoustically Balanced Singing

CHAPTER 6 — 119
Achieving Balance in Registration

CHAPTER 7 — 136
Understanding and Solving Middle Register Problems

CHAPTER 8 — 148
Balancing the Upper Passaggio

CHAPTER 9 — 163
Healthy Training of the Female Lower Passaggio

CHAPTER 10 — 179
Understanding the Physical Function Required for Legato Singing

CHAPTER 11 — 192
Applying Vocal Technique to Repertoire

CHAPTER 12 — 206
Achieving Acoustical Balance in Singing Onstage

CHAPTER 13   **219**

    Thinking Critically About Vocal Technique

CHAPTER 14   **244**

    Creating a Positive Learning Environment

CHAPTER 15   **253**

    The Importance of Psychology in Singing

CHAPTER 16   **262**

    Lesson Design: Organizing a Sequence of Exercises

RECOMMENDED READING   **281**

DAVID JONES RESOURCES   **281**

ABOUT THE AUTHOR   **283**

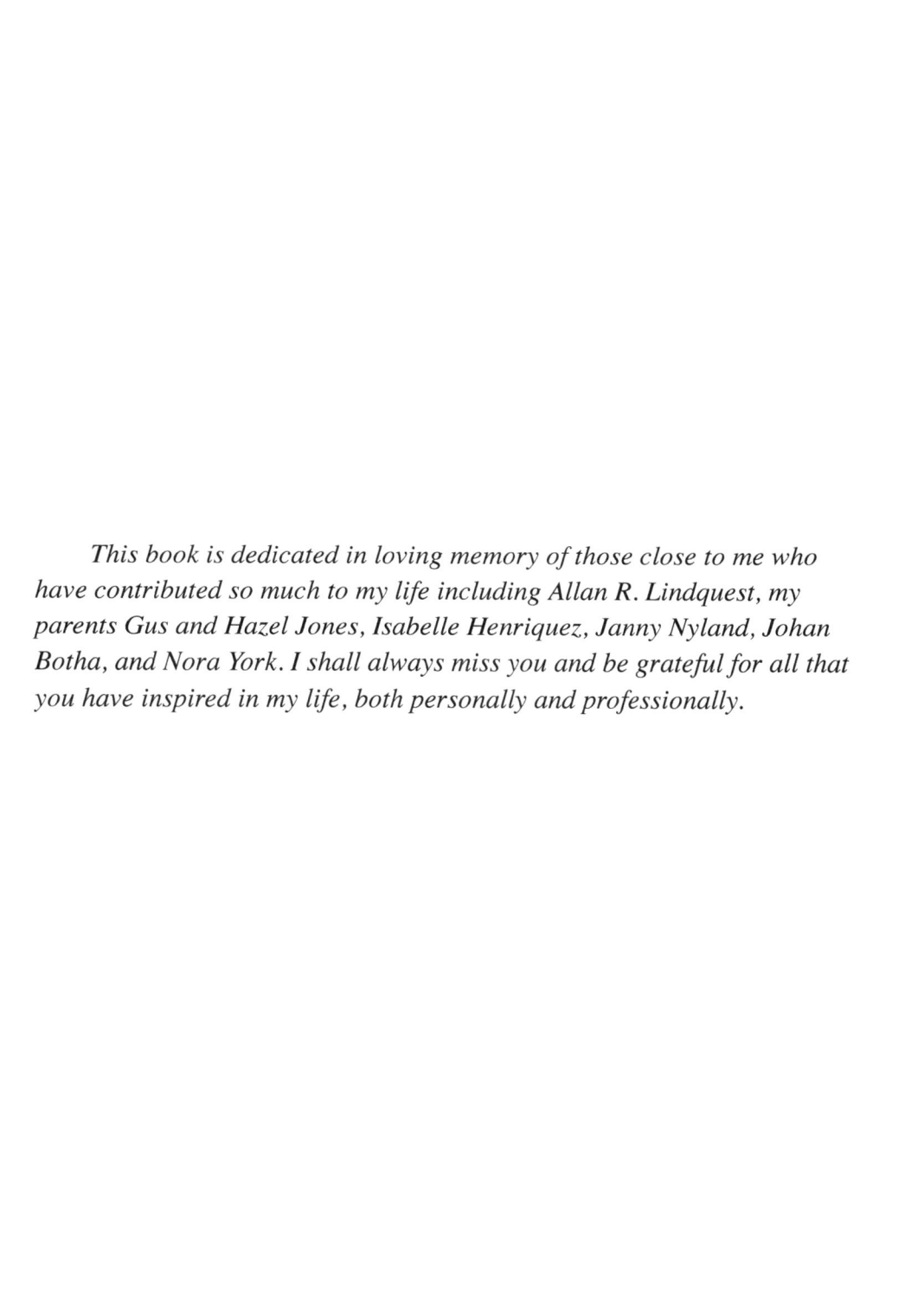

This book is dedicated in loving memory of those close to me who have contributed so much to my life including Allan R. Lindquest, my parents Gus and Hazel Jones, Isabelle Henriquez, Janny Nyland, Johan Botha, and Nora York. I shall always miss you and be grateful for all that you have inspired in my life, both personally and professionally.

CHAPTER 1

Allan Lindquest and the Swedish-Italian School of Singing

Background

In June, 1979, at the encouragement of my friend Martha Rosacker, I traveled to Santa Barbara, California, to study with Allan Lindquest. I remember exactly what she said to me on the phone: "He is really one of the last of the living Old Vocal Master teachers and this is a chance of a lifetime!" She could not have been more accurate in her evaluation, because when I worked with Allan Lindquest, an entire world of concepts was opened to me, things that I had never heard before. During my study with Lindquest, he shared the knowledge that he had collected over 70 years of experience as a singer and teacher.

I worked with Lindquest daily during that summer, sat in on his other lessons, and recorded all the lessons. For the next 30 years, I studied those recordings daily, in order to learn, digest, and thoroughly master Lindquest's teaching. These concepts form the core of my teaching today, and with this book I hope to make them more widely available, to carry on the Swedish-Italian school of singing, which is based on the Italian School, incorporating other concepts based somewhat on the German School, with the influence of the Swedish language.

Allan Lindquest

The name of Allan Rogers Lindquest (1891-1984) is largely unknown today; however, he is a link to the great singers and voice teachers in the Swedish-Italian school of singing that flourished in Sweden in the first half of the 20th century. Lindquest, born in Chicago to Swedish immigrant parents, had a successful and lucrative career performing in the lyceum circuit and Chautauqua tent shows, and in high-end vaudeville and operetta—genres that were highly popular into the first third of the 20th century, but which are largely unknown today, especially by singers and voice teachers in the classical realm. In addition to his successful career as a singer, Lindquest had a life-long passion for vocal pedagogy, and sought out the finest teachers of his time. He described his process: "I began by becoming an auditing student with outstanding European and American teachers. Spending several months with each of these masters, having almost daily personal lessons and auditing hundreds of lessons taught me much."[1]

Albert Karl Lindquest grew up in Chicago, and attended the University of Chicago, studying for a career in law. During his sophomore year, he was "discovered" by Alessandro Bonci[2], who heard him singing solos with a glee club. Using Bonci's connections, Lindquest left school and began to pursue a singing career, performing in concert and oratorio work, as well as touring.

In 1914, at an audition to record Swedish folk songs for Victor Records, he was introduced to Enrico Caruso, who gave him two coaching sessions and recommended that Lindquest go to Italy to study with his teacher, Vincenzo Lombardi. Instead, Lindquest traveled to France to study with Jean De Reszke. Unfortunately, his study was cut

---

1 Allan Lindquest, *The Total Response in Teaching Singing*, n.d.
2 Bonci was a tenor who rivaled Enrico Caruso at the Metropolitan Opera. As late as 1919, Lindquest's promotional materials mentioned Bonci as a sponsor.

short by the onset of the World War I: Lindquest was arrested in Paris as a German suspect, and was released only after singing an aria from Faust for the police, who readily recognized that he was American because of his French diction. He narrowly escaped from Paris via Brussels, London, and Canada.

Between 1913-1916 Lindquest made recordings for the Victor Talking Machine Company (precursor of RCA Victor). He was under management of the Wolfsohn Musical Bureau, whose roster also included Lucrezia Bori, Louise Homer, Alma Gluck, Mme. Ernestine Schumann-Heink, Efrem Zimbalist, and Jascha Heifetz. At one point Lindquest was offered a contract to sing at the Metropolitan Opera, which he didn't accept—a decision he later regretted.

In 1915, at the age of 24, Lindquest adopted the stage name Allan Rogers, and began to tour the vaudeville circuit. He continued to perform in concert and oratorios, touring with the New York Symphony Orchestra under the baton of Walter Damrosch, in works including *Elijah*, *Messiah*, and the Verdi *Requiem*. Between 1918 and 1921 Lindquest made a number of recordings for Thomas A. Edison, and was reputed to be Edison's favorite recording tenor.

A 1920 article in *The Lyceum Magazine* described Lindquest's career:

Among the list of high-class artists coming into the lyceum for an extended tour next season is Mr. Albert Lindquest, whom "Leslie's Weekly" referred to recently as "the distinguished American tenor with the golden voice." Mr. Lindquest has had wide experience in concert work, having been on the list of the Wolfsohn Musical Bureau of New York for six seasons. He is a young man and is just now coming into his own. The Edison people report that there is a larger sale for his records than for the records of any other tenor singer on their staff.

In addition to innumerable concert engagements, Mr. Lindquest has—during the past seasons—enjoyed twenty appearances with the New York Symphony orchestra (including three in New York City), four appearances with the Philadelphia Symphony orchestra; three times with the New York Philharmonic; three spring festival tours with the Minneapolis Symphony orchestra. . . . In fact Mr. Lindquest has appeared as soloist with most of the largest Oratorio societies in America.

The long list is a splendid tribute to his rare artistry. Everywhere his work has won highest commendation. Today Mr. Lindquest enjoys a place among America's foremost singers.[3]

During the 1920s he continued to tour with so-called "high class" or "polite" vaudeville in the B.F. Keith/RKO circuit, performing two shows daily, seven days per week, performing on the same bill with artists such as Sophie Tucker, the Marx Brothers, and Fred Allen. Lindquest also appeared in light opera (*Rose Marie* and *The Merry Widow,* as well as Gilbert & Sullivan operettas). In 1928 he appeared on Broadway in *White Lilacs*, a musical based on the life and music of Chopin, which required that he sing a high D nightly. The show closed in 1929 after 136 performances. In addition to singing in vaudeville, in the late 1920s Lindquest began to emcee vaudeville shows and conduct the stage bands.

In 1932, with the arts feeling the effect of the Great Depression, Lindquest relocated to California, where he worked in Hollywood at radio station KNX. He produced some of the earliest radio variety shows (with performers such as Jack Benny and Eddie Cantor), also conducting the orchestra and singing between acts. In addition to his radio work, Lindquest worked in Hollywood as a "studio tenor" for MGM and Paramount, providing singing voices for movie actors. His films include *The Merry Widow* (1934), in which he is the singing voice of Sterling Holloway; *Mrs. Wiggs of the Cabbage Patch* (1934), in which he sings on-screen; and *Every Day's A Holiday* (1938).

In 1935, using the name Allan Rogers Lindquest, he opened a vocal studio that quickly grew to be large and highly successful due to his professional reputation. Intrigued by the careers and vocalism of Swedish singers such as Kirsten Flagstad and Jussi Björling (and aided by

---

[3] *The Lyceum Magazine*, January 1920, 25.

his fluent command of Swedish), Lindquest contacted John Forsell, head of the Royal Swedish Opera in Stockholm, who arranged for Lindquest to study at the Stockholm Royal Conservatory. In the autumn of 1937 Lindquest moved with his family to Stockholm, where his major teachers were Joseph Hislop and Madame Haldis Ingebjart-Iséne, both of whom had studied with Dr. Gillis Bratt, and who had taught Kirsten Flagstad.[4] During this time, Lindquest became friendly with Jussi Björling, and they would get together and "talk shop". After 14 months of intensive study in Stockholm, the onset of World War II forced Lindquest and his family to return to the United States.

Once back in the U.S. Lindquest again dedicated his life to the study of vocal pedagogy and to teaching. Lindquest was a charter member of the National Association of Teachers of Singing. Along with his friend Lotte Lehman, he assisted in establishing the Music Academy of the West. Lindquest was a member of the American Academy of Teachers of Singing, an organization dedicated to vocal research, whose members also included colleagues Berton Coffin and William Vennard.

In 1955 William Vennard asked to sit in Lindquest's voice studio to observe his teaching; this led to Vennard having lessons with Lindquest. The primary focus of the work between the two was "balancing the registers."[5] In *Singing, the Mechanism and the Technic* (1967), Vennard includes an exercise that he studied with Lindquest, the *cuperto* exercise in the single-octave version.[6] (This exercise is the basis of the blending of the registers and it is one on which I focus with great concentration in my teaching).

Berton Coffin also studied with Lindquest during the summer of 1955 in Laguna Beach, CA. He was interested in working with Lindquest because he was "a student of the Swedish school which produced Hislop, Flagstad, and Björling."[7]

---

4   For the Swedish lineage, please refer to The Swedish-Italian Lineage Chart.
5   Lindquest told me about working with Vennard and Coffin when I studied with him in 1979. In 1993 I located Lindquest's widow, Ms. Martha Lindquest, who clarified the exact time and place that Lindquest and Vennard connected.
6   Vennard, *Singing: the Mechanism and the Technic*, 155.
7   Berton Coffin, *Coffin's Sounds of Singing*, 6.

In the early 1960s (when Lindquest was in his early 70s!), perhaps influenced by his interaction with Coffin, Lindquest studied with Madame Paola Novikova. (Coffin devotes the first chapter of *Coffin's Sounds of Singing* to Mme. Novikova's teaching.)

Lindquest taught actively until his death in February, 1984 at age 93 (after teaching two two-hour lessons). He was a master vocal pedagogue and a gifted psychologist in his teaching approach; he was a person who always put the interest of the singer first.

Lindquest's Philosophy of Teaching

"We teach the entire person, not just the voice. It is critical to work with a joyful and positive attitude, making learning a positive experience."

Teachers of Allan Rogers Lindquest

(approximate chronological order)

- Albert Borroff, bass
  Pupil of Manuel Garcia, II

- William Clare Hall, tenor
  Pupil of Jean De Reszke and Vincenzo Lombardi

- Enrico Caruso, tenor (2 coaching sessions)
  Pupil of Guglielmo Vergine and Vincenzo Lombardi

- Jean De Reszke, tenor
  Pupil of Antonio Cotogni and Giovanni Sbriglia. Teacher of Mattia Battistini, Beniaminio Gigli, Giacomo Lauri-Volpi, Giuseppe de Luca, Titta Ruffo

- Theodore Harrison, baritone
  Pupil of Manuel Garcia II

- Herbert Witherspoon, bass
  Pupil of Jean-Baptiste Faure, Jacques Bauhy, and G.B. Lamperti. Charter member, American Academy of Teachers of Singing.

Director, Chicago Lyric Opera. President, Cincinnati Conservatory. General Director, Metropolitan Opera.

- Enrico Rosati
  Pupil of Antonio Cotogni. Teacher of Beniamino Gigli, Giacomo Lauri-Volpi, Mario Lanza.

- William Wolf Vilonat
  Taught in Paris, later in New York and Philadelphia. Associated with Dresden Opera. Teacher of Leonard Warren, Todd Duncan, Beverly Wolff.

- William S. Brady
  Author of *Opera in Germany* (1901); taught singers at the Metropolitan Opera. Charter member, American Acadamy of Teachers of Singing.

- Joseph Hislop, tenor
  Pupil of Gillis Bratt. Teacher of Birgit Nilsson and Jussi Björling.

- Mme. Haldis Ingebjart-Iséne
  Pupil of Gillis Bratt. Teacher of Flagstad.

- Mme. Paola Novikova
  Pupil of Mattia Battistini. Teacher of Nicolai Gedda, George London and many others.

The Swedish-Italian Lineage

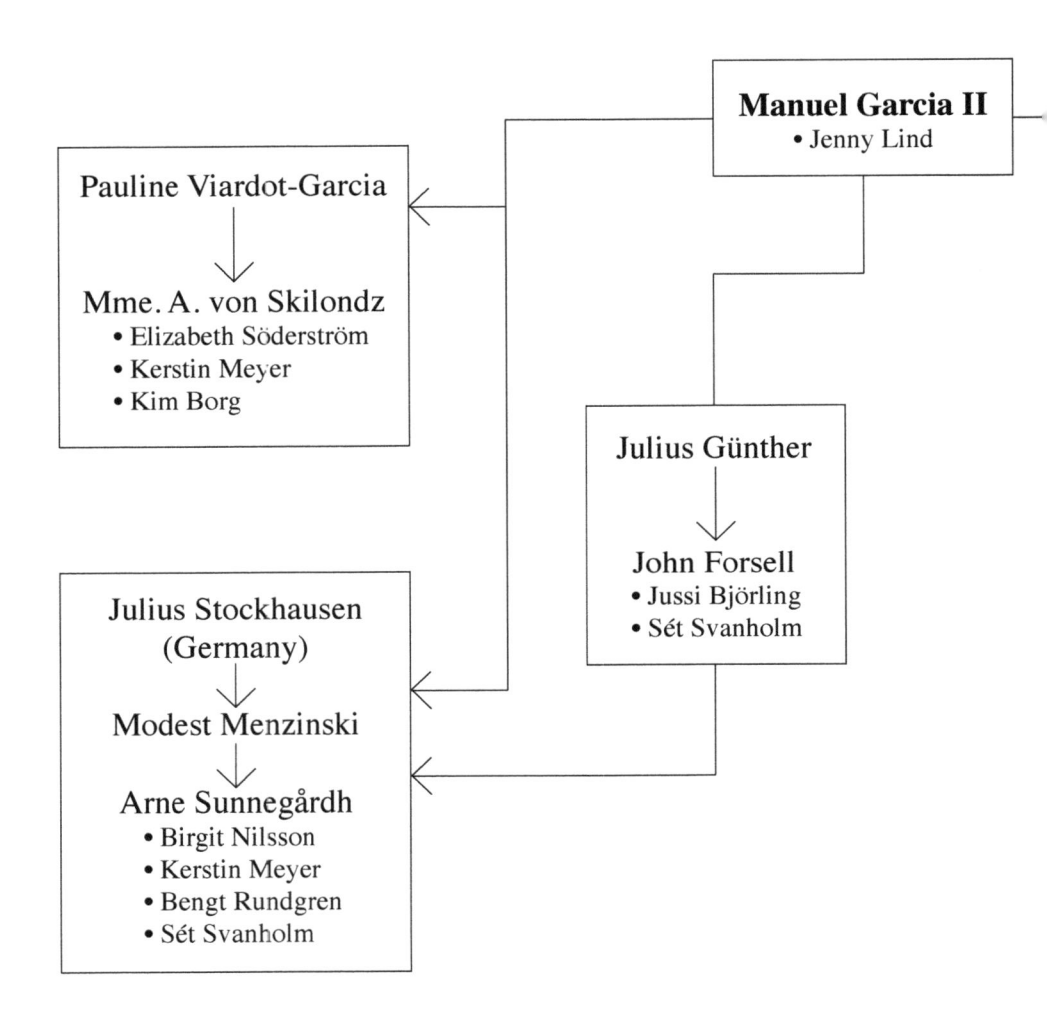

Manuel Garcia II
- Jenny Lind

Pauline Viardot-Garcia
↓
Mme. A. von Skilondz
- Elizabeth Söderström
- Kerstin Meyer
- Kim Borg

Julius Günther
↓
John Forsell
- Jussi Björling
- Sét Svanholm

Julius Stockhausen
(Germany)
↓
Modest Menzinski
↓
Arne Sunnegårdh
- Birgit Nilsson
- Kerstin Meyer
- Bengt Rundgren
- Sét Svanholm

Haldis Ingebjart-Iséne
- Kirsten Flagstad
- Torsten Ralf
- Aase Nordmo-Löfberg
- Allan Lindquest

Joseph Hislop
- Jussi Björling
- Per Grundén
- Birgit Nilsson
- Allan Lindquest

Lamperti Influence

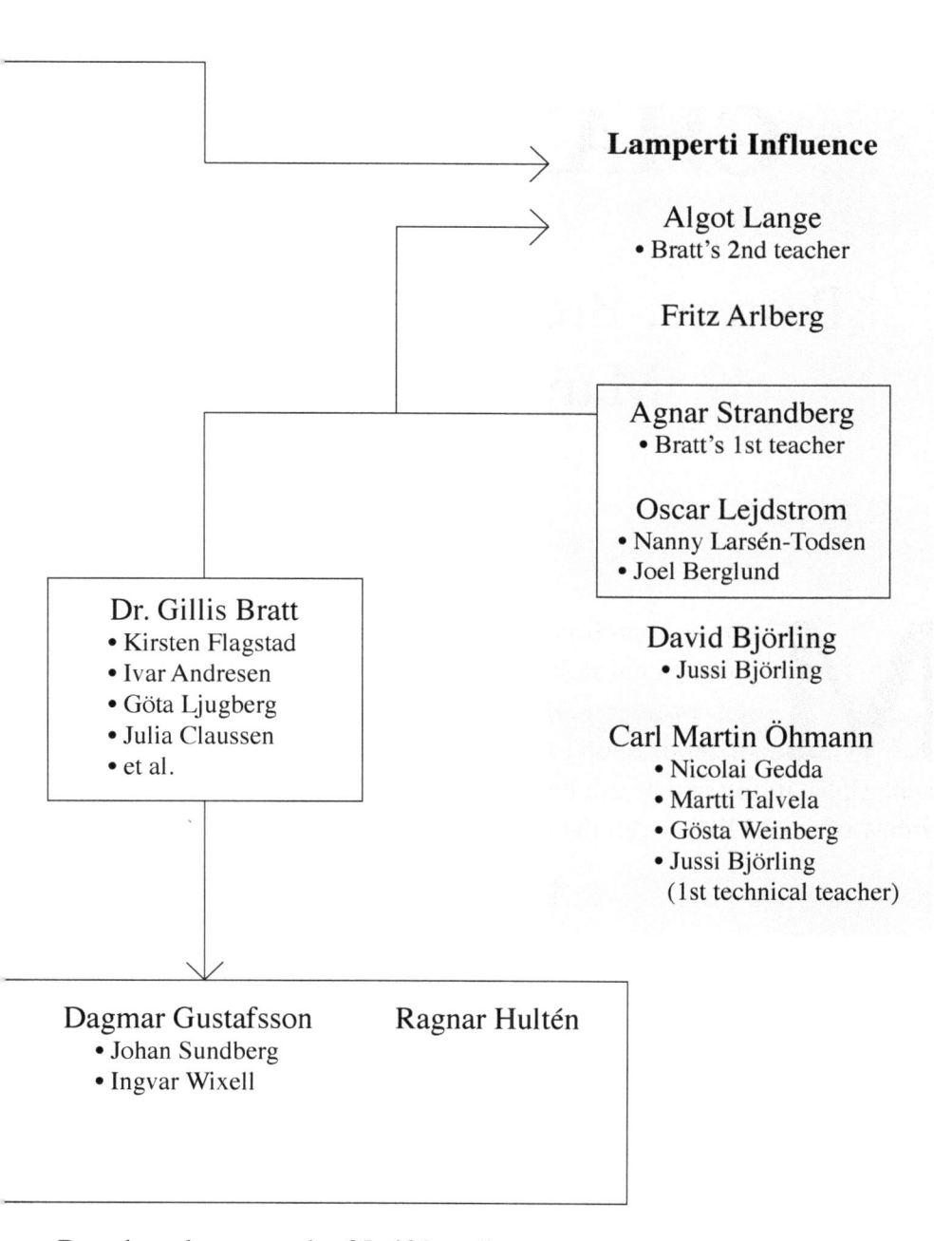

Algot Lange
• Bratt's 2nd teacher

Fritz Arlberg

Agnar Strandberg
• Bratt's 1st teacher

Oscar Lejdstrom
• Nanny Larsén-Todsen
• Joel Berglund

Dr. Gillis Bratt
• Kirsten Flagstad
• Ivar Andresen
• Göta Ljugberg
• Julia Claussen
• et al.

David Björling
• Jussi Björling

Carl Martin Öhmann
• Nicolai Gedda
• Martti Talvela
• Gösta Weinberg
• Jussi Björling
  (1st technical teacher)

Dagmar Gustafsson
• Johan Sundberg
• Ingvar Wixell

Ragnar Hultén

Based on the research of Leif Lundberg

Chapter 1 | Allan Lindquest and the Swedish-Italian School of Singing

CHAPTER 2

Posture, Breath, and Breath Management

Most vocal professionals realize that developing any professional skill requires discipline, knowledge-base, and self-awareness. Healthy vocal function requires that the singer develop a level of self-awareness regarding posture; breath (inhalation); and breath management, or the controlled, equalized outflow of what I like to call the small breath-stream.

Posture

Posture has a major effect on all aspects of singing. If the body is aligned efficiently, then the body coordination (including inhalation) will work efficiently. If the body is not aligned properly, then certain muscles tense, inhibiting healthy breathing, body engagement, and breath flow. For example, if the ribcage is compressed a singer cannot breathe properly. Nor can a singer breathe efficiently if the chest is pulled up too high, which compresses the back ribcage and this encourages high breathing. A singer who thrusts the head forward will struggle with a high laryngeal position.

Posture and breath in singing are directly affected by our habitual patterns in daily life. Many suffer from incorrect posture that is related to daily tasks such as driving, computer work, watching television, or interacting with other electronic devices. To move toward better body/breath coordination I recommend that all singers develop a mind/body awareness practice, or some form of movement awareness practice. I have studied the Alexander Technique for many years with John Nicholls in New York. I have also taken private lessons with Lynn Martin on Carl Stough's Breathing Coordination. Both disciplines have affected my singing and teaching positively through developing more self-awareness and becoming body-conscious.

The Alexander Technique is an excellent study in the alignment of the natural curves of the spine, encouraging a release from spinal compression related to daily life activities. With an excellent Alexander Technique practitioner, one is encouraged to discover the "springiness" in the spinal function. Other modalities that can assist in body/breath coordination include yoga, Feldenkrais Awareness Through Movement and Carl Stough's Breathing Coordination, among others. Each singer must find the personal practice that best fits his/her needs.

To assist in finding good body alignment for singing, Evelyn Reynolds uses a small trampoline (which fits under her piano). When a singer loses their posture, she has them move up and down a few times on the trampoline to find body balance. She also has the singer sing while sitting on an exercise ball; this engages the core of the body during phonation.

Healthy Posture

1. Tall spine, allowing for the natural 'S' shape.
2. Released hips and knees, which includes a slight bend at the hip sockets and knees.
3. Suspended ribcage, with special attention to the suspended back ribcage.

4. Rounded chest without hyper-extension (pulled-up chest).
5. Sitting bones above the heels.
6. Ears aligned somewhat over the shoulder area.
7. Shoulders released because of the suspended back ribcage. *Note:* shoulders should never be pulled back too far.

Postural Behaviors to Avoid

1. Hyper-extended front ribcage or a pulled-up chest. This cuts off the back connection and compromises the full motion of the diaphragm.
2. Either arching the lower back, or tucking under the tailbone area. This places too much pressure on the lower back area and creates a disadvantage at inhalation. I love John Nicholls' description—that the tailbone should fall away from the suspended ribcage—which is using gravity to assist in spinal alignment.
3. Belly-breathing—pushing down and out on the lower abdominal wall, which weakens the lower back and discourages back breathing.
4. Dropped chest position, which invites clavicular breathing.
5. Forward thrust of the head, which raises the laryngeal position.
6. Jaw tension, including the forward thrust of the jaw, which does not allow for healthy phonation.

The Act of Singing: Three Critically Important Functions

The three critically important stages in healthy singing are (1) free inhalation, which is enabled by correct posture; (2) controlled breath management through the musical phrase; and (3) body release at the end of the musical phrase. Body release at the end of a phrase is what inspires a healthy inhalation for the next phrase. Tension blockages in the body can inhibit this important sequence in healthy singing. Simply put, we need to know how to breathe, engage sound, and release, without a tight or tense body.

Inhalation

If the body is aligned properly with good posture, the singer can simply release the lower body muscles and allow for the new breath, without force. This must be accomplished without hyper-extending the ribcage—inhalation should feel more north-south in direction rather than east-west.[1] This thought can help the singer avoid over-breathing, or tanking up too much air. Of course, the intercostal muscles must be free and elastic, so that there is a springing open of the ribs at inhalation. Most know that we release the diaphragm at inhalation, which helps to draw air into the lungs, but many singers try to inhale by forcing large amounts of breath into the body, which is inefficient. My feeling is that forced inhalation inhibits a full expansion of the lungs. If the singer is flexible in the intercostal muscles, the back ribs will be more in motion, allowing for a freer inhalation. Incorrect posture can block healthy inhalation. Some singers are taught to over-breathe by thrusting the ribs too wide at inhalation. Opening the ribs abruptly or forcefully in an east-west direction leads to the push reflex. If the singer takes too much breath, the body will instantly try to blow it out quickly; however, if less breath is taken efficiently, the body tends to sustain its buoyant posture and the singer can more easily sustain the slow, even exhalation. I consistently use the concept of breathing in the north-south direction in my teaching, which discourages over-breathing.

Over-Breathing

An overly-inflated body is a tense body. Years ago, I observed the great singer Arleen Auger teach a master class at the Mannes College of Music in New York. She used an incredibly efficient tool with these young singers: she advised them to measure how much breath they needed for each phrase. The singers would create a space between their hands to

---

[1] For more information, see my instructional CD, *An Introductory Lesson With David Jones: A Resource for Voice Teachers and Singers*. www.cdbaby.com/david

accomplish this; it brought to their awareness that if the phrase was short, one need not take so much air. I often quote Lindquest in his statement, "Take a smaller amount of breath and imagine you are putting it in the tailbone!" Other great singers have voiced concern about over-breathing. When Lindquest sang for Caruso in 1914, Caruso told him, "I take no more breath than to have a casual conversation with a friend!" The famous soprano Nellie Melba said "One only need as much breath as to set the cords a-vibrating." Contralto Ernestine Schumann-Heink once said, "It is not how much breath I take, it is how I manage the outflow!" I am sure that these artists' understanding of breath varied somewhat, but the one major idea that they had in common was not to over-breathe.

Phonation/Body Connection

Controlled phonation in the act of singing requires a coordination of the lower muscles of the torso. Establishing a connection to elastic lower body resistance, such as laughing, coughing, sneezing, or hissing, is essential to accomplishing vocal balance. The idea of "support" is a flexible engagement of the body. The muscles that assist in holding back breath pressure are the pectorals, the intercostals, (front, side, and back) and the lumbars. You may note that all these are related to posture. On the other hand, the muscles that regulate the equalized outflow of air are the upper abdominals (epigastric area) and the lower abdominal muscles. Evelyn Reynolds called this an "antagonistic pull," or a relationship between these two sets of muscles that regulate a slow, even outflow of air on which to pronounce healthily.

When we hold back breath pressure, the resulting sensation is elastic, as though the body is gently stretching outward. This *must* be gradual and elastic, performed with a great deal of body self-awareness. In addition, the singer may feel an east-west pull in the lumbar muscles; a flexible east-west stretch at the upper abdominal area (epigastric area directly under the lower front ribs); and a slight forward, wide and upward stretch of the lower abdominals.

The Role of Appoggio in Body Support

I often tell students, "The forward stretch of the sternum is the key to a healthy onset!" Appoggio is often described as a forward leaning of the body. After the onset, this slow forward stretch of the sternum inspires the lower body muscles to engage, assisting in achieving the healthy tiny breath-stream. The lower abdominals are inspired to move slightly forward, wide and upward.

The Christa Ludwig Experience

Years ago, I frequently attended the concerts of Christa Ludwig. I would often request a seat toward the front and on the side, so that I could observe her profile as much as possible. Many thought this to be a bad seat, but in fact it was one of the best locations to observe this great artist. When taking breath (inhaling), I noticed that Ms. Ludwig would lean slightly back on her heels. Then, when she began the onset, she would stretch slowly forward, leaning slightly on the front of the feet. When she finished the phrase and breathed for the next phrase, she would lean slightly back once again. These body movements were extremely subtle and masterfully efficient. Her inhalation was both subtle and free and she did not force large amounts of breath into the body.

Compression and Release/ A Duetto in Breath Usage

Two vital factors in breathing and breath usage are compression and release. In other words, we cannot sing well on too much loose air, and we cannot sing on a tight body that does not allow enough breath to flow. There is the wonderful coordination of compression and release that give us the beauty of balance in breath, balance in healthy singing.

Under-Compression

We sing using compressed breath, not loose air. Some singers are too loose in their body, and this results in under-compression of the breath.

The result is usually a high larynx, loose vocal folds, imbalance in registration, and forced expulsions of breath pressure. I remember that Allan Lindquest once said to me, "David, you have too much loose wild air through your larynx and vocal cords!" At that time, I had little understanding of the body or how to use it properly in singing. I had previously been taught to pull inward at the onset, which over-blows the vocal folds at the onset—then there is no hope of finding a healthy compression in the body. One vital part of healthy sub-glottic compression is the healthy closure of the cords after inhalation. If the cords do not close after inhalation, then the body will quickly collapse and the singer will suffer from under-compression in his/her tonal production.

In 1979 I observed a lesson that Lindquest taught my friend Martha Rosacker. She had suffered loss of both her high and low ranges. Previous instructors tried to take her down in range because her high voice was difficult, but this was the wrong approach. Allan Lindquest discovered that she was under-supporting or under engaging the body to sing. Because she was suffering from using too much loose air, her high notes were throaty and shrill and her low range simply disappeared.

The solution: Lindquest realized that Ms. Rosacker was suffering from too much under-compression, so he instructed her to engage both the pectoral muscles and the upper gluteal/lumbar muscles directly after inhalation. This immediately increased her range because the vocal folds could stay together and work efficiently. This was due to her accomplishing a healthy sub-glottic compression. The ring came into her tonal production and Lindquest then said, "You can go about twice as far on a focused tone as opposed to an unfocused tone!"

Over Compression or "Over-Support"

The opposite issue to Ms. Rosacker's is that of over-compression of breath, or what I like to call "over-support." Some singers are simply too tight in their bodies, often forcing a large inhalation and then locking the body in an attempt to "support" tone. The result can be catastrophic to the voice. Resulting issues include (1) a locked solar plexus; (2) locked tongue-root, which compromises healthy phonation; (3) compressed or "pulled-down" back ribcage; (4) leaning on the heels; (4) high chest position; (5) forward thrust of the jaw; and (6) pushing "down and out" on the lower abdominal wall. One dangerous concept that is taught today is the idea that one needs to support as in "lifting a heavy object," such as a piano. The results are catastrophic to the voice and healthy vocalism.

The solution to over-compression is often posture-related. Again, I recommend that such singers research and study the Alexander Technique as a way of finding the tall, suspended ribcage and the healthily lengthened spine. This will assist in releasing massive tension blockages that result from pulling down on the ribcage.

Body Connection/A Visual Confirmation

Simply from observing a singer onstage I can tell whether he/she is body-connected. It is easy to detect by studying the shape of the lower laryngeal area. If a larynx shape is narrow, then I know that there is a certain amount of "laryngeal squeeze," which can only come from a high laryngeal position. If the lower laryngeal muscles are beautifully released wide, then I know that the throat is open and that the body is finding the duality of holding back the breath pressure, while allowing for the small, controlled air stream. Lindquest once said, *"Good singing is next to good laughter, and one who cannot feel free enough to laugh cannot be free to sing well!"* I shall never forget this statement, because it reflects that the lower body muscles must be engaged yet elastic in function.

Body Release: The End of the Phrase

In 1914 when Lindquest worked with Enrico Caruso, Caruso taught him what he called the "cough-off"—the release of old breath pressure that often builds in the body after singing several dramatic phrases back to back. This was a vital lesson because it allows the singer to release what I would call over-compression of the breath. When the body has built an excess of breath pressure, then the singer must learn how to break the cycle. The answer is what Lindquest later called the "puff-off" (I think this term invites a less abrupt approach). To accomplish this, the singer must allow the ribcage to collapse quickly. After this is accomplished, the body will re-breathe on its own—no thought of inhalation is necessary. A good inhalation is often a result of a good exhalation.

Exercise 2.1 Hissing Breath Sitting in a Chair

This exercise helps to balance the outflow of breath, regulating speed by training the lower abdominal function, while sustaining a tall spine. Use a straight or folding chair for this exercise.

1. Sit in a straight chair that is the right height to bring the bend in your knees to a 90-degree angle. (If the chair is too high, you can place books under your feet to achieve the correct height). Sit toward the front of the chair. Your feet should be slightly apart, with your feet flat on the floor.
2. Bring your awareness to a tall posture, from the hip sockets to the top of the head, with the feeling of a long back rib cage.
3. Take a slow breath until you feel an expansion of the lower back, creating the sensation of breathing between the hip sockets.
4. Lean forward from your hip sockets, and inhale. You will feel anchored to the chair through the "sit bones" and you will feel the back ribcage expand gently without thrusting too open. (This is the back-breath described by Flagstad). Do this several times.
5. Next, while pivoting or rocking slowly forward from the hip sockets, make a strong hissing sound. Do this several times, returning to your tall posture in between hissing. Observe what you feel in the lower body, paying special attention to the lower back (lumbar region) and the area around the waist. You will most likely gain a sensation of resistance surrounding the body, especially around the waist area. Notice that the lower abdominals do not pull inward and they do not push down and out. Rather, the abdominal muscles stretch slightly forward, wide, and upward. Study the solar plexus area under the line of the front ribs. You will notice that it stretches in an east-west direction. The ribs remain flexible and in movement.

6. **Variation**: Pivot slightly forward from the hip sockets as you sing a five-tone scale (/a/ /o/ /u/ /o/ /a/, two notes per syllable) and then return to your tall posture.

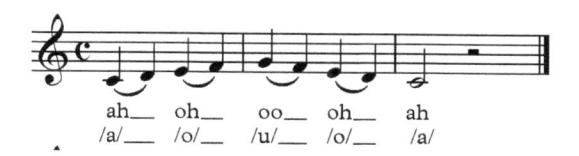

ah__ oh__ oo__ oh__ ah
/a/__ /o/__ /u/__ /o/__ /a/

Exercise 2.2 Strong Consonants While Sitting in a Chair

This is an exercise I learned from Allan Lindquest. Be sure to use strong consonants.

1. Sit tall in a straight chair, and pivot slightly forward from the hip sockets so that you can feel your lower lumbar region more easily.
2. Inhale/exhale several times, paying attention to the motion of the lower back and the back ribs.
3. Speak "*ka ka ka*," or "*ka ke ki ko ku*," using strength at the consonant /k/. Feel the reaction of the lower body (the lower body resistance). You may feel a kicking motion in the lower lumbar region in the back.
4. Now speak such sounds as "*ga ga ga*", and "*da da da*." Make certain that the consonants are strong.
5. Repeat this sequence several times to feel the reaction of the lower body resistance.

Exercise 2.3 Hissing Breath Lying on the Back

This exercise brings awareness of the role of the lower back while engaging sound.

1. Lie on the floor in a comfortable position, facing upward. Bend your knees to protect the lower back. Inhale gently and slowly and feel a relaxed inhalation and exhalation. Do this

several times. Notice that the lower back expands gently during this motion.

2. Begin a strong hissing sound with the teeth closed. As you feel your body engaging, notice that the lower back presses slightly into the floor. Do this several times in a row to feel the stretch of the lower back.
3. Now sing a short 5-tone scale on any comfortable vowel. Make certain that you feel the lower back press gently into the floor. Notice the elastic movement of the back ribcage.
4. Next sing an ascending phrase of a song or exercise. As you go higher in pitch, press the lower back more and more into the floor, because going to higher pitches requires that the body hold back more breath pressure.
5. Sing the phrase again and bring your attention to the neck area. If your head is lifting off the floor, you are experiencing intense neck pressure. Sing the phrase using the engagement of the lower body, while relaxing the shoulder and neck area.

Exercise 2.4 Hissing Breath Lying on the Front

This exercise is designed not only to align the body for good posture in singing, but also to engage the lower body at phonation. It will show you how to feel the deepest sensation of internal resistance in the lower body.

1. Find a comfortable posture on the floor, lying face downward. Place your hands under your forehead to protect the nose area.
2. Inhale and exhale several times comfortably.
3. Make a strong hissing sound, creating a firm resistance at the teeth and tongue. Concentrate on the resistance in the body. Use the thought that your lower abdominal muscles are slightly lifting the body weight away from the floor. Feel the lower back stretching toward the ceiling.
4. At first, hiss strongly and loudly; then try different dynamics, and

crescendo and decrescendo. You may also use voiced consonants /v/ or /z/ in this kind of exercise. Choose the sound that is most comfortable for you.

5. Start by hissing, then move from hissing to a vowel sound, keeping the same body resistance as you open to the vowel.
6. Do this exercise several times until your body learns that the intensity of the resistance in the lower body changes with different levels of vocal intensity.
7. Sing a part of a song that goes at least to the upper *passaggio* range. Notice that the neck is freer in the face down posture than in the face up posture. Repeat this step several times and let your body memorize the feeling of engaging elastically without neck tension.

Exercise 2.5 Finding Core Support

This exercise will educate your body on how to support sound from the deepest muscles, making the exhalation/phonation function more controlled and efficient. You will also learn to take less breath at inhalation. Repeat each step many times to memorize the feeling.

1. Sit in a straight chair that is firm and supportive. Inhale/exhale several times observing that the ribs are free enough to move flexibly.
2. Now blow out about 70% of your breath, then make a sudden and very strong hissing sound. Feel the contraction of the deepest muscles in the core of the body. These are the true support muscles.
3. Stand up, making certain that the hips and knees are not locked, that the ribcage is suspended with an open back, and the chest is open without being pulled upward.
4. Blow out about 70% of the breath and then make a very strong hiss.
5. Next, blow out about 70% of your air, then sing a glissando that moves from low register to middle register to upper *passaggio*

range; a glissando moving from /a/ to /o/ to /u/ is the recommended vowel sequence.

6. Finally, after blowing out about 70% of your breath, sing a musical phrase, or part of a song or aria, while engaging the core muscles. Use music that is memorized, so that your concentration can be fully focused on the body response.

Exercise 2.6 Hissing While Standing Against a Wall

1. Stand with your back against a flat wall area. Make sure that the feet are slightly away from the wall, and that the shoulders and lower back are against it.
2. After finding this posture, inhale low in the body, feeling the lower back expand.
3. Make a hissing sound while pressing the lower back against the wall. To train flexibility in the support muscles, create a pulsation in the hiss function. This will help your body to remain elastic while achieving lower body engagement. You may find a mirroring width in the side waist muscles when this is employed fully.

Exercise 2.7 Finding a Performing Posture

This exercise is designed to find correct performing posture for stage or concert work. This exercise should be done only after exercise 2.6 has been practiced repeatedly.

1. Stand with your shoulders and hips against the wall while the feet are slightly apart and slightly away from the wall.
2. Open and expand the arms outward at shoulder height, flat against the wall.
3. Bring your arms forward, as though you are embracing a tree. Allow the arm weight to bring your body forward until you catch and balance your body weight on the front of your feet. Observe that this posture allows for a springing motion in the knees and hips, and develops buoyancy in the upper body while the lower

body feels engaged. It is also helps to feel lengthening in the back rib cage.

Exercise 2.8 Hissing with One Foot on a Chair

This exercise is especially good for those individuals who have difficulty finding the strength of the lower back and the long spine. Use a straight chair for this exercise.

1. Put one foot up on the chair; the other foot is on the floor. You may notice that your back feels long and open.
2. As you inhale, feel the lower abdominal muscles release.
3. Begin to make strong hissing sounds. Notice that when you are making a hissing sound, the back muscles and the abdominal muscles activate.
4. Now step away from the chair and stand with the feeling of length in the back. You will feel a newfound strength in the lower back muscles and engagement of the lower abdominal muscles.

Variations for Hissing Exercises 2.7 and 2.8

(1) Exhale on a hissing breath while imagining a five-note scale; memorize the feeling. Then sing the five-note scale on "alleluia," keeping the same body feeling.

(2) Sing a five-note scale on a /v/ sound, memorizing the feeling. Then sing the five-note scale on the syllables *da me ni po tu*.

(3) Sing the five-note scale on /ŋ/ ("ng"), memorizing the feeling. Then sing the five-note scale on the syllables /kjo/ /u/.

ng_____ kyo_____ u_____
/ŋ/_____ /kjo/_____ /u/_____

(4) Sing a five-note scale on the syllables *la le li lo lu*.

la le li lo lu lu lu lu lu_____

Exercise 2.9 Engaging the Lower Back Ribs

This exercise is designed to teach engagement of the lower back ribs, while releasing the neck.

1. Lie face upward on the floor, with the knees bent.
2. Slowly take several breaths, noticing the feeling in your lower back. As you inhale, feel that the hip sockets widen and the lower curve of the back moves a little more toward the floor. Feel your lower body open more and more with each breath. The feeling of expansion in the lower back will also encourage width in the back rib cage.
3. Next, take six to eight sniffing breaths through the nose, noticing the feeling of breath even lower in the body.
4. Make a sustained hissing sound and feel the lower back resist downward toward the floor as the lower abdominal muscles resist in an upward and wide direction.

Exercise 2.10 Panting with a Tall Rib Cage

The purpose of this exercise is to isolate the free movement of the diaphragm from large movements of the ribs, offering an opportunity for the body to stay tall and open, yet not hyper-extended or locked. Singers who sing with a quickly descending rib motion usually over-blow the vocal folds. However, a slow elongation of the ribs *is* desirable.

1. Stand with one foot in front of the other (step position), placing your hands on the slightly suspended rib cage (Dr. Evelyn Reynolds uses the image that the front ribs sit wide on top of the upper abdominal or solar plexus area). Take a very small amount of breath.
2. Pant, feeling motion in the lower abdominal muscle area, near the pelvic area. The ribcage should move only minimally. (If you have difficulty isolating the rib cage from the panting function in the standing position, try lying on the floor face up with the knees bent).
3. Make a strong hissing sound, pivoting forward from the hip sockets as you lean slowly forward onto the front of the feet. This will assist in regulating the motion of the breath.

Exercise 2.11 Finding the Suspended Rib Cage

Lindquest said that we need to breathe 90% in the back and only 10% in the front. This exercise also brings awareness to the back rib cage. It is crucial to educate the muscles of the torso to engage and relax quickly. This exercise is designed to train this quick engagement and relaxation reflex, which is the basis of quick recovery between phrases while singing repertoire.

1. Extend your arms in front of your body, forming a curved shape as though you are wrapping them around a large beach ball. Feel a slight bend or looseness in the hip sockets and knees.
2. Inhale slowly with the feeling of the hip sockets opening and the pelvis tilting slightly backward at inhalation. You will feel the breath motion open the lower back area. As you inhale, feel the upper back rib cage open in the shape of a cobra head, feeling slightly rounded, yet suspended. Do this without tension, making it more a breath response than a muscular response.
3. Now speak a series of very short "*ah*" /a/ vowels repeatedly (like a laugh reflex) and feel a slight open bouncing motion in the

lower back muscles. This feeling will achieve the sensation of the lower back opening repeatedly. Make sure to relax between the short staccato vowel sounds. This is closely related to the laugh reflex. (You may also use a repeated series of short hissing sounds, making them very short so that you can feel the motion of the lower back and lower abdominal muscles.)

4. Repeat this exercise until you feel the lower back muscles achieve openness and flexibility.

Exercise 2.12 Exploring Proper Head and Neck Posture

Most teachers have worked with younger singers who thrust the head forward when they sing, a posture that closes the throat by raising the laryngeal position. To demonstrate the importance of head and neck posture to healthy singing, this exercise works with both incorrect and correct posture, and demonstrates the dramatic contrast between an open pharynx for healthy singing and a closed pharynx, which creates a closed tight-throated vocal production.

1. While sitting in a chair, find a tall posture (Exercise 2.1). Make sure that the ears align approximately over the shoulders. You can check this posture by placing fingertips at the edge of the ears and then touching the shoulders. It should be obvious when the ears and the shoulders are properly aligned. The neck will feel long, but without completely taking out the curve of the spine. Repeat this step as necessary, until you achieve a balanced head and neck posture.

2. Start to sing a tone, and while sustaining the tone, thrust your head forward. You will immediately feel a shrill, thin, throaty sound. When the head is forward, tension is created in the neck muscles, the larynx rises and the pharynx closes.

3. Move the head back so that the ears are positioned approximately over the shoulders. Sing the same tone again, using the same vowel. You will notice more color, warmth, and roundness in tonal quality.

4. Repeat these two steps, varying the vowel and pitch.

CHAPTER 3

Defining Factors of the Open Throat

Voice science has shown that a resonant sound can only come from an open acoustical space. The open throat is a major factor in the development of optimal overtones that create the resonance (ring factor) necessary to establish a competitive, polished, and professional-level vocal sound. When used with sufficient equalized breath-flow, an open throat offers the singer the vocal control required for achieving nuances in musical expression and the stamina required to function at a more professional level. Since volume is enhanced through expansion of the acoustical space, there is little need for the singer to employ the push reflex. I often work toward helping singers replace the push of breath pressure (which closes the throat by driving the larynx toward a high position), with the open acoustical space, cord closure, and ring.

The Primary Resonator: an Open Pharynx

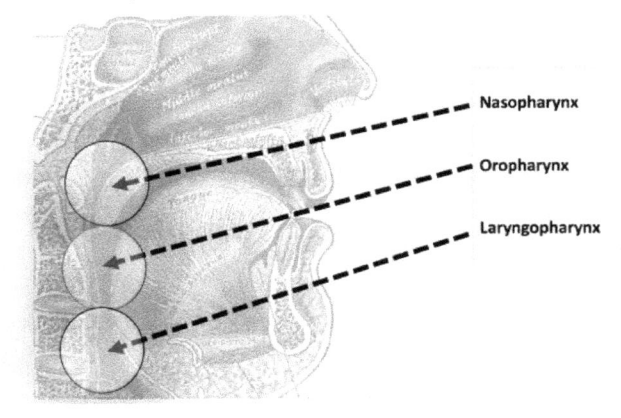

Nasopharynx
Oropharynx
Laryngopharynx

The primary source of resonance in the voice is an open pharynx. The pharynx is comprised of three parts: the nasopharynx, which lies behind the nasal port; the oropharynx, which is located behind the mouth (from the level of the uvula to the hyoid bone); and the laryngopharynx, which forms the bottom part of the pharynx, extending from the epiglottis to the larynx and esophagus.

Achieving an Open Pharynx

Inhalation provides a major opportunity for opening the pharynx. Each separate chamber of the pharynx must achieve maximum space without hyperextension of the laryngeal muscles. The *nasopharynx* is expanded by feeling a wide, east-west stretch of the soft palate. This reflects widening the pillars of the fauces. The *oropharynx* expansion requires a feeling of space between the tongue-root and the back wall of the throat behind the mouth opening. The *laryngopharynx* is released by breathing the larynx slightly down and wide at inhalation ("pre-vomit" feeling at the base of the larynx). The down-and-wide pull of the larynx at inhalation allows the lower laryngeal muscles to expand in an east-west direction.

Pharyngeal Vowels = Vowel Strength

The study of pharyngeal stretch is directly related to the concept of vowel origin. Lamperti said, *"A singer pronounces vowels in the pharynx, not the mouth!"* Allan Lindquest once said, *"A singer's strength of technique is in the strength of their pharyngeal vowels!"* He was speaking of the integrity of the vowel-form in the pharynx. Lindquest often focused on the concept of vowel strength within the width of the soft palate, which allows the larynx to be stimulated to release naturally, and avoids over-stretching the throat muscles.

This approach to vowel strength, in which the singer uses a stretch of the pharyngeal wall, is quite the opposite of the "placement" or "forward" technique commonly taught by some schools of singing today. The pharyngeal vowel strength allows the singer to feel residual frontal vibration (mask resonance) *as the result* of an open acoustical space and a forward tongue position. When the tongue is arched and forward, frontal vibration results from the duality of the open pharynx and the healthy closure of the vocal folds. Again, this is only possible when the tongue sustains a forward and arched position with a released or softened tongue-root. The strong pharyngeal vowel approach reflects the concepts that many well-known singers who studied the Swedish-Italian School adopted.

If the concept of vowel strength is taught carefully, the voice will take on more impressive color, freedom, ring, and lightness in the muscles. The color is a direct result of the free ring factor in the voice, something Lindquest taught me years ago. It took me a long time to realize that the full ring factor in the voice is substantially enhanced by free, open laryngeal muscles and a released tongue. When the acoustical space is open, the voice will sing or thread on the resulting ring, assisting the singer in navigating the voice from register to register. This ring must be fueled by a small controlled equalized breath-stream. This was a concept that Evelyn Reynolds reinforced during my study with her in New York. In teaching vowel strength, I often use Lindquest's idea of feeling the vowel in the wide stretch of the soft palate, while simultaneously releasing the lower laryngeal muscles at the base of the larynx. The concept of a wide palate discourages depression of the larynx with the tongue-root, and discourages heavy singing.

A Flexible Approach

Singers sometimes need to adjust their approach to vowel origin, depending on what they may need at a specific time in vocal development. For instance, if a singer's voice is too weighted or dark (often the result of tongue depression), then the open, wide soft palate with a slightly forward arched tongue posture can help to counter that problem. However, the problem of high-larynx singing often requires a different approach. Using the image that the vowel is formed under the base of the larynx, or directly at the vocal folds, can help in freeing and grounding the voice. This concept is most useful in the middle and lower registers of the voice and is sometimes a short-term study.

Enrico Caruso told Lindquest in 1914 that he visualized that his vowels originated "under the vocal cords". He also stated that he never felt as if he pushed breath through his vocal folds, but that he sang *under* them. There was only a small, even breath stream. These images helped Caruso sustain an open pharynx and healthy closure of the vocal folds, and to achieve a bigger sound without pushing breath pressure. Caruso's image is directly related to the concept of "drinking in" or "inhaling" the voice (*inhalare la voce*).

For singers who have a history of pushing too much breath pressure through the larynx and vocal folds, the image of vacuuming the breath below the cords (which, of course, is not physically possible) works especially well. It also works for those who are confused about how to achieve sufficient subglottic compression. During my study with Allan Lindquest, he encouraged me to feel the vowels at the glottis, or directly at the vocal cords. I had a history of singing with a high larynx and with the cords slightly apart or over-blown. Using the concept of the "vowels *at* the cords" was a large factor in helping me to find and sustain my open throat and my fuller resonance. Other singers have used the image of the vowels originating all the way down at the solar plexus area—another way of accomplishing an open throat and a lower, more rooted feeling in the body.

Another concept that helps maintain an open throat is the use of the "ng", when accompanied by an open acoustical space. Flagstad vocalized each musical phrase of an aria on the "ng" /ŋ/. In an interview, she said that she felt an "uh" /ʌ/ vowel at the base of her larynx at the onset and while sustaining vowels. The resulting stabilization of the larynx is obvious when one listens carefully to her recordings. This concept helped Flagstad achieve a lower laryngeal position in text. Flagstad added, *"This concept only works properly if the tongue is free, and if the body connection and posture are fully and correctly developed."* Luciano Pavarotti also used this idea as a foundation of space under the Italian vowels.

Imagery—while often scientifically inaccurate—can be another powerful tool in directing the singer's vocal energy. Using imagery to direct sound toward an area or direction can often help a singer find balance in singing. The direction may change depending upon what the singer needs at a given point in development. I often say to a singer, "This is what you need in order to find balance today! We may need to add a little more of [......] if you go too far in this direction."

Additional Tools for Achieving Pharyngeal Stretch

In addition to the concept of vowel strength, there are several other images that encourage the development of the open pharynx, including the *pre-yawn*, the *pre-vomit reflex*, the *joyful surprise breath*, and Lindquest's concept of *drinking water from a giant glass*. Dixie Neill used the image of *vacuuming under the cords*, which in truth is the sensation of breath usage when we are body-connected and laughing.

The "Pre-Yawn" Feeling

Many Old World teachers used the image of the "beginning of the yawn", or "half-yawn", in their teaching. This can be very useful in opening the throat, as it avoids over-spacing or over-stretching the laryngeal muscles. At the beginning of the yawn, notice that the muscles at the base of the larynx widen elastically without force or tension, creating a gentle east-west stretch. Slow practice in achieving this feeling will serve the singer well. Avoid the use of the full yawn reflex, as this encourages too much tension in the outer laryngeal muscles and in the tongue-root, often inviting tongue retraction. Be aware that locking the exterior laryngeal muscles diminishes interior pharyngeal space.

The "Pre-Vomit" Throat Response

Some teachers in the Old Italian School used the "pre-vomit" feeling (*vomitare*) as a tool for releasing an east-west stretch of the laryngopharynx. Be sure to keep the tongue position forward and arched in order to not over-stretch the laryngeal muscles, and to avoid the gag reflex at the tongue-root. Previous narrowing of the laryngeal muscles can be reversed with the careful use of this concept. This concept can also be very useful for those who have a history of singing with a closed throat and a high laryngeal position. However, *vomitare* should be used judiciously because, as with the "full yawn," taking the concept too far can be counterproductive.

The Joyful Surprise Breath

Allan Lindquest employed what he called the "joyful surprise" breath to encourage the development of the open pharynx and pharyngeal vowel formation. Correct employment of the joyful surprise breath also includes a slight forward movement of the tongue, plus a slightly down and back jaw position. Cradling the jaw with the hands during the joyful surprise breath encourages the larynx to drop more easily and releases the back of the neck. Some singers describe the resulting sensation as an "up-and-down" feeling, combining a high, wide soft palate and a lower larynx position. It should never simply be a muscular response, as this encourages throat tension. "Breathing the larynx down and wide" is very different from a forced, muscular throat heave.

Drinking Water from a Large Glass (Upper Passaggio and High Range)

To encourage development of the open pharynx in the upper passaggio and high range, Lindquest used the image of drinking from a large glass. When using the image of preparing to drink water from a giant glass, the neck should remain long, and the head should only move slightly upward. The back of the neck remains somewhat tall and free, not crunched. It is as if the skull lifts away from the jaw to open the mouth, resulting in more acoustical space for the upper passaggio and high range. This allows for the acoustical space to open more efficiently, and encourages the larynx to "hang" with gravity rather than rise. Lindquest also referred to this as the "Caruso head posture." I have found it to be extremely successful when a singer is having difficulty in sustaining the open acoustical space in the upper passaggio and high range.

Vowel Alteration in the Upper Passaggio and High Range

It is impossible to sing pure vowels in the upper *passaggio* and high range without closing the throat. This is an acoustical scientific truth that all teachers, singers, conductors, and coaches need to study and understand. In a 1938 interview, Kirsten Flagstad said, *"Over-pronouncing in the upper range has destroyed more throats and careers than practically any other factor in singing!"*

Without careful vowel alteration, the acoustical space cannot open sufficiently, nor can the singer sustain a free higher tessitura. The altered vowels must sound acoustically clear to the listener; this is accomplished by keeping the integrity of the vowel in the tongue posture. There are two approaches to opening the throat in the upper *passaggio* and high ranges: either alter the vowels, and the throat will open; or open the throat (pharynx) and the vowels will be altered. Each singer needs to use whichever approach works for his/her individual needs.

Ninety percent of excellent diction is a result of strong pharyngeal vocal release. Two factors are involved: the vowel is altered in the pharynx, while the tongue maintains the shape (integrity) of the vowel. Correctly altered vowels produce more acoustical space. When the correct tongue position is in place for each vowel, altered vowels are more understandable than unaltered vowels.

Vowel Distortion

Several factors can be responsible for vocal distortion. It is frequently caused by a retracted tongue position, and/or a bunched or narrow tongue-root. This can be a result of a too-high larynx position and/or the use of too much breath pressure in tonal production. A brighter, purer sound can be achieved by using a wider, arched tongue position. For example, if an /i/ vowel sounds dull or dark, bring the tongue toward an arched, wide position. This brightens the vowel while maintaining a rounded embouchure and an open throat.

I have taught many singers who had developed the incorrect habit of using the tongue to assist in altering the vowels. A bunched tongue plays a major role in (1) vowel distortion, (2) registration imbalance (3) dysphonia (4) locking of the breath flow, compromising clarity of language and resulting in muddy non-resonant tone. I frequently tell singers to alter the vowels with the pharyngeal shape, keeping the integrity or purity of the vowel with the correct tongue position.

Two important points about embouchure (mouth shape):

- First, never instruct the singer to spread the mouth shape to brighten a vowel—this will close the pharynx by raising the laryngeal position.
- Do not employ a forward pursing of the lips to achieve a

rounded *embouchure*. I often quote Lindquest: *"Tight lips tie up the throat!"*

Two Types of Vowel Alteration

Careful employment of vowel alteration is fundamental in achieving both the proper laryngeal tilt, and the release of the tongue. I employ two types of vowel alteration: first, pharyngeal vowel alteration, to open the acoustical space; and second, French nasal vowel alteration, to release the tongue-root.

Pharyngeal Vowel Alteration

For the throat to open when moving toward the upper *passaggio*, the closed vowels need to alter toward /œ/. The open vowels, /a/ and /o/, must alter from the pure vowel sound in the middle voice, to an "aw" /ɔ/ feeling in the head voice transition, and then toward an /ə/ or /ʌ/ (neutral *schwah*) in the upper *passaggio*. To free the high range, the root of the tongue must lift higher in order to release any tongue pressure at the vocal folds. Singing /æ/ (as in "*cat*") at the tongue-root will assist in achieving freedom in the upper register. Tenors and sopranos need the /æ/ by high A natural above the staff, mezzos and baritones at high F-sharp, and basses and contraltos at high D or sometimes E-flat, depending upon the weight of the voice. However, this must be achieved without spreading the *embouchure*.

Exercises in Pharyngeal Vowel Alteration

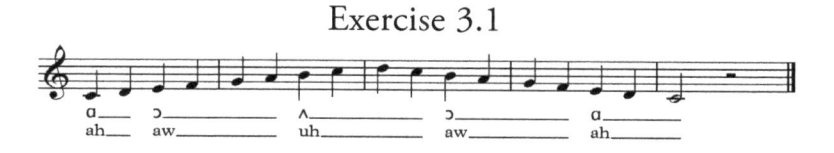

Exercise 3.1

a___ ɔ___ ʌ___ ɔ___ a___
ah___ aw___ uh___ aw___ ah___

Exercise 3.2

a ɔ___ ʌ ɔ___ a
ah aw___ uh aw___ ah

Exercise 3.3

ɑ	ɔ	ʌ	ɔ	ɑ
ah	aw	uh	aw	ah

French Nasal Vowel Alteration

Lindquest taught French nasal vowel alteration, and I also learned a great deal about it during my study with Dr. Suzanne Hickman. This concept is especially effective in releasing the root of the tongue in the high range. It reflexively encourages the tongue to move further up and arch out of the pharynx, increasing the acoustical space behind the tongue root. French nasal vowel alteration is most useful in the upper *passaggio* and high range, where the tongue has a tendency to retract, tense, or bunch (narrow). This approach is especially effective for those singers who have difficulty with high notes, and results in more balanced resonance and a freer approach to higher pitches.

When you speak the pure Italian /a/ vowel, and then speak the French /ɛ̃/ (as in *plein*, *main*, or *fin*), you can observe the difference in the position of the tongue: when employing the French nasal, the tongue moves further out of the pharynx, allowing for more high overtones to be released. Since the forward tongue is a large part of achieving an open acoustical space, this vocal concept is of fundamental importance in helping the singer to achieve a more open pharyngeal space. French nasal vowel alteration will not create a nasal tone if the larynx is released and appropriate acoustical space is employed behind it.

Vowel	French nasal alteration
/i/ /e/ /ɛ/ /ɪ/	/ɛ̃/
/ɑ/ /ɔ/ /o/ /u/	/œ̃/

The recommended alteration for the closed vowel sounds such as /i/, /e/, /ɛ/, and /ɪ/ (as in *bit*) is the French *ain* /ɛ̃/. The Italian /a/, /o/ and /u/ vowels must alter toward the French /œ̃/ (as in *chacun*, or as in the English word *uncle*).

Be aware that vowel alteration can be taken too far, to the point of distorting the acoustically clear vowel. Concepts in singing are subtle and should be employed carefully.

"Primal Sound" and the Open Throat

Laughter. While the use of spoken sounds is not always the best way to find a fully open throat, the study of primal sounds can be helpful to certain singers. Lindquest once told me, *"Good singing is next to good laughter, and one who cannot laugh cannot sing!"* He was comparing full-bodied, supported singing to the natural reflex of laughter, a primal function that engages the body and opens the throat. Laughter can be an extremely helpful tool in helping singers experience the open throat needed for singing. You need only observe the base of the throat when someone is laughing to see that the lower laryngeal muscles open and expand wide. I once had a singer go from laughter to singing for approximately six months before moving into singing without first laughing. He happened to have a beautiful quality in his laugh, a quality that later blended beautifully into his singing.

Other Primal Sounds. Dr. Evelyn Reynolds uses the comparison of the body engagement in sneezing, grunting, coughing, and moaning. In recent years, I have worked a great deal with the *deep moan* exercise. It teaches a singer the primal connected sound that is often described in the Italian School, without sacrificing healthy breath flow. In getting to a primal sound, the singer must feel the proper expansion of the body. When the moan or deep cry is engaged, the lower laryngeal muscles expand, yet remain flexible.

The /ʊ/ sound (as in *book* or *could*) can be extremely useful in helping a singer find full sound and body connection simultaneously, especially in the upper *passaggio*.

Taking the Open Throat Concept Too Far (Heave Reflex)

It is all too easy to take concepts too far, resulting in a negative effect rather than a desired one. I have witnessed some singers taking the concept of the open throat too far to the point of the 'full vomit' reflex. It is possible to over-widen the exterior laryngeal muscles to the point that the gag re ex is engaged at the root of the tongue, distorting healthy phonation. The negative results of overdoing the open throat concept can include loss of ring, high range, and flexibility in the voice. This is related directly to retraction of the tongue when the laryngeal muscles are over-stretched. One reason that many singers go too far with this concept is that they are over-compensating for years of closed-throated singing.

Some singers employ this destructive heave reflex by using a strong "lifting reflex," as though they are lifting heavy weight. A singer should never sing while compressing the rib cage (as in heavy lifting) because this places undue pressure directly at the vocal folds. (This is the reason some vocal professionals discourage heavy weight lifting for singers). It can sometimes take years to reverse this destructive vocal habit. The rib cage must be expanded, lengthened, and achieve a flexible floating sensation in order for breath flow to be realized healthily. Individuals who use over-compression through pulling down on the ribs are more subject to loss of vocal function in a shorter time. This "pulled down" motion of the rib cage creates a large, heavy sound, but the sound is weighted and muscular, and vocal longevity is sacrificed. While larger-voiced singers are the most likely to suffer from hyperextension of the laryngeal muscles, it can also occur in lyric singers.

Correcting the Heave Reflex

The primary solution to over-compression (which employs the heave reflex) is a suspended, floating open rib cage. This is accomplished by working toward correct posture in singing, and I strongly recommend that singers study the Alexander Technique to help with this issue.

When the suspended rib cage (including the *back* of the rib cage) is sufficiently mastered, the next step is for the singer to vocalize with a feeling of a flexible elastic width at the lower laryngeal muscles (at the base of the neck). It is critical that this width be achieved with softness (not rigidity) in the lower laryngeal muscles. A free, loose feeling in the back of the neck must be maintained while sustaining the "ng" /ŋ/ tongue position, to avoid retraction of the tongue.

I often use the image of a pyramid. The wide base of the larynx represents the foundation of the pyramid, and the "ng" /ŋ/ ring (under the upper part of the septum bone) represents its upper point. Work with these concepts slowly, using a mirror.

You will notice that the suspended rib cage plays a large role in releasing the root of the tongue. The singer can also be encouraged to gently move the head from side to side while vocalizing, so that the neck muscles are not locked in position. This movement must be a small motion in order not to disturb healthy phonation.

Emotional Reactions. It can take some time to reverse the negative effects of the heave reflex in the throat, and there can be a negative emotional response as the singer releases it, because tension feels like control. The Alexander Technique not only helps to achieve a floating open rib cage, but is also instrumental in releasing the back of the neck, the root of the tongue, and the jaw, all contributing factors in blocking healthy singing. Work slowly and carefully, isolating the function of the rib cage, larynx, tongue, and jaw. Remember that the sternocleidomastoid muscles must not over-widen at inhalation. (***Note:*** *Some instructors teach support through the grunt reflex. You can only grunt healthily when the rib cage is suspended and tall*).

Finding Correct Tongue and Jaw Posture

Many singers feel content with their approach to vocalizing, but experience difficulties when moving into singing text. Gaining a full understanding of correct tongue, jaw, and facial posture can assist in sustaining vocal consistency in language. Learning to control the tongue, jaw, and facial posture begins to establish the acoustical foundation of consistent resonance in the voice.

Employing the "NG" Tongue Position

To inspire maximum resonance or ring in each vowel, the Italian and Swedish-Italian Schools encouraged the use of the *ng* /ŋ/ as home position for the tongue. Note that this tongue posture is a flexible home base: locking the tongue in one position is not the goal. This concept is intended only to encourage and sustain high overtones while singing various vowels. Notice that the *ng* tongue position has a forward front half of the tongue, while the tongue-root relaxes with the sensation of a down-and-forward direction. This allows the singer to sustain a lower laryngeal position.

For maximum results, the *ng* /ŋ/ tongue position should be encouraged directly after each consonant, resulting in more acoustical vowel alignment. Even though the *ng* /ŋ/ brings a singer's concentration more toward focus in tonal production, the back of the pharynx must remain open. The tongue tip must be free to move to the different positions of the five Italian vowels. I encourage every singer to remember that healthy vocal sensations are subtle, intensifying only during crescendo. Kirsten Flagstad vocalized on the *ng* /ŋ/ when first learning an aria or role, before inserting text.

While use of the *ng* /ŋ/ tongue position is a practical way of bringing the tongue more forward and out of the pharynx, it must be carefully produced with the middle of the tongue, not the back of the tongue or tongue root. Tongue retraction on the *ng* can cause a choking sensation. For the younger singer, achieving the *ng* /ŋ/ may be practiced by vocalizing on such English words as *singing* or *hanging*.

Correct Tongue-tip Positions and the Open Throat

Correct tongue tip position will also help the singer to achieve and sustain the open acoustical space behind the tongue-root. If the tongue-tip is not in the correct position for a given vowel, the root of the tongue can become tense and it is then difficult to release the laryngeal muscles or sing clear vowel sounds. The study of tongue-tip positions involves developing an awareness of the front of the tongue during vowel change in the middle and lower registers. These tongue tip positions are most effective in the middle registers—they are basically for on-the-staff singing only. Toward the upper *passaggio* and into the high range, the tongue-tip position must be deep below the gum line for all vowels, which works as an anchor for the tongue-tip, enabling the back of the tongue to lift out of the pharynx for high pitches.

When working on tongue-tip positions, the jaw should unhinge slightly down and back. If you stabilize the jaw slightly down and back and speak the five Italian vowels without closing the jaw, you will feel the proper position of the tongue-tip for each vowel sound naturally. Work slowly, practicing the proper tongue-tip position for each vowel.

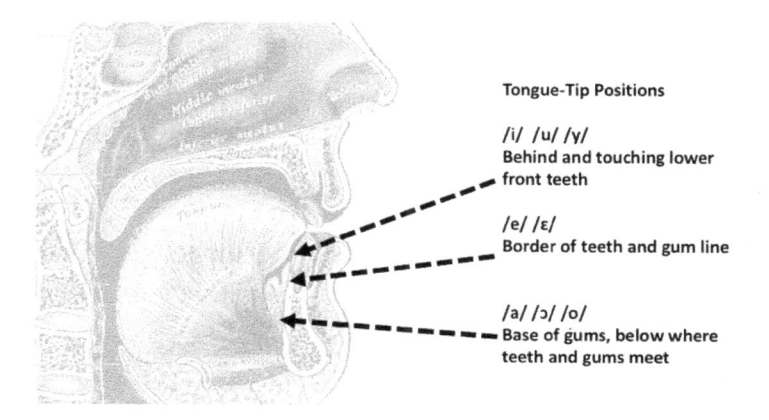

Tongue-Tip Positions

/i/ /u/ /y/
Behind and touching lower front teeth

/e/ /ɛ/
Border of teeth and gum line

/a/ /ɔ/ /o/
Base of gums, below where teeth and gums meet

- In forming the /i/ and /u/ vowels the tongue-tip should be positioned directly behind (and touching) the lower teeth.

Chapter 3 | Defining Factors of the Open Throat

- The vowels /e/ and /ɛ/ require the tongue-tip to be positioned approximately at the ridge where the lower teeth and gums meet.
- The correct tongue-tip position for the /a/, /ɔ/ and /o/ vowels is at the base of the gums, quite a bit below the point where the teeth and gums meet.

It is important to note that a technique that locks the tongue-tip behind the teeth for all vowels causes tension and/or bunching in the root of the tongue, resulting in throaty singing. It should also be added that the tongue should never be held stiffly behind the upper teeth, as this also tenses the tongue-root.

Tongue Exercises

Exercise 3.4

Use the fingertips to stabilize the jaw position slightly downward and back. Speak the five Italian vowels, /a/, /e/, /i/, /o/, and /u/, allowing the tongue-tip to assume its correct position for each of them.

Exercise 3.5

e a e a e a e a e

Stabilizing the jaw in a slightly downward and back position, speak and/or sing the vowels /e/ /a/ /e/ /a/ /e/ /a/ in a legato line.

It is important that the tongue move independently of the jaw. The jaw should remain in a stable position. Notice that the tongue will relax slightly back for the /a/ vowel, so you will need to allow this motion. The tongue will move forward automatically for the /e/ vowel. Speak or sing this repeatedly, thinking that the vocal folds stay together during the vowel change.

This exercise is designed to simply strengthen the front of the tongue, lessening the tendency for the root of the tongue to pull back into the pharynx.

Exercise 3.6

did-dle did-dle did-dle did-dle   did-dle did-dle did-dle did-dle
/dɪ/ /dl/ etc.

Stabilize the jaw slightly downward and back (but mainly back), without locking it in position. Say the word *diddle* /dɪdl/ over and over. As you speak longer, you may find that the tongue will sometimes begin to tense. If this happens, slow down the tempo of this spoken exercise.

did - dle   did - dle   did - dle   did - dle   did - dle

When you have achieved enough freedom in the tongue to speak this word quickly, then add a five-tone scale, either ascending or descending. Keep the mouth shape rounded. If the tongue tenses, begin speaking again slowly and then start singing at a slower tempo.

Exercise 3.7

Speak the Italian syllables, *la le li lo lu*, without the jaw moving. Make sure the tongue is wide, *not* narrow. The jaw should be slightly unhinged down and back, but not too open. Pronounce the syllables again with tongue movement only, allowing the tongue to flip for the /l/ and keeping the jaw still. Then, using varying *tempi*, sing the syllables on various scale patterns. Be sure to voice the /l/ under the cheekbones, not at the tongue root.

la   le   li   lo   lu

Chapter 3 | Defining Factors of the Open Throat

Exercise 3.8

Achieving resonance in vowels using the ng. Remember to produce the /ŋ/ feeling with the middle of the tongue, not with the root of the tongue. In forming the *ng* /ŋ/, keep the tongue root wide, never bunched.

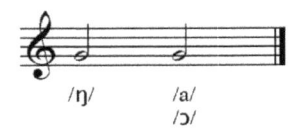

/ŋ/   /a/
      /ɔ/

First, sustain a note on the /ŋ/ and slowly move toward an open vowel such as the Italian /a/ or /ɔ/. As you move toward the vowel, imagine that you are going to open the sound by elevating the soft palate high and wide, away from the tongue-root. Never allow the tongue-root to crash suddenly downward. A sudden dropping of the tongue position distorts the higher overtones, which intensifies the register shifts or breaks in the voice.

Next, work a five-tone descending scale in the middle register using *ying yeng yang yong yung*. Notice that the front of the tongue moves toward the hard palate behind the upper teeth when reaching the *ng* /ŋ/.

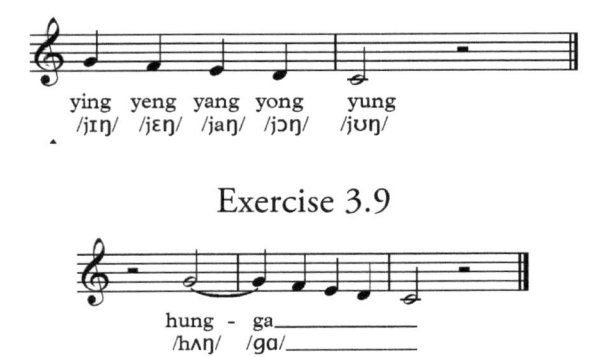

ying   yeng   yang   yong   yung
/jɪŋ/ /jɛŋ/ /jaŋ/ /jɔŋ/ /jʊŋ/

Exercise 3.9

hung - ga_____
/hʌŋ/ /gɑ/_____

Using the syllables hung-gah (/hʌŋ gɑ/). The /g/ is a reflexive consonant, assisting the singer in opening the soft palate, or upper space, while achieving efficient closure of the vocal folds. Keep in mind not to over-blow the /g/ by using too much air pressure. Avoid using the feeling of blowing breath out of the mouth space; instead, imagine channeling the breath directly up toward the soft palate. This will help achieve the correct sound without over-blowing.

Sing a descending five note scale: start with *hung* on the first note, then change to *gah* and sing down the scale.

This is useful when a singer has a history of pulling down on the palate or the root of tongue, especially in the upper *passaggio*.

Vowel Distortion and Tongue Position

Excessive vowel distortion diminishes the acoustical space, as well as language clarity, no matter how exceptional a singer's instrument. If left uncorrected, this will hinder an otherwise fine performer from being able to compete as a professional. How can singers remain unaware of such a large problem as vowel distortion? They are deceived by a distorted auditory perception of tonal quality, which I refer to as *"distorted inner hearing."* A person can become so conditioned to hearing distorted vowels as pure sounds that he/she cannot tell the difference.

With correct guidance, vowel distortion can be corrected. It is important to get external feedback, and finding a good vocal teacher with an excellent diagnostic ear is an excellent first step. An extremely useful tool is for the singer to consistently record, and listen, to his/her voice.

Vowel distortion is usually caused by a bunched tongue-root. To clear up the problem the singer needs clear concepts and exercises that will release the tongue and develop sufficient acoustical space. Below is a comprehensive list of causes of vowel distortion.

Causes of Vowel Distortion

1. Imitating recordings of famous singers when one is young.
2. Speaking in a regional dialect that distorts pure vowels.
3. Pushing too much breath pressure through the larynx, resulting in a gag reflex at the root of the tongue and/or tongue retraction.

4. Misinterpretation of the concept of open throat by over-stretching the outer laryngeal muscles (heave reflex). When laryngeal muscles are over-stretched, the tongue can become tense or retracted, resulting in the distortion of vowels.

5. Use of too much breath pressure when singing consonants, which can result in retraction of the tongue position at vowel function. This also distorts the even outward breath flow on which one pronounces healthily.

Correct Jaw Function in Pronouncing Text

Finding the correct jaw motion in singing text is a key study in healthy singing. Many singers are aware of tension in the jaw, but most are not aware of the correct motion of the jaw. Many schools of singing technique work toward a loose and/or relaxed jaw. However, it is also important to study the "back" jaw position after each consonant in text, which is necessary to pronounce text with an open throat.

In the middle and lower registers, the jaw should rarely open downward, but instead should release more toward the back. (As always, this must be accomplished without locking the jaw in a back position.) When approaching the upper *passaggio* and higher range, the jaw then must drop more.

Of course, the jaw must be in motion during language function, but jaw motion is different in singing than in speaking. When singing, the jaw must wrap gently back and down (without locking), after each consonant in text. Lindquest compared this jaw motion to the down and back motion of a trap door or a gentle up and down chewing motion, as in chewing soft food. A singer can feel this "back" jaw posture by looking upward toward the ceiling, leaning the head back, and then allowing the jaw to drop with gravity. Notice that the jaw falls downward and back, not down and forward.

Several years ago, I had the opportunity to observe Olga Borodina from the wings of a major opera house. She was singing the role of Dalila.

It was interesting to study the freedom of her jaw: it wrapped gently back (not down) after each consonant in text. She did not open the mouth too much in the middle register. She waited to open the jaw toward the upper *passaggio* and high range. This kept high overtones present in her middle register and when singing lower pitches. Placido Domingo is another singer who wraps his jaw back gently after each consonant when he sings text. It is helpful to study videos of these singers, especially in profile shots, as you will see that this concept is of fundamental importance.

Dangers of the Down and Forward Jaw

Many singers hyperextend the jaw down and forward, sometimes to the point that it moves forward out of its socket. This not only raises the larynx position, but it also disturbs healthy vocal fold adduction and causes the tongue to retract. The jaw should never thrust forward, because this disturbs healthy phonation. A strong downward thrust of the jaw is a major factor in loss of resonance, and it diminishes acoustical efficiency in the voice. Many singers think that an unhinged jaw is a relaxed jaw. They do not realize that if the jaw unhinges down-and-forward, then the pharynx gets smaller due to the resulting high larynx position.

The down-and-forward thrust of the jaw is a common problem for baritones and bass-baritones. It leads to what is often called the "baritone bark," or singing without vocal protection. "Barking" is a direct result of thrusting the jaw downward and forward at consonants, which closes the acoustical space. The Italians call this *voce aperta*, meaning that the voice is too open in the mouth cavity and too closed in the pharynx. A healthy acoustical protection cannot be achieved employing such a down and forward thrust of the jaw. This problem most often occurs in dramatic passages of music.

The negative side effects resulting from forcing the jaw downward and forward include: lack of legato line, expulsion of too much breath pressure at the consonants, diminished breath control, lack of ring in the voice, imbalance in registration, closed acoustical space, and distortion of vowels.

Correct Diction: Jaw and Tongue Independence

Most native English speakers pronounce with the tongue and jaw connected in function, which tends to elongate the consonants and shorten the vowels. This is the exact opposite of what is needed for healthy legato singing. Italian speakers have an advantage in pronouncing words, as independent function of jaw and tongue is built into the Italian language, making it much easier for Italians to pronounce with an open throat when singing.

In order to sustain an open throat while pronouncing, a singer must be able to separate the functions of the tongue and jaw so that they can work independently of each other. This can be studied using the flipped /l/ and /n/, and dentalized /d/ and /t/. These consonants must be exercised while keeping a slightly open jaw position. Correct function requires that the tongue produce these consonants independent of the jaw.

Exercises for Jaw/Tongue Independence

Exercise 3.10

Speak the Italian syllables: *da me ni po tu*.

Rest the fingertips on the chin during this exercise to discourage the jaw from moving during pronunciation.

Pronounce slowly at first, and allow the jaw to only move with minimum motion. Then gradually increase the speed of pronunciation, keeping the motion of the tongue separate from any jaw motion.

Exercise 3.11

Speak the Italian word *dentale*, keeping the jaw slightly open and back during pronunciation and keeping the tongue and jaw working independently. The /d/, /t/, and /l/, should all be produced by flipping the tongue-tip up behind the upper teeth. This motion must be accomplished quickly.

First, slowly speak this exercise. Then sing it on a 3-tone scale or triad, maintaining this jaw-tongue separation.

de— nta— le   de— nta— le

Exercise 3.12

Speak the syllables *kona lona luna* without moving the jaw. Allow the tongue tip to flip for the /n/ and /l/. The goal is to achieve separation of jaw-tongue function. Then sing the syllables on one pitch. Stabilize the jaw with your fingers; do not allow it to close during this exercise. Again, produce the /l/ and /n/ sounds by flipping the tongue-tip up behind the upper teeth.

ko na lo na lu na   ko na lo na lu na   ko na lo na lu___ na

Jaw Release and Registration

How far should a singer open the jaw when pronouncing text? While there are varying opinions on this subject, the degree of opening the jaw is completely related to registration. Some singers lock the jaw in a closed position, making both low breathing and an open acoustical space difficult to achieve; others lock the jaw too open in the low range, resulting in a gag reflex at the tongue-root, which cuts high overtones. Locking the jaw either too open or too closed will never produce free resonance.

In fact, we actually need less acoustical space in the middle range in order for ring to be realized in that register. The higher the person sings, the more the jaw must open, using a fuller range of motion down and back. This gradual increase in opening the jaw allows for more acoustical space to be realized in order to accommodate higher pitches. In the very highest range, the singer may be required to make more space by tilting the head slightly upward, which opens the wide soft palate. The jaw will hang open from this head position.

Jaw Exercises and the Open Throat

Exercise 3.13

Use a mirror when doing this exercise, or use two mirrors at a 90-degree angle so that you can study your profile as you sing.

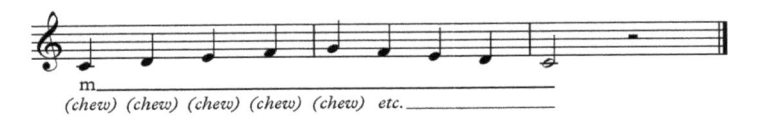

m___
(chew) (chew) (chew) (chew) (chew) etc.___

Close the lips and sing a five-tone ascending scale while chewing downward and back (not side to side) on every pitch of the scale.

It is critically important that the jaw muscles move slowly and gradually, not abruptly. Avoid any sudden downward thrust of the jaw. Remember that the goal of your study is to achieve a jaw position that is back and down, accompanied by a slow gradual jaw motion as in gentle chewing.

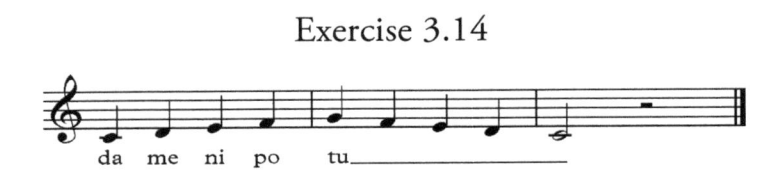

Exercise 3.14

da me ni po tu___

Cradle the jaw with both hands, allowing it to fall into your hands. When you have totally relaxed it, sing a five-tone scale using the Italian syllables *da me ni po tu*. Monitor the jaw motion, making sure that it is down and back.

Exercise 3.15

m___
(chew)(chew) etc.___   da me ni po tu___

Combine the gentle chewing hum (lips gently sealed) with the free jaw to achieve balance in vowel-consonant relationship. First sing a five-tone scale using the chewing hum, making sure that the jaw muscles move in a slow elastic up-and-down motion. Then add text (as in the previous exercise) without adding jaw pressure. Continue to do this until you can feel the sensation of a loose jaw. This exercise will require slow practice and patience.

Correct Facial Posture

Facial posture plays a major role in balancing high and low overtones in a singer's tonal production, because it directly influences the internal posture of the throat space (pharyngeal space). Most people have seen performances where the artist made unusual faces, sometimes pulling the facial muscles downward, or singing out the side of the mouth (which often happens with baritones). These unusual facial habits can create a negative effect on vocal acoustics, requiring the singer to push too much breath pressure and work harder to produce his/her sound. It is important for the singer to study the effects of facial posture on vocal acoustics. If the correct facial posture is not employed carefully, then the singer can find neither acoustical balance, nor balance between upper and lower overtones.

Each singer's physical structure is unique, so there is no single facial posture that is right for everyone. Different adjustments may be required to establish balance in upper and lower overtones. Because every singer is individual, the instructor must determine what works for each singer. However, there are some aspects of facial posture that consistently help singers find more acoustical balance.

Factors in Facial Posture that Enhance Acoustical Efficiency

- ***Jaw gently back and slightly down,*** allowing for a slightly low larynx position.

- *Slight lift of the cheek muscles under the outer cheekbone area,* which spreads the soft palate wide. This allows for the enhancement of upper overtones, a result of a line of stretch from the sides of the nose all the way under the outer cheekbone area. The jaw must be relaxed, suspended from this stretch of muscles under the cheekbones. This is subtle and should not be overdone. (**Warning:** *if the cheek muscles directly under the eyes are over-stretched upward, then the larynx will rise.*)
- *Lower lip relaxed over the lower teeth.* Showing lower teeth usually pulls down the soft palate and is an indicator of jaw tension. Never show lower teeth unless they are particularly long in structure and the lower lip cannot cover them efficiently, as this pulls down the soft palate. Avoid wrapping the lower lip over the lower teeth, as this creates unnecessary tension.
- *Show at least a little of the upper teeth* without spreading the embouchure (mouth opening). This is accomplished by slightly lifting the cheek muscles until a small portion of the bottom edge of the upper teeth is exposed. Try to do this while sustaining a rounded or oval mouth shape.
- *Sunken cheek muscles at the back teeth,* which opens more internal pharyngeal space. This encourages the development of pharyngeal vowels rather than mouth vowels, adding another tool for opening the throat.

Incorrect Facial Posture and Distortion of Acoustical Efficiency

- *Pulling the upper lip downward over the upper teeth.* This tends to pull down the soft palate.
- *Showing lower teeth by pulling down the lower lip.*
- *Jaw to one side or forced downward.* Pulling the jaw too far downward to the point that the facial muscles are pulled downward cuts high overtones. Note: opening the jaw too far downward and forward distorts acoustical efficiency, and shortens the high range.

- ***Spread mouth position,*** which raises the larynx and closes the throat space.

The best kind of practice for correcting facial posture is to use a mirror. It is the single most important tool besides using a video camera, which is also an excellent and helpful tool. Use of the video camera not only gives physical feedback, but it also shows clearly how facial posture affects vocal sound.

Singing in the Incorrect Vocal Fach

Singing in the wrong vocal *Fach* or wrong *tessitura* can disturb a singer's ability to achieve and/or sustain an open throat. As a lyric baritone who was first trained as a tenor (and sang as one for 20 years), I experienced many severe vocal problems.

Singing in a higher *tessitura* when the voice is naturally a lower voice results in such problems as a high larynx position, a closed pharyngeal space, irritation of the vocal folds; tension and/or bunching at the tongue root at phonation or at the preparatory breath; over-blowing of the vocal folds due to lack of correct approximation after breathing; unprotected spread vocal tone, as a result of a high larynx position; imbalance in registration; intonation problems; and shaking laryngeal muscles, jaw, or tongue. It is critically important to realize that if a singer's throat cannot sustain a higher tessitura, then he/she may belong in a lower vocal category, especially if the laryngeal tilt is not established properly in the middle register. The wise approach would be to work in the middle voice for a period and see what vocal timbre develops after the laryngeal muscles fully release.

At the opposite extreme, there are higher-voiced singers who force their voice into a lower vocal *Fach*, which is often accomplished by depressing the larynx with the root of the tongue. It is my personal concern that some schools of training actually encourage this type of depressed larynx vocal production, an extremely dangerous practice. Singing with a depressed larynx is created by inducing muscular pressure on the larynx with the root of the tongue. Singers who perform in a lower vocal *Fach*, when they are a higher singer, often develop (1) loss of both high range *and* low range, shortening the voice in both extremities, (2) intonation problems, (3) imbalance in the upper *passaggio*, (4) lack of sufficient breath flow through the vocal folds (singing on a gag reflex), (5) cracking in the voice, (6) insufficient ring in the voice, and (7) possible vocal damage due to bursting capillaries or vocal hemorrhage.

Daily Practice Concepts for the Open Throat

To develop vocal consistency, every singer needs a healthy daily routine of vocalization, one that inspires a healthy opening of the laryngeal muscles. At inhalation, the singer must feel the larynx release about halfway down, while simultaneously keeping a forward and arched tongue position. Lindquest called this "preparing the throat to sing." The lower laryngeal muscles will widen, the soft palate will become slightly elevated and wide, and the oropharynx (space behind the tongue-root) will expand in a straight back direction. To accomplish this the jaw must first release slightly down and back in order to inspire a low breath, a major factor in accomplishing an open acoustical space.

1. Inhale, feeling the muscles at the base of the larynx slightly widen. These muscles must remain flexible.
2. Loosen or unhinge the jaw slightly before inhalation. Then feel a wide soft palate as you inhale. This corresponds to the Old Italian image of the "inner smile", which consists of a wide soft palate stretch.
3. Arch the tongue in the forward "ng" /ŋ/ position at inhalation. Be sure that the "ng" /ŋ/ is produced with the middle of the tongue, *not* the back.
4. Spread the root of the tongue at inhalation as it arches and moves toward the "ng" position. This helps to avoid bunching (narrowing) at the tongue-root, which leads to pressure at the vocal folds.

[musical notation: "i___"]

5. Vocalize an ascending major third in the middle register, allowing the larynx to "pivot" slightly down and forward. Use the rounded /i/ vowel at first. Remember that the embouchure (mouth opening) should remain oval, as in speaking "oh" /o/ or "aw" /ɔ/. The lips should be rounded yet relaxed, not protruded forward. You will feel the vowel deepen as you ascend to the upper pitch. Repeat this exercise. After you achieve freedom in the larynx sustain the upper pitch and sing the Italian syllables *da me ni po tu*. This begins the correct training of the laryngeal muscles in vowel-consonant relationship. Notice that you feel the larynx drop after each consonant.

[musical notation: "i___ da me ni po tu___"]

6. Breathe, feeling the back wall of the pharynx (area behind the tongue-root) stretch open beyond the root of the tongue. Also imagine that you are breathing the tongue-root forward and the vertebrae open in the back of the neck.

I also recommend the Sieber *Vocalises,* composed by the Viennese Italian-trained vocal teacher Ferdinand Sieber (1822-1895). These exercises are a useful bridge between vocalization and singing repertoire; they can help the singer in applying open-throated, flexible laryngeal function in vowel-consonant relationship (*da me ni po tu la be*). In executing the Sieber *Vocalises*, remember the importance of separating the tongue-jaw function by employing both dentalized (/d/ and /t/) and flipped (/l/ and /n/) consonants, which will allow the jaw to remain in a slightly loose and lower position. The larynx should drop slightly after each consonant as the jaw moves slightly back after each consonant.

Exercises for the Open Throat

In my experience of teaching the principles of both the Italian and Swedish-Italian singing schools for over 35 years, I have found the following sequence of simple and basic exercises to be a way to most efficiently and easily access the open throat.

Exercise 3.16: Use of the Pre-yawn Sirening Stretch

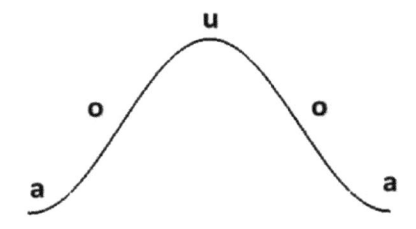

```
        u
      /   \
    o       o
   /         \
  a           a
```

An important preliminary exercise in establishing an open acoustical space is to have the singer "stretch through the registers," using the pre-yawn sensation. Lindquest called this exercise "sirening through the registers." It is an ascending glissando from the low range (using the /a/ vowel) to the middle range (using the /o/ vowel) and into the upper *passaggio* range (using the /u/ vowel), and descending glissando through the same series of vowels. It must be employed as the singer simultaneously concentrates on pharyngeal stretch and body connection. It is a good idea to cradle the jaw with the hands when doing this exercise in order to keep it relaxed.

You will notice that the /o/ vowel encourages the larynx to tilt in the middle register, allowing the correct head voice transition from the upper middle register into the higher range. Sirening through the registers needs to be exercised with a healthy body posture and a rounded or oval mouth shape. Use of a mirror can be helpful when first learning this exercise, because it helps in monitoring the jaw position and the mouth shape. This specific exercise awakens the voice early in daily vocalization, and it helps the singer feel the increase of throat space as he or she ascends higher in pitch.

Exercise 3.17: Use of the Open-Throated Hum Applied to Pharyngeal Vowels

This is an exceptionally effective exercise that I use for the development of the open throat.

m m m m m

- Place the tongue between the lips.

- Hum a descending five-tone scale on staccato, imagining a vowel-stretch directly behind the tongue-root and in front of the back wall of the oropharynx. Feel the hum vibrate under the sternum, as this anchors the sound to the body and creates a more natural vocal protection.

i e a o u

- Next, with the tongue in a normal position in the mouth, and keeping the same open feeling of vowel stretch behind the tongue-root, sing a five-tone descending staccato scale, using the five Italian vowels, /i/ /e/ /a/ /o/ /u/. **Note:** *It is important to image the vowel-origin space behind the tongue-root for this exercise to be successful.*

m m m m m   i e a o u

This exercise works extremely well for the majority of singers, and it works especially well for those who have a history of a closed-throated vocal production.

Exercise 3.18: Employing the Laryngeal Pivot

Use the interval of an ascending major third for this exercise, which is designed to acquaint the singer with the *tilt* or *pivot* of the larynx. Use of this exercise directly assists the singer in the release of the upper *passaggio*. In working with the laryngeal tilt, remember that the back of the neck must be free of tension.

Before the onset, breathe the larynx about half way downward, while keeping a forward, wide, and arched tongue position. As you breathe the larynx slightly down and wide at inhalation, make sure that you also breathe with the tongue in an "ng" /ŋ/ position, keeping the tongue-root wide. This avoids depression of the larynx with the back of the tongue. Use of the *ng* /ŋ/ will encourage a natural arch of the tongue, which produces higher overtones. Make sure that the front of the tongue achieves a wide position as well, as this increases the ring factor and discourages bunching of the back of the tongue.

- Using a rounded /i/ vowel, sing the interval of a major third up, and then back down again. Check that the /i/ embouchure is rounded in an oval /o/ shape (not spread), and that the jaw position is back.

- As you ascend to the upper pitch of the major third, concentrate on the vowel dropping slightly lower in the pharynx. When moving toward the upper pitch, you will feel a small movement of the larynx slightly down and forward. This movement is often referred to as the *laryngeal tilt*, a factor necessary to open sufficient acoustical space for correct head register transition.
- After the laryngeal tilt is mastered, go through all five Italian vowels using the major third. Feel the same slight downward and forward motion of the larynx for all the vowels.

Exercise 3.19: The Pre-vomit Reflex

i_____

This exercise should only be used in the middle register upward toward the upper *passaggio* range. Be sure to do this exercise using an oval or rounded mouth shape and a slightly back and down jaw.

Use a pitch sequence involving ascending thirds for this exercise. As you move upward on intervals of thirds, feel the base of the larynx expand slightly wider. This encourages what is sometimes called the pre-vomit feeling at the base of the larynx.

In this exercise, the pharynx wall expands in an east-west direction. This sensation should be accompanied by a feeling of width in the root of the tongue, as well as an east/west stretch at the soft palate. The east-west image assists in achieving a more open acoustical space without over-stretching laryngeal muscles.

In Summary: Characteristics of Closed-Throated Singing

The following factors are commonly present in closed-throated vocal production.

1. High larynx position at inhalation, or at the onset or attack. This often results from locking the jaw at inhalation and/or insufficient body connection or support.
2. Dropping or collapsing of the rib cage at phonation, resulting in pushing too much breath pressure through the larynx.
3. Using mouth vowels instead of pharyngeal vowels. This can be a result of studying a speaking-level training for the upper range instead of adopting an open-throated training, which involves full- throated open vowel forms and careful vowel alteration, especially when approaching the upper *passaggio* and the high range.

4. Spreading the mouth position (*embouchure*). This use of a "smile" technique raises the larynx. Notice that a "smile" technique also creates a false sense of ring, which in the upper range results in shrillness.
5. Using a flat or retracted tongue position, which fills the oropharynx with the tongue root, thereby distorting full resonance. This can also be a major cause of vowel distortion.
6. Forward jaw position, which raises the larynx and encourages a retracted and/or flat tongue position. It also does not allow for a healthy closure of the vocal folds and closes the acoustical space.
7. Forward thrust of the head posture, which also raises the larynx and disturbs healthy vocal fold closure.
8. Breathing under the rib cage instead of allowing the lower abdominal muscles to release straight downward and the lower back muscles to expand.
9. Thrusting of the jaw downward dramatically at consonant function in text. This engages the gag reflex at the tongue-root, which stops the breath flow, and disturbs pure legato line.
10. Opening the mouth too much in the middle and low registers, often cutting the ring factor in tonal production. This is caused by a retraction of the tongue, which also weights the voice, causing imbalance in registration.
11. Use of a collapsed soft palate, causing occasional nasality.
12. Bunching (narrowing) the tongue-root at inhalation, which tends to close the pharynx and can also contribute to nasality in the voice.
13. Over-lifting the outer cheek muscles. This can result in a locked jaw, high breath, and a high larynx position.
14. Over-stretching the soft palate vertically, often leading to a depression of the tongue-root, causing a false sense of color in the voice.

In Summary: Characteristics of Open-Throated Singing

It is always important to not go to the extreme in applying these concepts. It is possible to over-space the throat, which can create other vocal issues (for instance, a retracted tongue and hyperextension of the laryngeal muscles). Even though these are excellent concepts, they must be applied judiciously, and under the supervision of a good diagnostic teacher.

1. Opening of the nasopharynx, the oropharynx, and the laryngopharynx at inhalation. This includes a wide soft palate, wide laryngeal release, and forward arched tongue position.
2. Tilting or pivoting of the larynx slightly down and forward in the upper middle register, allowing for an easy transition into head voice.
3. Release of the larynx (slight dropping and widening of the base of the larynx) at inhalation and after each consonant in text.
4. Slight wrapping of the jaw straight back after each consonant in text in the lower and middle registers. This encourages the larynx to drop slightly after each consonant, thereby opening the pharynx. (*Note: the jaw must be relaxed, never locked in position.*)
5. Pharyngeal vowel alteration and French nasal vowel alteration when ascending toward the upper *passaggio* and high range. The pharyngeal vowel alteration is designed to open more acoustical space, while nasal resonance vowel alteration is designed to release the tongue. (*Note: French nasal vowels are not produced with a nasal sound, but must be accompanied by sufficient acoustical space.*)
6. Breathing with a rounded mouth position and sustaining it throughout text in repertoire. This requires that the singer use a more oval shaped embouchure for vowels and consonants during the pronunciation of text. This mouth position needs to be opened

more for the highest range, depending upon the individual singer's physical structure.

7. Low breath at inhalation, using the breath to inspire the opening of the acoustical space. This requires a released jaw. *(**Note:** the lower back should expand at inhalation.)*
8. Perfect onset (attack), which results from properly resisting breath pressure with the lower body support muscles (i.e. lumbar muscles), coordinated upper and lower abdominal muscles, pectorals, and suspended, open intercostal muscles in both the front and back rib cage.
9. Correct facial posture, which includes a subtle lift of the muscles under the outer cheekbone area (this widens the soft palate), sinking of the cheek muscles at the back teeth (this opens the oropharynx), and jaw slightly down and back (this allows the larynx to release downward).
10. Proper suspended body posture, which includes a tall spine and open rib cage. This also inspires an open lower lumbar area, allowing the singer to access lower back strength.
11. Use of the "ng" /ŋ/ tongue position as home base in pronunciation of text. This allows more space in the oropharynx by bringing the tongue mass up and forward out of the pharyngeal space. *(**Note:** This is only an approximate tongue posture used as "home position." The tongue must be allowed to move freely during pronunciation of text.)*
12. Correct employment of the basic tongue-tip positions for the 5 Italian vowels, which releases tension in the tongue-root. Use this concept only in the middle and low registers.
13. Correct head posture, which includes approximate alignment of the ears over the shoulders. The head may need to release slightly upward from upper *passaggio* into the higher range, depending upon the singer's physical structure. A tall open neck must still be sustained, while keeping the gentle curve in the back of the neck.
14. Separation of tongue/jaw function when pronouncing text. This includes use of Italian dentalized and flipped consonants in text,

such as d, t, l, and n. The tongue tip must touch behind the upper teeth to pronounce these consonants properly.

Final Words

"Never tell a singer to place the voice forward! The mask vibration or "ng" /ŋ/ feeling will reflect there as a result of an open throat and forward tongue position."

"Put a thread of "ng" /ŋ/ over the vowel, but not a rope. This will keep the sensation subtle and healthy!"

"If you crash your tongue, you will crash your registers and close the throat. Breaks will become very prominent in the voice."

  - Allan R. Lindquest

"We sing with the feeling of one vowel in the throat."

"A singer needs to accomplish the ability to move from pitch to pitch in the middle register without the throat moving. This needs to first be accomplished on a hum function."

  - Giovanni Battista Lamperti

CHAPTER 4

Lindquest's Perfect Attack—Defining Garcia's Coup de Glotte

There are numerous advantages to mastering healthy vocal fold adduction at the onset (beginning of tone, or attack): first, achieving Lindquest's "perfect attack" creates an immediate access to healthy, resonant tone; second, the compressed sub-glottal breath allows the vocal folds to vibrate on what Lindquest called a "pillow of breath," rather than large, pushed expulsions of air pressure; and third, it allows the acoustical space in the throat to stay open, because the larynx sustains a lower position. This lower laryngeal position is a direct result of balance in the sub-glottal breath control. When the concept of cord closure is mastered correctly, the singer can sing more freely for longer periods without suffering vocal fatigue.[1]

I will frequently ask a singer, "How do you start your first note?" The result of this question is often an empty look coming from across the

---

1   Please note that cord closure is a temporary study, until the cords learn to close automatically after inhalation.

studio! Many singers have never taken the time to study or analyze what happens in the body at the onset, which is the absolute core beginning of healthy phonation. Efficient onset (beginning of tone) has been described in several ways. Allan Lindquest called it the "perfect attack", William Vennard referred to it as an "imaginary /h/", Lamperti promoted the idea of a small amount of "breath before tone," while Garcia taught the *coup de glotte*.[2]

Allan Lindquest described the *coup de glotte:* "*The vocal cords gently close directly after inhalation, allowing a healthy subglottic compression of breath. Then the singer employs the body connection to move the perfect amount of air through the vocal folds.*" The body/breath coordination encourages the perfect small breath stream present in healthy phonation. By encouraging the vocal cords to begin to vibrate at the exact instant that the support muscles of the lower body begin to engage, the *coup de* glotte is a useful tool for the singer who has historically over-blown the vocal cords.

Mastering the perfect attack takes an investment of time. Allan Lindquest befriended Jussi Björling in 1938 while studying in Stockholm. The two singers were fascinated with vocal technique, and they spent long periods discussing various aspects of technical study, frequently focusing on which concepts achieved the most spontaneous, healthy result. Björling told Lindquest that it took him almost four years to master his "perfect attack." However, the timeframe for mastering this varies depending upon the singer's background of study, and his/her mind-body coordination.

The Body Connection

Lower body engagement is the primary source of regulating the sub-glottal air pressure, inspiring and balancing the movement of the small, equalized breath stream on which we speak and sing healthily. Healthy phonation is related to several natural functions of the body,

---

[2] It is unfortunate that Garcia's term translates as "*stroke* of the glottis." Garcia himself eventually regretted using the term because many teachers and singers took the concept too far and employed a thick, glottal attack, which can be injurious to the voice.

including laughing, sneezing, coughing, grunting, and moaning. But what muscles move in what direction?

There are several responses in the body at the onset or "attack":

- The lower abdominal muscles stretch slightly forward, wide and upward;

- The lower back (lumbar) muscles stretch wide and slightly downward;

- The solar plexus stretches in an east-west direction (never locking in the middle area);

- The sternum stretches straight forward (not up or down);

- The side waist muscles stretch in a gradual, east-west direction; and

- The ribs begin a slow elongation (a concept described in the research work of Carl Stough, and reflected in the Italian *appoggio)*.

When all of these responses are present, the lower laryngeal muscles naturally expand rather than constrict, allowing the beginning of what many refer to as open throat.

Appoggio

The *appoggio* plays a huge role in guiding the even breath-flow, through the slow, forward leaning of the body, beginning with a forward stretch of the sternum. The forward stretch of the sternum inspires the lower body muscles to engage (resist) elastically, resulting in healthy phonation without either over-blowing or under-fueling the vocal folds. This is the body/breath connection that allows a musical phrase to be fueled with the perfect small breath stream.

Lindquest used the concept of *appoggio* in his teaching, requesting in addition that the singer begin the tone with a slight grunt reflex at the lumbar muscles (lower back). He would always remind me that healthy sub-glottal compression is dependent upon correct body posture, which included a tall spine, a suspended back rib cage, a slight looseness or bend at the hip sockets and knees, and the slight engagement of the upper-gluteal muscles.

For singers who suffered under-compression of breath (or too much loose breath through the larynx) Lindquest requested that they engage the upper gluteal muscles, which inspires the lumbar muscles to engage, offering the singer a better breath compression. The slight upper gluteal-lumbar response is a result of the body weight being slightly forward on the front of the feet. The tall spine stretches from the hip sockets to the top of the head, with a suspended (not hyper-extended) ribcage.[3] I often tell singers to stretch tall in the spine, as though there were space between each two vertebrae. For the singer who over-blows, this seems to inspire the lower body muscles to engage, inviting a more balanced sub-glottal compression.

Cord Closure

Lindquest's perfect attack allows the vocal folds to gently come together (adduct) after inhalation. This action automatically encourages a more perfect subglottal breath compression, a requirement for accomplishing steadiness of tone, registration balance; it is the basis for the development of ring, or maximum resonance, in the voice. Lindquest described breath and ring as partners traveling at the same rate of speed. If breath dominates ring, the result is often a breathy, over-blown, unfocused tone. If ring dominates breath motion, then the singer often manufactures a squeezed tone with a closed throat and too much tension at the vocal folds. Neither extreme is desirable. What we need is the balance of the two factors working together.

---

[3] This is somewhat related to the principles of the Alexander Technique.

Lindquest referred to the study of vocal fold closure as the process of "sealing the vocal cords." He presented a number of approaches to finding the perfect coordination of healthy cord closure. During my study with him, he would asked me to imagine that I had taken a breath to say something and then had forgotten my thought. He would also ask me to say "uh-oh", as if I had dropped something on the floor; or he would have me gently speak the words "every orange" and feel the very gentle glottal closure. Included in my instruction was to "click" the vocal folds gently with hardly any sound (Caruso called this the "silent cough"). When these techniques are employed carefully they create a perfect closure of the vocal folds on the thin-edge function. Lindquest often spoke of using only the "thin edges" of the vocal cords at phonation. This is a powerful image that discourages vocal weight, which is the use of too much cord mass too high in pitch.

Another concept Lindquest used was "capping the breath":

"You will first feel the larynx drop and widen as the tongue moves forward toward the /ŋ/ position. The soft palate widens somewhat like the shape of a dome. Then, you will feel something "cap" the breath. This "capping" is the perfect closure of the cords after inhalation. Then you are ready to begin to speak, leaning on the musical phrase using the forward sternum resistance, which inspires what many call support between the abdominal muscles and the lower lumbar muscles in the lower back. The appoggio, or leaning forward of the sternum, will inspire the first note to phonate correctly. You will always feel a thread of /ŋ/ over the beginning tone if the tongue is in the correct position. This helps to encourage movement of the small breath stream."

This forward stretch, or appoggio, is what I often find missing in a singer's technique.

After the perfect onset was more fully integrated, Lindquest would then ask me to repeatedly speak the closed /e/ vowel, using a firm yet elastic closure of the folds. The body would automatically pulsate as I spoke the vowel repeatedly at the vocal folds. This body response assists in regulating the healthy flow of air. He invited me to visualize Caruso's concept of feeling the vowels "under the cords", which brought my attention to a deeper sensation of vowel origin. Lindquest would say, "Let the cords speak the vowel deeply." He would often use Caruso's quote: "I feel the vowels below my vocal folds. I also always feel as though I am singing under my vocal cords, never pushing through them with too much breath." The concept of vowel depth is an especially useful tool for singers who have had a history of singing with a high larynx, accompanied by over-blowing the vocal folds.

The next step was to speak, alternating closed vowels and open vowels, without leaking too much breath, matching the vocal fold adduction between the two vowels. Lindquest used /e/ /a/ /e/ /a/ /e/ /a/, and /i/ /o/ /i/ /o/ /i/ /o/, etc., spoken at first on the same pitch. This exercise sustained the gentle closure of the vocal folds while moving from closed vowel to open vowel function. It enabled my throat to sustain tone on healthily adducted vocal folds, even though, generally, the cords tend to vibrate further apart on the open vowel sounds.

After the cords gently come together, they can begin to vibrate in coordination with the lumbar muscle expansion. Concentrating on the lumbar stretch also inspires the lower abdominal engagement. It must be emphasized that the breath is controlled slightly at the glottis, in conjunction with the body support system. But this glottal control is very slight and should not be taken to the extreme. We all need to sing with a healthy, small stream of air, but with the folds healthily approximated. This balance can be experienced in producing voiced consonants such as /v/ or /z/.

Avoiding the Hard Attack, or "Glottic Shock"

The perfect onset must never be confused with what is called "glottic shock". Glottic shock is a hard attack resulting from over-adduction (over-squeezing) of the vocal cords, which then requires the singer to begin the tone with a large expulsion of breath pressure, resulting in over-blowing. In considering glottic shock, there will often be a slight noise (an unvocal sound) right at the onset. A perfect onset is silent and body-connected, producing little or no noise. It is extremely important that teachers discuss the difference between these types of onset early in a singer's training in order to avoid confusion and potential future vocal problems.

To overcome the habit of the hard attack, teachers in the Old Italian School often spoke of "drinking in the voice" (in Italian, *inhalare la voce*). Although not a scientific description, the idea of "drinking in the voice" is a useful concept for singers who tend to over-blow their vocal folds at the onset. The feeling of "vacuuming the breath below the vocal folds" can also be a useful tool to help resolve the issue of the hard attack. The vacuuming sensation is a direct result of the *appoggio* (sternum connection), a natural response that we feel in body-connected laughter.[4] Caruso shared this concept with Lindquest in 1914 during their sessions together.

Evelyn Reynolds used the hum function that was started with a puff of air through the nasal port. This guarantees that the body connects under the perfect onset. Another approach is to laugh with the lips closed and the jaw unhinged or slightly open down and back. This avoids glottic shock. I also recommend that voiced consonants such as /ŋ/, /v/, or /z/ be used temporarily until the vocal folds learn not to over-adduct after the breath or at the onset. The process of correcting this issue can take time, but the resulting vocal health is well worth the process.

Avoiding the Breathy Attack

Lindquest referred to the breathy attack as a "leaky" attack, which tires the voice quickly and can easily lead to hoarseness.[5] A breathy onset can be injurious to a singer's technique over time, resulting in a high larynx position, a shrill upper range, lack of registration balance, and lack

---

[4] Lindquest often compared the correct onset with the laugh reflex.
[5] Those who speak with a breathy tone will experience vocal fatigue. When we hear someone speak with a resonant voice, this indicates that the person is speaking with healthy cord closure and an open pharynx, free of breathiness.

of pitch control. As a result of the higher laryngeal position the pharyngeal space is compromised and resonance is diminished.

Breathy onset can result from a lack of cord closure after inhalation, and/or a body that is too loose, with a lack of resistance in the lower body muscles (which holds back breath pressure and regulates the small breath stream). When the body is not engaged sufficiently to maintain a strong, tall posture, the result is the over-blowing of the vocal folds (lack of healthy adduction).

Flagstad said, "*If I achieve a perfect onset on the first note, then I have no difficulty singing a musical phrase of almost any length on one breath. But if my attack is incorrect [breathy] without enough closure of the folds, then I cannot redeem myself until I breathe for the next phrase.*" When Flagstad first auditioned for Dr. Gillis Bratt in 1916, he told her that her tone was so immature and breathy that it reminded him of the voice of a child (!), but that it was possible to resolve the vocal fault with hard work. During her study with him, this vocal issue was solved using specific exercises that helped her to feel a healthy closure of the vocal folds and to feel the body connect to the sound.[6]

Connoisseurs of classical music know the name Jenny Lind, a world-famous 19th century Swedish soprano. At one point in her career, Ms. Lind began to develop vocal technical issues: she became quickly vocally tired from employing too much breath pressure at the onset. She traveled to Paris to study Manuel Garcia, who limited her to two, 20-minute, supervised sessions per day, working almost exclusively on healthy vocal fold closure. Once Lind had regained proper vocal cord coordination after inhalation, she was able to continue her career for years afterward.

"Freeing the Breath"—A Cause of Breathy Tone?

Many have heard the term "freeing the breath" in voice studios. If employed with a healthy image of proper breath usage, the concept can be of benefit in some circumstances. However, if applied incorrectly, it

---

[6] Howard Vogt, *Flagstad: Singer of the Century*. London: Sacker and Warburg, 1987, 48.

can result in a lack of healthy sub-glottal breath compression, leading to throaty, unhealthy singing. In addition, some singers are confused by the belief that if they "free the breath," then the laryngeal muscles will relax completely. Again, in some circumstances this concept can be helpful, especially if the singer has developed a habit of clutching or grabbing at the laryngeal muscles. But for others it can be disastrous, leading to the over-blowing of the voice.

Defining "Free Breath"

The concept of free breath refers to the small, compressed breath stream that fuels the overtones of healthy singing. In other words, it refers to finding the balance of holding back breath pressure with the lower body muscles (as in body-connected laughter), while allowing the tiny breath stream to flow. This duality is critical for healthy singing, and it must be taught in the body carefully in order for the singer to find balance.

"Free Breath" and Body Connection

Some singers employ too much loose (uncontrolled) air through the vocal folds at the onset, which makes it difficult for them to make it through a musical phrase. Lindquest once said to me, "David, you have too much wild loose air thrusting through your larynx and vocal cords!" This was due to my lack of body connection and incorrect posture. The perfect attack (onset) is *only* effective when total postural balance and body connection are achieved.

Directing the Breath Flow

Use of the term "freeing the breath" without proper explanation of how to direct the breath flow, or how to connect to the body, can be counterproductive. In some cases, it can encourage breathy, pushed, throaty singing. After the perfect onset is achieved, the singer should never direct a push of air pressure out of the mouth cavity: this produces an unhealthy, unprotected tone (sometimes called a "mouthy" tone or a "'belted'" sound). When tone is produced this way, the singer has no true foundation for healthy breath compression, nor can they achieve a protected tone.

Lamperti instructed singers to imagine that the small breath stream moved inward, up beyond the uvula, and then through the nasal port. Lamberti used the image of spinning the breath and resonance back and up beyond the soft palate, which assists in sustaining healthy cord closure and protected tone throughout the musical phrase.[7] If the instructor tells a singer to move the tiny breath stream inward beyond the soft palate or uvula area (instead of out the mouth), the problem of over-blowing at the onset is often avoided. Of course this is scientifically impossible but, like the concept of *inhalare la voce*, it brings a desired result, helping the singer to find vocal balance.

Using the sensation of "ng" (/ŋ/)

To close the cords without glottic shock, Lindquest would frequently request that the singer employ "a thread of 'ng' /ŋ/" over a starting tone, which closes the cords without glottic shock. The /ŋ/ was imaged with the middle of the tongue, not with the back of the tongue (to avoid tongue-root tension). Taught in conjunction with the concept of the airflow moving beyond the uvula, this encourages the singer to feel tone circulating in the head before moving out to the listening audience. In teaching this concept, Lindquest was referencing a Lamperti concept that works effectively in the majority of cases.

The use of /ŋ/ is a fundamental idea that introduces residual frontal vibration (ring), which is a result of the open pharynx and the forward tongue position. This resulting ring has nothing to do with "placement", because it has been scientifically proven that we cannot place sound.[8] If studied carefully, with laryngeal release and an open acoustical space, the /ŋ/ can act as a guide for the singer in navigating registration. The /ŋ/ is a solid tool for achieving Lindquest's perfect attack or onset; however, if

---

[7] This is a concept that Dixie Neill used during my study with her in 1983.
[8] It has been scientifically proven that we cannot "place" sound. See *The Science of the Singing Voice* by Dr. Johan Sundberg.

a singer cannot produce the /ŋ/ with vocal freedom, I suggest replacing it with the single consonant /n/.

Diagnosing Onset Problems

Many singers come into a voice lesson dealing with the concept of onset from one of two extremes—either they are over-blowing, using a breathy attack; or they are over-squeezing the vocal folds, frequently employing a hard attack. In terms of vocal health, neither is acceptable. It is up to the vocal instructor to train his/her diagnostic ear to determine the nature of the singer's onset. I also recommend that teachers study the shape of the larynx carefully to determine if the singer is narrowing or squeezing the laryngeal muscles. If the singer is squeezing the laryngeal muscles, the base of the neck will take on a reversed parenthesis, or half-moon)(shape rather than expanding slightly, which is the desired stretch of the lower laryngeal muscles.

What are the characteristics of an incorrect onset? If there is a lack of vocal fold approximation (closure) at the onset, there is often breathiness of tone or flatness in pitch. When the singer over-squeezes the vocal folds in an attempt to control the breath at the glottis, the result is a thin tone, a result of a closed throat or a high laryngeal position. If there is too much glottal pressure, there will often be a small "noise" before the tone begins an indication that too much muscular effort is engaged. Again, to find the feeling of correct glottal closure, I recommend that the singer speak the words *"every orange"* gently, as Lindquest suggested.

Restoring Vocal Health

I have taught many mature singers who have enjoyed long careers, singing well over a period of many years. I have also worked with those who developed major vocal problems over the years due to the absence of healthy vocal fold adduction. In many cases, the singer had simply not learned to close the cords after inhalation.

A carefully employed sequence of cord closure exercises can bring the singer to the point of experiencing the voice as feeling freer and younger. It is often a short-term study until the onset becomes healthy and balanced. I have witnessed how Old World concepts can help singers from both extremes to regain healthy vocal function. Whether the singer comes from a history of singing with a vocal wobble (wide, slow vibrato) or a tremolo (fast vibrato), these problems begin to disappear with employment of a healthy thin-edge vocal fold adduction. The voice then begins to vibrate in a healthier function. Balance in registration develops quickly, and the singer again becomes more capable of artistic expression.

Case Study: Lyric Soprano

I worked with a young Swedish lyric soprano who had sung for years professionally in opera houses, was popular on stage, and had appeared in several opera videos. She enjoyed early professional success, much like Jenny Lind in the previous century. At age 32, she was forced to give up singing due to major vocal problems. When we started our work together there were no obvious symptoms of breathiness or unfocused tone in her voice. It took little time to realize that her throat was closed and her larynx position was too high. Her laryngeal muscles were inflexible and she had no access to the laryngeal tilt in the upper middle register. Working approximately four times per week, it took six weeks to release her laryngeal muscles. This process required a lot of concentrated work on the laryngeal tilt, pharyngeal vowels, and the release of the larynx at inhalation.

However, once her throat had opened, the true source of her vocal problems was revealed: when her throat was open, she could only produce a breathy tone because her vocal folds were not closing after inhalation. Since her past technique had involved squeezing her laryngeal muscles in order to close her vocal cords, we found that her cords could not approximate well when the pharynx was open and the laryngeal muscles released. Her high-larynx technique had also created a false resonance, generated by squeezing the interior laryngeal muscles. This kind of squeeze is less obvious and more difficult to diagnose in some high soprano singers. Her past vocal study had never revealed the difference between her squeezed, false resonance and a healthily ringing tone. *Note:* True open-throated resonance reflects warm color and ring (higher overtones).

Many singers make the mistake of closing their throats so that they can hear the sound more clearly and loudly in their inner hearing. With the cords gently closed and the throat open, the singer frequently perceives less inner volume—in fact, the sound can seem somewhat distant and far away. When the throat (pharynx) is open and the larynx released with the laryngeal tilt, the singer must then learn to guide the voice through sensations rather than sound. This is why Lindquest consistently reminded his singers to feel, rather than listen to themselves.

In the case of this Swedish soprano, as soon as she was able to open her throat, we could proceed to the second step in her vocal alignment: adding gentle cord closure exercises. I used the same exercises that Lindquest had given to me in 1979, based on the work of Dr. Gillis Bratt, who was the last technical teacher of Kirsten Flagstad. The positive results were immediate. This retraining allowed her to achieve her full vocal function. In turn, we were able to apply this vocal coordination to her repertoire, and she was able to resume her career. The process required intense work, but the rewards were well worth the effort. She sang two world-premiere operas the following summer without experiencing any vocal difficulties.

Case Study: Lyric Soprano

A few years ago, an internationally known lyric soprano came to me for technical work. She had sustained an international career for over 25 years; however, she was experiencing a lack of adduction of the vocal folds in the middle register. This made it extremely difficult to tune pitches or employ fuller volume in the mid-range. The primary issue was the lack of the laryngeal tilt in the middle register. The laryngeal tilt stretches the vocal folds appropriately in order for the light mechanism (head voice) to function correctly. When the middle register started to respond, her first question was, "Why have I not heard of these concepts before?" She was referring to the lack of vocal fold adduction and how infrequently it is discussed in many vocal circles.

Because she was excellent at self-supervision, her retraining process involved only a total of about seventeen hours of instruction. After the first three lessons, there was a dramatic change in vocal fold approximation, mainly because of the laryngeal tilt. And after learning the laryngeal tilt, she quickly accomplished the perfect attack (onset). Two months afterward, she sang a recital to rave reviews. I remember that she called me on the telephone saying, "This was the first positive review I have had in seven years!"

Case Study: Bass-Baritone

Several years ago I was contacted by a professional bass-baritone who was concerned about having developed some vocal problems. He had been singing for over 25 years in major opera houses in Europe and the U.S. At our first meeting, it was easy to hear that his primary issues involved pitch, and he was suffering the beginning stages of a vocal wobble (wide, slow vibrato). His vocal issues were directly related to the fact that he did not close the cords on the thin edges after inhalation—his onset was based on a large expulsion of breath pressure, which thickened the vocal folds.

The first step toward resolution of this problem was to correct his old habit of taking too much breath at inhalation (preparatory breath), and employing too much breath pressure at the onset. Accessing the thin-edge function of the vocal folds enabled easier access to head voice function, and in decreasing his use of too much vocal weight. He soon realized that when he employed the fine edges of the vocal folds, he did not need to use so much breath pressure at the onset or attack. After one month of vocal work, he began to regain the tautness and the thin-edge function in the vocal fold folds, which we accessed through the use of specific staccato exercises.

This process can be more challenging for larger, lower-voiced singers. Within a three-month period, this bass-baritone's voice began to reestablish high overtones, and the vibrato began to increase in speed to a normal rate. He resumed his career, performing major dramatic roles, including Wagnerian roles. He would still come into the New York studio for lessons periodically to check his vocal balance.

Exercises to Access Healthy Vocal Fold Closure

While the subtle aspects of Garcia's *coup de glotte* may be challenging to explain, it can be an even more daunting task to find exercises that encourage healthy employment of this vocal behavior. I have found the following exercises useful in achieving perfect onset and cord closure.

Exercise 4.1

Make several strong hissing sounds, bringing your attention to the slight secondary expansion of the body when the sound begins. This should be trained as the body's response at the onset or attack. This resistance is the function that assists in creating a perfect closure of the vocal folds. It is accomplished through controlled, flexible lower body resistance.

Exercise 4.2

Use the concept that vowels are formed below the vocal folds. Place a fingertip at the base of the larynx and speak the vowels *a, e, i, o, u,* as though the strength of each vowel is at the approximate location of the vocal folds.

Exercise 4.3

Unhinge the jaw slightly, using the weight of your fingertips. Using the same concept as Exercise 4.1 above, speak the five vowels without changing the position of the jaw. Allow the tongue tip to move in order to produce clarity in the vowels. Think the vowels under the cords. Notice that the body engages when this concept is employed. Make certain that there is sufficient breath-flow as the vowels are spoken.

Exercise 4.4

ev' - ry___ or - ange

Unhinge the jaw slightly as in Exercise 4.2 above and speak the words *"every orange."* Notice the very slight glottal closure at the beginning of each word. The unhinging of the jaw should allow you to feel the cords come together, creating a firmness of the vowels at the glottis. Then add a 5-tone scale using these words, keeping the same sensation. It will give the singer the feeling of the proper coordination.

Exercise 4.5

uh oh uh oh___

Speak the sound *"uh-oh,"* as though you have dropped something on the floor. You will feel a flipping together of the vocal folds at the glottal closure and then you will feel the sound sustain on the perfect stream of air on the "oh". Then speak the "uh", suspend the sound for a second, and then sing a descending 5-tone scale on the "oh", using sufficient breath-flow.

Exercise 4.6

Speak the /e/ vowel repeatedly at the glottis. This may feel like a tiny cough without breath. Then alternate speaking /e/ and /a/, keeping the same closure of the folds. Work back and forth from the /e/ to the /a/ without losing tautness at the vocal folds. Then sing a 5-tone scale using the two contrasting vowels.

Exercise 4.7

Imitate the sound of a cow mooing.[9] Use this idea with an open jaw and lips closed. Keep the chest posture low and feel the back rib cage open. As you "moo," you feel a deep moan, accompanied by the resistance in the lower body muscles. This integrates the ring factor and the body connection simultaneously. The vocal folds pull perfectly together for healthy singing and the deep "moo" or "moan" assists in producing the perfect air stream for healthily singing a musical phrase.

Final Thoughts

"Singing with the vocal cords apart is like a cellist trying to play without enough rosin on the bow or like playing an expensive clarinet with a split in the reed!"

- Allan R. Lindquest

---

[9] If you are not familiar with this sound, numerous examples may be found on the Internet.

CHAPTER 5

Vocal Protection: Its Role in Acoustically Balanced Singing

The purpose of vocal protection is to help the singer to establish and sustain stamina in singing. Acoustical protection has also been referred to as the *vocal cover*, *coperto*, *cupo*, or what Allan Lindquest called the *voce cuperto*. Having its roots in the Old Italian School, it is a concept that is the foundation of establishing and sustaining head voice development.

Voce Cuperto Defined

Lindquest defined the *voce cuperto* as singing a tiny Italian /u/ vowel with a slightly unhinged jaw and with a fully opened acoustical space (open throat). He used the term *voce cuperto* to refer to an expanded /u/ vowel in the pharynx, accompanied by the ring of the "*ng*". It is a fundamental principle that is at the core of the Italian and Swedish-Italian singing schools.

The *voce cuperto* is established and stabilized through training a sufficient stretch of the walls of the pharynx. This stretch begins at inhalation and further expands at the onset (attack). It must be taught in combination with the correct alteration of the vowels in the pharynx in order for the singer to reap maximum benefits. The tongue should always speak the integrity of the vowels as the pharyngeal stretch alters the vowels. This develops clarity in language while sustaining an open acoustical space.

Benefits of Voce Cuperto

If employed correctly, the open space of *voce cuperto* can protect the voice and discourage over-singing, or pushing too much breath pressure through the vocal folds. It is achieved by singing through a small embouchure with an open pharyngeal space and a strong /u/ vowel at or below the glottis. The strength of the vowel at the glottis, a Caruso concept, helps in maintaining an open throat by assisting in the control of the subglottic breath pressure. Caruso employed this as a fundamental part of his vocalization.[1]

A Therapeutic Tool. Because the *voce cuperto* also encourages the use of the thin or fine edges of the vocal folds, it has been instrumental as a therapeutic tool in restoring vocal health to damaged voices, and in realigning voices that have been poorly trained. It is also a major factor in registration balance. When Dr. Van Lawrence (who was the designated laryngologist for the Houston Grand Opera for many years) first saw the *voce cuperto* function with a fiber optic camera, he said it looked as though the cords were receiving a massage on the thin edges. Dr. Lawrence made this observation during the course of scientific research of Dr. Barbara Mathis, whose doctoral dissertation demonstrated the therapeutic value of the Lindquest vocal exercises over a five-year period.[2]

---

[1] Caruso told this to Lindquest in 1914.
[2] Barbara Mathis, *Selected vocal exercises and their relationship to specific laryngeal conditions: a description of seven case studies*. 1990: University of North Texas.

Vowel Alignment. The *voce cuperto* assists in developing strength of resonance through exercising the smaller, connected, yet lighter part of the voice. Aligning all of the vowels in a similar pharyngeal space creates an overall professional tonal quality. Applying the release of the pharyngeal /u/ vowel to the other vowels is fundamental in achieving this, and it is basic to the Swedish-Italian and Italian schools. Lindquest called this acoustical result the "vowel line-up." Lotte Lehmann, who was a colleague of Lindquest, believed in mixing vowels to achieve balance and/or the acoustical protection. She once told Lindquest, "the /a/ vowel is the most dangerous vowel of all; it needs a bit of /u/, /i/, and /e/ mixed in it." Notice that she first used the /u/ vowel. This was her approach to mixing vowels in order to help create a vocal protection and clarity of vowel sound, especially on open vowel sounds. If you vocalize on a sustained single pitch using this vowel sequence, you will notice a more aligned acoustical balance in the /a/. There will also be an acoustical release which allows this tiny /u/ to fill a theater.

Equalizing the Voice. Use of the *voce cuperto* can assist in solving such problems as a wide vibrato (wobble) and registration imbalance, especially in the female middle voice and upper passaggio. Additionally, it is an exercise that is instrumental in lengthening the vocal tract, encouraging more closure of the vocal folds and creating more overall resonance.[3]

Float Function. Monserrat Caballé demonstrates great control in her high pianissimo through use of the *voce cuperto*, a basic training of the Italian School. I gave this exercise to Shirley Verrett in 1994. It can be best described as a small yet open-throated /u/ vowel that achieves and sustains the float function in the voice while simultaneously expanding the resonance factor.

Professional Sound. The *voce cuperto* training is at the very core of the development of a protected, professional sound. Many singers feel their voices go through growth periods, sometimes experiencing the

---

3   Lindquest also used the term "sweet spot" to describe the sensation of the voice working more automatically, especially in the upper *passaggio* range.

voice as becoming too large or out-of-control. As the voice matures, the singer is tempted to sing loudly, rather than continuing to exercise the small part of the voice with an open acoustical space, and with correct body connection. Birgit Nilsson once said at a master class in New York, "I get my big relaxed sound from my small, body-connected, free sound." We may wonder why so many great Italian singers sang so consistently directly after the turn of the twentieth century. Since the small Italian /u/ was at the heart of the Italian School, it is understandable that many great singers developed their voices with great power and control through the use of this concept, achieving a large tone from the small open throated tone.

Finding Vocal Protection

Finding a vocal protection that engages the proper balance between the frontal ring and the appropriate pharyngeal space accompanied by the Italian *appoggio* can be a challenge, but it is fundamental to free singing. A number of factors are involved in the proper development of acoustical release. In order to be fully effective, they must be employed carefully and in balance.

Open pharyngeal chambers, including the nasopharynx, oropharynx, and laryngopharynx. This must be accomplished without rigidity in the external throat muscles.

A forward, arched tongue position, forming the "*ng*" /ŋ/ shape with the middle or forward half of the tongue, and allowing the tongue-root to release. Correct employment of this tongue position creates sufficient acoustical space between the root of the tongue and the back wall of the oropharynx. The singer may feel the sensation that the tongue root is releasing slightly down and forward.

A relaxed, slightly down and back jaw position for the five basic Italian vowels. This encourages a more open acoustical space and an efficient vocal fold approximation.

A wide soft palate, which, along with the /ŋ/ tongue position, encourages the release of upper overtones and discourages depression of the larynx with the tongue-root. The resulting wide tongue-root takes pressure off the vocal folds and encourages healthy phonation.

Sinking and slightly forward stretch of the cheek muscles at the back and side teeth (molars). These cheek muscles are sometimes called the sucking muscles. Coordinated with the wide soft palate stretch, this reflexively opens the acoustical space beyond the tongue root and encourages a lower laryngeal position. When employed carefully this allows the tongue root to remain free.

Laryngeal tilt in the upper middle register, allowing a smoother transition into the head voice register.

Use of the appoggio, including development of the sensation of the forward stretch of the sternum, the wide stretch at the solar plexus (epigastrium), and the forward, wide, and upward stretch of the lower abdominal muscles.

Holding back the breath pressure with the lower lumbar muscles (lower back muscles) and regulating the outflow of air with the antagonistic pull between the upper and lower abdominal muscles.

A more closed mouth position in the middle register in order to sustain the pharyngeal /u/ vowel, a major factor in accomplishing the pharyngeal stretch. Round the embouchure only as far as you can keep the tongue root wide (over-rounding can narrow the pillars of fauces, narrowing the pharyngeal space). In early training, the singer often needs to close the mouth more, in order to feel more internal stretch in the pharynx. Later in development, once the soft palate has established a wider stretch and the larynx has integrated the tilt, the singer can open the mouth more (although some singers need to unhinge the jaw earlier in their development).

Chiaroscuro

Singing with the vocal protection results in what the Italian school calls *chiaroscuro* (bright-dark tone), a tone that is total and balanced in both upper and lower overtones. Old World training embraced the *chiaroscuro* because it was a way of accomplishing balance in singing that protected the voice over time, offering both stamina and longevity. The correct employment of the *chiaroscuro* requires that the singer use the full depth of pharyngeal vowels and body connection without hyperextending the outer laryngeal muscles. Brightness, or ring, is accomplished through the wide soft palate and the forward arched tongue position. Darkness, or color, is accomplished through the employment of the open pharynx, using a slightly lower laryngeal position, the release of the tongue root, and efficient use of the small breath stream on which we sing healthily.

Vocalizing either too dark or too bright leads to vocal imbalance. Healthy singing involves both color and ring, not just one or the other. We need to embrace both the bright and the dark aspects of the voice in order to create the next generation of healthy singers. Currently there seems to be an epidemic of high, light, bright, and unprotected singing, under the confused impression of "light and healthy" singing. It is costing many singers their vocal health and career opportunities as a direct result of a lack of laryngeal release. When singing, the vocal timbre should mirror a timbre similar to that of one's speaking tone.

Kirsten Flagstad's Experience

One of the most efficient approaches in achieving the vocal protection consists of balancing two basic sounds: the /ŋ/ and the expanded /u/ in the pharynx. Kirsten Flagstad spoke of finding the balance of ring and space by vocalizing musical phrases on the "ng" /ŋ/, while sustaining an open acoustical space behind it. She was also a proponent of a reflexive exercise using both the /e/ or /a/ vowels and the /ŋ/ interchangeably. Flagstad also described her use of the /ŋ/ as a tool to facilitate the narrow ring in her voice without closing the throat. This is a way of accomplishing focus or ring in the voice without closing the acoustical space. Lindquest referred to this as the "sweet spot."

Flagstad described the engagement of the *chiaroscuro* and the *appoggio* as a sensation of "dropping the voice into the body, a feeling that the voice and body become one entity." She also stated that she sang with a feeling of resistance under her sternum area—she called it "the resistance of a breastplate" on her chest.[4] Flagstad is describing the action of the sternum moving slowly forward at phonation, while maintaining the rounded, barrel chest shape. (This must be accomplished without pulling upward on the chest). It can feel similar to the Italian "deep cry" in the body, which encourages a long back rib cage and an open chest. Healthy vocal protection requires full coordination of the total body, a major factor in diminishing the "reach reflex" when moving toward the higher range.

You can hear Flagstad using this combination on a video of the great soprano's life, produced by the Flagstad Museum in 1995. It is especially evident in a clip of a rehearsal at the Mermaid Theater in London in 1950. Since most audio technology was unable to capture the full dimension of dramatic voices at that time, it is refreshing to hear Flagstad's voice recorded in a theater instead of a recording studio. The rehearsal excerpt is not more than 30 seconds in length, but her voice is heard in its totality within an excellent acoustical environment. The quality reflects a complete balance of space and ring, the two major factors that establish and sustain a vocal protection.

Establishing Longevity in Singing

Stamina in singing—the ability to sing for longer periods with little or no vocal fatigue (what Lindquest referred to as "full and light" singing)—is the core foundation of a longer performing career. Long careers are based on knowing how to consistently employ acoustical protection both in vocalization and repertoire. Professional singers who achieve the vocal protection enjoy years of free singing, often sustaining

---

4   This is not to be confused with hyperextension of the chest, or the chest pulling upwards too high in position, as this can lock the rib cage and tongue-root, and it can collapse the back ribcage.

careers covering decades. Mezzo-soprano Christa Ludwig is a fine example of a singer who mastered the vocal protection, avoiding any kind of spreading or pushing of the voice. It is obvious in her singing that her vocal longevity resulted from healthy self-monitoring, especially during the maturing process of her voice. Hans Hotter and Sir Thomas Allen are two more examples of singers who enjoyed long careers as a result of singing both with the vocal protection and full body connection. Helen Donath is another singer who has carefully supervised her voice over fifty years of excellent singing, keeping the light, connected part of her voice well exercised.

Vocal longevity and singing with a healthy vocal protection are unmistakably linked. My most recent teacher, Dr. Evelyn Reynolds, is a dramatic mezzo who has been singing for well over sixty years, and her voice still sounds healthy, young, and shimmering. She has sustained the healthy vocal protection (*chiaroscuro*) as taught in the Old Italian School throughout her career, singing with such international artists as Birgit Nilsson and Jussi Björling. She has had a great influence on my teaching career in regard to helping other singers to achieve this phenomenon.

A few years ago one of my students attended a lecture by Leontyne Price. During the question and answer session, he asked, "Ms. Price, how do you keep your voice in such wonderful condition?" She quickly answered, "Well, my dear, I vocalize every single day, paying close attention to *how* I am exercising my voice." There is no doubt that the aging factor in the voice has a lot to do with misuse, or singing with a lack of the vocal protection. I sometimes call the *cupo* the space that is the shock absorber for the vocal cords.

What some call "natural" singing is often high-larynx singing and is unsafe for the voice over time. I once taught a famous lyric soprano who had a career as a light singer; however, unlike Helen Donath, she never allowed her voice to open and expand naturally with maturity. This led to premature aging of her voice and the end of her career, mainly because she did not embrace the full vocal protection or the open throat. When I led her toward her mature, balanced sound, she could not deal with the change psychologically.

Dangerous Misconceptions

The concept of cover (acoustical protection) is designed to assist the singer in accomplishing vocal freedom; however, its incorrect application can have exactly the opposite effect. Many go too far in their pursuit of this concept, and the result can be devastating to a singer's vocal health. Unfortunately, some approaches to the vocal protection are based on manipulation of the throat muscles and tongue depression, rather than a more complete understanding of vocal acoustics based on pharyngeal vowel formation.

As a result of these extreme techniques of "cover," singers either tend to drive their voice too forward, or they over-space the throat, depressing the larynx with the tongue root and/or retracting the tongue. When this happens, phonation requires that the singer drive too much breath pressure through the larynx. Exercising the upper passaggio and high range without proper breath flow or with too much push of air pressure can be injurious to the voice over time. Singing in extremes, or what some would call either "too frontal" or "too back" creates a great amount of stress for the singer both vocally and emotionally. Developing healthy sensations of the physical coordination is the basis of establishing tonal consistency.

Voce Aperta or Voce Chiusa?

Confusion regarding the vocal protection can lead to tonal production that is too open or spread (*voce aperta*)—usually involving a wide, spread embouchure and a resulting high larynx position. Another extreme in approaching the concept of the vocal protection is known in Italian as *voce chiusa* (closed or darkened voice). When taught improperly, this technique employs tongue retraction or bunching, which can result in depression of the larynx with the tongue-root. *Voce chiusa*, in the correct meaning of the term, describes creating a vocal protection through balancing upper and lower overtones, a result of a more total understanding of balancing the acoustical space.

Singing Without an Acoustical Protection

In truth, it is injurious to the voice to sing without vocal protection and the results can be catastrophic, leading not only to technical problems but, in extreme cases, vocal damage. I have worked with many singers who had developed polyps, hemorrhages, bruises, nodules, and other kinds of vocal damage stemming from singing without vocal protection. When the vocal protection is absent, the singer must push breath pressure through the larynx in order to force phonation. Again, I quote Lindquest: "Breath pressure is the enemy of the vocal cords!"

The following problems can result from singing without the vocal protection:

Confusing laryngeal muscular pressure with open-throated singing. This includes heaving or the hyperextension of the external laryngeal muscles, sometimes called over-spacing. This sudden *"aggiustimento"* (or "cover") is in fact muscular manipulation of the throat.

Pushing too much breath pressure through the larynx to produce tone, an attempt on the singer's part to hear more volume.

Development of the "vocal wobble" or a wide, slow vibrato, often a result of pushing too much breath pressure through the larynx, which also disturbs registration balance.

Inability to produce pure vowel sounds, resulting from tension or bunching of the tongue. Tension at the tongue-root can also require that the singer push too much breath pressure through the larynx.

Loss of upper range due to the use of a high larynx position. This is yet another negative result of the use of too much breath pressure through the larynx.

Use of a depressed larynx position, often the result of a singer trying to create a warmer or darker internal sound. This is a trap arising from "listening" instead of embracing vocal sensations and it distorts resonance in the voice.

Development of a false and/or "pushed ring" in the voice. The resulting shrillness is a result of forcing too much breath pressure through the larynx. Shrillness should not be confused with resonance.

Inappropriate engagement of the laryngeal muscles in an attempt to shift the voice from register to register. (Note: This abrupt change of the tongue and laryngeal position often heard in male singers, is a futile attempt to access the high range through the use of *over-covering*, especially at the upper *passaggio*.

Taking Vocal Cover to the Extreme

The muscular cover leads to a myriad of frustrations and a vast array of vocal problems. It has also been called "the hook" or "turning the voice over", among other terms. Once this muscular "over-covering" has been learned and employed, it can take years to overcome this vocal fault. Over-covering is often employed in the upper *passaggio* range (especially in male voices) when too much emphasis is placed on darkening without employing the "ng" /ŋ/ tongue position or the wide release of the tongue root. In this case, the interior acoustical space closes, even though the muscular sensation may be one of opening. Resonance is then muted, forcing the singer to employ too much breath pressure.

The most negative side effect of overindulging in the concept of the cover is imposing a radical muscular adjustment, which engages the outer laryngeal muscles (full vomit reflex), and tongue pressure, which depresses the larynx. This leads to an imbalance in registration, vowel distortion, and locking the breath with the root of the tongue, especially in the upper *passaggio* and high range. I reiterate that it also diminishes the internal acoustical space—the exact opposite of a singer's primary goal. If a singer's laryngeal function is balanced, registration transitions will happen both naturally gradually without the need for sudden muscular adjustment.

I have found that achieving the healthy vocal protection is more challenging with male singers than with female singers, although some female singers with more dramatic voices have also ventured too far with the concept of vocal cover, often employing too much breath compression. It can sometimes be more difficult to hear when a female singer is producing an unprotected tone because the higher octave and the higher overtones can disguise the primary issue.

Occasionally some lighter-voiced singers try to sing heavier repertoire by employing an overly covered sound, which usually involves depressing the larynx with the tongue root, and pulling downward in posture. This is a misguided attempt to compete in a world that often promotes the belief that "bigger is better." Unfortunately for a singer who employs a muscular cover, the result is a smaller sound to the listener, even though it is a larger sound in the singer's inner hearing. Contrary to the desired effect, this type of tonal production does not carry well in the theater because it is acoustically inefficient.

Retraining the Inner Hearing: Embracing Ugly Sound

When first finding the acoustical protection the singer often has an urge to push too much breath pressure, in order to hear a bigger sound internally. This is a huge mistake and is a major factor in shortening careers. When singing properly, the singer usually hears a smaller internal sound. During my lessons with Allan Lindquest, he repeatedly asked me to "feel and not listen." When balanced singing is aligned with an internal feeling, the sensations of singing become much subtler (this usually happens as the singer becomes more advanced). Singers must rely 90% on resonance and internal sensations in order for the proper acoustical protection to be developed and sustained. The other 10% of the internal hearing must be used for intonation purposes.

When producing tone with a protection, most singers describe singing as a sensation that is contained in the body, mirroring the Old Italian term, *inhalare la voce* ("inhale" or "drink in" the voice). Singers also describe the sensation of resonance and breath flow spinning in the soft palate area. Never should the sensation be that of singing out the mouth.

The responses of singers who achieve the vocal protection range vary: from *"I can't hear any sound inside my head at all—is any sound coming out?"*; to *"My voice feels far away, with a sensation of a noisy rattle in front of my face"*; to *"This sounds so ugly in my inner hearing, especially in the higher pitches!"* These descriptions are most common when a singer achieves the proper acoustical balance and full release of resonance in the voice. In one of my lessons with Lindquest, he reflected on a quote by the great teacher Lamperti: *"Oh, that someone could give us the gift of hearing our own voice!"* The quote indicates his belief that when we sing well, we get a distorted sound inside the head.

Every singer needs to develop sensation as the true guide toward establishing and sustaining healthy vocalism. This takes time and patience, and a good instructor with a disgnostic ear. I also recommend that singers record their practice, so that they can familiarize themselves with the reality of the outside sound. Because voices can sound brittle and sharp in a small room (yet in the theater the tone warms and darkens to its natural beautiful timbre), it is better to record the voice from another room, so that the singer gets more of the faraway sound. This mirrors more of the correct acoustical release.

Case Study: Bass

I once taught a bass who was singing in opera houses internationally. He was pushing too much breath pressure through his larynx, resulting in less internal acoustical space. His vowel production was shallow, using mainly mouth resonance. Over a period of months, we worked toward releasing his voice, and he learned to employ resonance instead of breath pressure. His initial response was that he had no voice left, because he couldn't hear it. He had formerly conditioned his singing based on internal sound rather than on sensation. When we worked through the full realignment of his voice, achieving the complete acoustical vocal protection, he began to be hired for more and more leading roles. Let me clarify one point—from that point on, he never enjoyed the sound of his own voice. Every singer must face the reality that he or she will never hear the true sound of his/her own voice. We all need to embrace sensation, not sound, and we also must embrace this reality.

Techniques for Teaching the Cuperto as a Vocal Protection

Allan Lindquest employed the *cuperto* exercise using both one- and two-octave leaps to accomplish what he called "separation and reintegration of the registers." Its primary purpose was to strengthen the weaker register in order for all of the registers to match in color and timbre. Another benefit of this exercise was a vocal protection that resulted in gradations of tone in the upper *passaggio*, making singing in that range much easier.

In male voices, exercising with the *cuperto* in falsetto mechanism strengthens the thin edges of the vocal cords, making the opening at the glottis gradually smaller. The Italian School taught that the process of this vocal fold closing in the low falsetto allowed easier access to the upper range in full-voice mechanism. Lindquest also believed that the female voice had a falsetto, and that its development enhances vowel alignment, acoustical balance, and assists in easily accessing the upper *passaggio* and high range. It is important to understand that the protection of the upper *passaggio* should never be a sudden adjustment, but rather an acoustical release that occurs gradually as the singer moves up the grand scale. I refer to this as achieving "shades of gray" in tonal production, especially after transitioning into the upper head voice range from the middle register. It requires a full understanding of vowel formation and vowel alteration in the pharynx, a free tongue and jaw, and a full understanding of how to sustain this function throughout a musical phrase.

There are several exercises that can help a singer access the *voce cuperto* function. The primary goal is to produce a tiny Italian /u/ vowel with a small mouth opening, a healthy vocal fold closure, accompanied by opening the acoustical space (pharynx). A word of caution: some singers close the throat when approaching the small /u/. Most native English speakers produce /u/ with a bunched root of the tongue, which results in pressure directly at the vocal folds, and creates a more closed-throated tonal production. This is a very dangerous approach to the *cuperto*, and should be avoided. A singer can avoid this tight approach to the /u/ vowel by insuring that the root of the tongue is wide rather than bunched. The lower lip must be relaxed slightly over the lower teeth. Additionally, the lips should not over-shape the /u/ vowel to the point that the tongue tenses. The lips must be rounded without forward protrusion.

Exercise 5.1 Tongue Trills

Many teachers already use this exercise. It is only the beginning of a singer's journey to the thin edge function of the vocal folds. Although a good way to release tension, this exercise will not produce the acoustical phenomenon of the tiny /u/ vowel. Tongue trills can be taught on scales or arpeggios.

Exercise 5.2 Tongue/Lip Trills—Vibrating both the tongue and lips simultaneously[5]

This is also a wonderful exercise to encourage the singer to work with the concept of lower body support. It also promotes access to the thin edges of the vocal folds, and loosens the tongue root. Again, scales and arpeggios are both effective.

Exercise 5.3 The Tiny /u/ Vowel

In order to be effective, the tiny /u/ must be produced with a wide soft palate, a low larynx, and a wide tongue-root. Depressing the larynx with the tongue root can be injurious and can encourage a closed acoustical space (pharynx). I recommend that the singer work in the middle register

---

[5] This is also known colloquially as the "Bronx cheer" or the "raspberry".

using a small hum with the tongue gently extended between the lips, and then slowly moving to the tiny /u/ vowel. Visualize the tongue as wide at the back (at the root). Work this exercise on descending arpeggios at first, and then combine it with descending and ascending arpeggios.

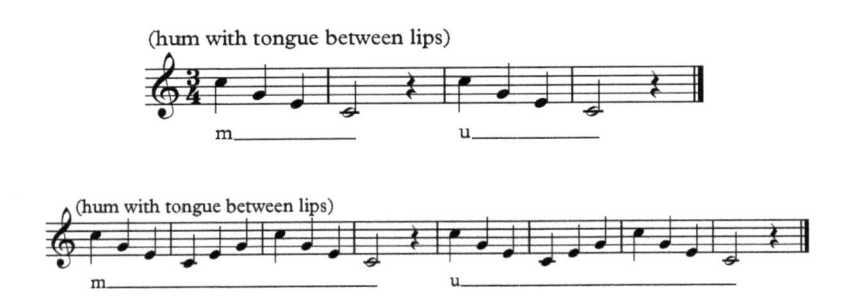

Notice that if the integrity of the vowel (vowel strength) is maintained in the pharynx, the vocal weight will drop off the voice.

Exercise 5.4 Using the /v/

Use of the /v/ is a wonderful way for many singers to access the thin edge function of the vocal folds. One exercise that helps to find this thin edge function is the octave swing (sliding on the interval of an octave) on the voiced /v/. As the singer gains freedom and ease in the octave swing, have them move toward the tiny /u/ vowel. The voiced /v/ will assist the singer in producing the small /u/ without squeezing the root of the tongue or constricting the laryngeal muscles.

Use of the Cuperto in Repertoire

I have often been asked, "What does the *voce cuperto* have to do with full-voiced singing? My answer to this question is, *everything*!! It creates a healthy acoustical and vocal preparation for full-voiced singing, integrating a full resonance factor when it opens to the full-voice function. Pavarotti used the concept of the *cuperto* in orchestrating his voice in new music. He first worked the small /u/ vowel before expanding to the other vowel sounds. Then he added consonants without disturbing the throat space.

Process

First work the repertoire using the tiny /u/ to feel the open space in the pharynx. Then proceed to sing the repertoire using just the vowels; then bring in the consonants. In order to find the free *cuperto*, there must be some space between the teeth as the lip muscles shape the tiny /u/. When the *cuperto* is free, there is a resulting slight buzz or vibration at the lips. Remember that the lips should never be tensed, but rather, rounded without protruding forward, as in covering a yawn in public. It may take time to find the open throat in coordination with the small mouth opening, so I recommend slow, concentrated study.

Singers with a history of squeezing the laryngeal muscles may find it more of a challenge to find the *cuperto* function than those without such a vocal history. Considering the acoustical benefit that this exercise offers, the *voce cuperto* is worth serious and careful study. Even the lowest voices can access the thin edges of the vocal folds using the *cuperto*, making high pianissimo singing more accessible, and balancing registration.

Case Study: Dramatic Soprano

Several years ago in my New York studio I taught a dramatic soprano who suffered from a faulty vocal technique, which included a high larynx position, a spread embouchure, a forward thrust of the jaw, and a dropped soft palate. Because multiple technical issues needed to be addressed, I decided to keep the instruction as simple as possible, drawing on the basic principle of *voce cuperto* that Lindquest had so carefully taught me in 1979. Within the first ten minutes of her first lesson, she found an acoustically balanced tone that filled the room with overtones, a pure, ringing sound that could carry in any opera house. In the first hour she found the *cuperto* (small Italian /u/) without squeezing the laryngeal muscles. Her *cuperto* function was amazingly beautiful and colorful.

Exercise 5.5

[musical notation: /ŋ/____ /u/____ ; ng____ u____]

How to "Cover" or Protect Without Damaging the Voice

I often have requests from singing teachers to address the issue of the acoustical cover, especially in male voices. I rarely use the term "cover," which I prefer to call *vocal protection*. The acoustical protection consists of a coordination of several functions, both in the lower body and in the laryngeal area, in order to shield or protect the voice from over-singing, or from "classical belting."

Each body function described in the list below must be studied individually and then coordinated. After this coordination is achieved, the singer can then perform without thinking so intensely about vocal technique. Lindquest once said, "We study technique to forget about it in performance!"

1. ***A lower larynx position.*** No singer can master the vocal protection until a slightly lowered larynx position is achieved. This laryngeal position must be accomplished at inhalation *without depressing the larynx with the root of the tongue (**Note:** attempting a "cover" with a flat or depressed tongue is extremely dangerous)*. Simultaneously the lower laryngeal muscles must slightly widen. This is accomplished through employment of both the laryngeal pivot or tilt in the middle register, in coordination with the "ng" tongue position.
2. ***The "ng" /ŋ/ tongue position.*** As stated previously, the tongue must assume the /ŋ/ shape as home position, a tool designed to avoid a depressed larynx using the tongue-root. The "ng" must be produced with the middle or frontal arch of the tongue, never

with the back (or root) of the tongue. Of course, vowels cannot be formed clearly from this exact tongue position, but the idea should predominate as a general rule to promote healthier singing, allowing for a more perfect mixture of upper and lower overtones.

3. *A slightly downward and back jaw position.* If a singer has a forward swing (thrust) of the jaw, the larynx lifts, and the tongue often pulls back into the throat. When the tongue retracts as a result of a forward thrust of the jaw, resonance is muted. The vocal folds do *not* completely approximate when the jaw thrusts forward. This is especially true in the middle voice, where an over-opened jaw can cause retraction of the tongue and loss of higher overtones.

4. *Sustaining a healthy curve in the back of the neck, without crunching the head into the spine.* Since full resonance cannot be achieved without an open acoustical space, it is important to keep the neck free. Realize that the head should never crunch down on the neck. The spine has a natural curve in the back of the neck, which must be maintained so that the back of the neck may remain free and relaxed, allowing for a more open pharyngeal wall (back of the throat). Freeing the neck also allows for a lower larynx position.

5. *Support (balancing subglottic breath pressure using the lower body muscles).* The term "support" is often used without full explanation. When a singer resists the outflow of air with the lower body muscles, the larynx can then sustain a lower position. But when too much breath pressure is employed in singing, the result is a higher laryngeal position resulting in a pushed tone. The consistent production of a well-supported tone directly contributes to the healthy protection of the voice, as a result of a stabilized laryngeal position.

The three sets of muscles that comprise the support system are (1) the lower back (lumbar) muscles; (2) the epigastrium area (the muscle mass directly below the front ribs), which stretches in an east-west direction; and (3) the lower abdominals, which resist upward and wide, not in or out. In addition, there must also be an elongation of the rib cage while sustaining tone. The use of *appoggio* (sternum resistance) encourages the lumbar muscles, solar plexus, and abdominal muscles to coordinate, which is critical to finding balance of tone. Kirsten Flagstad said that there should be a sensation of the sound "washing down the sternum" while singing.

6. **The rounded or oval embouchure.** Facial posture plays a major role in the internal posture of the throat. In the Swedish-Italian School of vocal training, the idea of maintaining a more rounded or oval mouth shape was encouraged to assist in sustaining a more open throat. Sunken cheek muscles (between the upper and lower molars) helps to expand the acoustical space.
7. **Keeping the feeling of the /u/ vowel in the pharynx.** The use of the *voce cuperto* is a basic concept of the Swedish Italian School. The *voce cuperto* is created through the use of the small Italian /u/ vowel at the embouchure, accompanied by a large throat space. Remember that the /u/ vowel must be shaped without too much tension at the lips.

Exercise 5.6

Close the mouth for upper notes and use the same vowel feeling for the turn to the 9-note scale.

Begin with *cuperto* /u/ in full voice opening gradually to fuller sound.

Exercise 5.8

nyuh_____
/ɲʌ/_____

Sing this exercise with an "uh" /ʌ/ in the wide soft palate and base of the larynx. It assists in establishing a vocal protection.

Exercise 5.9

a o__ u____ a o__ u____

On the ascending intervals, feel a slight dropping of the sternum and an elongation of the rib cage.

Exercise 5.10

"*Give yourself a hug.*" Wrap your arms around your body (below the shoulders) and feel expansion across the back ribs. As you inhale, feel the breath drop down into the body. This is an exercise I learned from Dr. Evelyn Reynolds.

Exercise 5.11

ah   aw   uh   aw   ah
/ɑ/ /ɔ/ /ʌ/ /ɔ/ /ɑ/

Use this vowel sequence to help establish the wide soft palate space.

Exercise 5.12

i____ i____ i____

Use this exercise to feel laryngeal tilt in the middle register and then upper *passaggio*. You will also feel the lower laryngeal muscles widen as you ascend in pitch.

Exercise 5.13

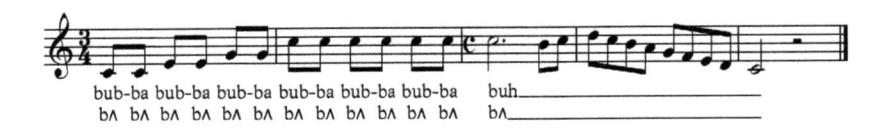

bub-ba bub-ba bub-ba bub-ba bub-ba bub-ba   buh_____
bʌ bʌ bʌ bʌ bʌ bʌ bʌ bʌ bʌ bʌ bʌ bʌ   bʌ_____

Notice a feeling of vibration down the sternum while ascending in pitch. There will be a darker tone as the singer ascends.

CHAPTER 6

Achieving Balance in Registration

Register definition, strengthening, and blend play a major role in the development of healthy singing, offering the singer one unified vocal sound. Stated simply, registers represent different ranges of the voice that are controlled by separate muscle groups. The chest register, or to use Vennard's term "heavy mechanism," is controlled by the thyroarytenoid muscles. The head register, or what Vennard called "light mechanism", is controlled by the cricothyroid muscles. During my study with Lindquest he referred to the basic two-register approach, although he also described smaller sub-registers. Sub-registers have historically been called "flip points," or "acoustical shifts." They help singers access the upper range more easily without vocal weight when body connection is sustained.

Registers and Sub-Registers

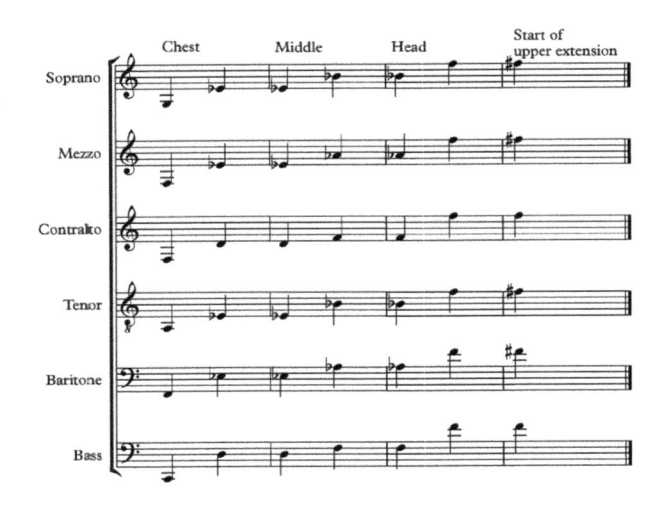

[Musical notation showing register ranges for Soprano, Mezzo, Contralto, Tenor, Baritone, and Bass voices, with columns labeled: Chest, Middle, Head, Start of upper extension]

Upper Register Extension Shifts
These are the same for all voice types.

[Musical notation ending with "and higher"]

Some instructors voice concern about the use of register definition and register blend, fearing that the singer will create register transitions by tensing throat muscles. Realize that we must simply allow for these register changes to occur without falsely creating or manipulating register adjustments.

Factors that Negatively Affect Registration Balance

When laryngeal muscles manipulate pitch, the resulting imbalance in registration can make navigating through the registers difficult. This often results in the singer developing the sound of several voices instead of one uniform vocal sound. Laryngeal manipulation (sometimes referred to as "laryngeal bobble") is a common problem developed by many experienced singers, but it can also be present in younger singers as well. It is a characteristic often found in choral singers.

Insufficient acoustical space and/or lack of pharyngeal vowel formation can also contribute to registration imbalance. Keep in mind that the acoustical space must expand more as the singer goes higher in pitch. Taking that into consideration, it is only logical to conclude that the middle and low registers require slightly less acoustical space than the upper *passaggio* and high range.

Imbalance in registration can also be caused by a number of other factors, including (1) uneven breath flow; (2) jaw tension, including forward thrust of the jaw; (3) tongue tension and/or tongue retraction: (4) incorrect posture, either hyper-extension of the sternum, which collapses the back rib cage, or dropping of the sternum, which drives too much breath pressure through the larynx; (5) over-compression of breath, resulting from pulling down the rib cage; (6) incorrect facial posture, often involving a spread embouchure or a pulled down overly-narrow facial posture; (7) lack of flexible lower-body muscle resistance between the upper and lower abdominal muscles, resulting in a breathy unfocused attack or onset; and (8) the use of inner hearing as a guide rather than using physical sensations.

Balancing the Registers

Lindquest once said to me, "Singers often come into the voice studio using their voice in one of two extremes. Either they have too much chest development, revealing the depression of the larynx with the tongue-root, or too much head development, reflective of singing with a high larynx position or a laryngeal squeeze." This includes the sternocleidomastoid muscles on the sides of the neck. Isolating whichever register is weaker, strengthening it, and then reintegrating it with the other stronger register is fundamental in achieving register balance. The reintegration process is greatly dependent upon the release of the larynx (the laryngeal tilt). The release of the tongue is greatly dependent upon employment of the gentle laryngeal tilt in the middle register as well, making it easer for the singer to ascend higher in pitch.

To help the singer achieve register balance, Lindquest masterfully employed what I call reflexive exercises that inspired faster vocal progress without over-complicating the approach. Because they work efficiently without extraneous muscular tension or manipulation, I still use these exercises in my teaching today. Many of Lindquest's exercises involved a sequence of vowels that helped the singer to navigate efficiently from the low register through the middle register and upper passaggio, and into the high range, without the use of too much breath pressure or vocal strain.

He frequently used staccato exercises in his teaching, asking the singer to imagine touching only the "fine edges" of the vocal folds on the staccato notes. Strengthening the thin-edge function of the folds while encouraging the "ng" /ŋ/ tongue position is key in the development of higher overtones throughout the voice. The purpose of threading the different vowels on the "ng" /ŋ/ ring was also to drop vocal weight while sustaining a light yet body-connected tone. The "ng" must be produced with the middle and front of the tongue, never the tongue-root. Both the Swedish-Italian and Italian Schools emphasize vocalizing from higher pitches downward, using the *voce cuperto* function (the small Italian /u/ vowel with the open acoustical space).

Exercise 6.1 Lindquest's One-Octave Cuperto

This is the one-octave version of an exercise Lindquest used for balancing the registers. It encourages mixing chest resonance (body connection) into the head register, while sustaining a slightly low larynx position; and then mixing head resonance or higher overtones (which requires a wide soft palate position) into the chest voice range. Mixing head resonance into the chest register is assisted by employing the "ng" /ŋ/ tongue position in the low range. The warmth of the chest register remains in the /u/ vowel if the singer sustains the feeling of the vowel deep at the base of the larynx, or Caruso's image of feeling the vowel under the cords. The Italian School calls this "connecting the head to the chest, and the chest to the head." Dixie Neill encouraged the singer to sustain tracheal vibration in higher pitches.

Begin by singing a three-note scale using a body-connected tone lightly in chest register, on the vowel "ah", keeping the "*ng*" /ŋ/ tongue position and the thin edge function of the vocal folds intact. It involves the use of strong, yet un-pushed chest (heavy) mechanism and the use of light yet body-connected head (light) mechanism. The singer begins this exercise using a solid gentle chest tone on the Italian /a/ vowel. If the /a/ is too heavy or thick, it may be altered toward "aw"/ɔ/. Sung on a three-tone scale, this works as a foundation for establishing the sensation of an open throat before ascending to the upper pitch an octave higher.

Keeping the same throat space, cord closure and body connection, sing a tone an octave higher, in head register on the vowel /u/, and then a descending scale on a small Italian /u/ vowel, while sustaining an open acoustical space behind the small mouth shape. The lips must be rounded but never protruding forward (as this tenses the tongue-root), and the "ng" /ŋ/ tongue position (with wide tongue-root) must be maintained in order to sustain ring throughout the descending scale. The jaw must also be loose in order for sufficient acoustical space to be released.

Sustaining the ring discourages the singer from developing the habit of using too much vocal weight (thicker cord mass), and to bypass muscular involvement. This can be accomplished by employing a slight French nasal (which is *not* nasal).

Adding Resonance Within a Register

There is a difference between the chest mechanism and chest resonance; as there is between head mechanism and head resonance. The description of head or chest resonance simply describes where the sympathetic vibrations are felt in the body. Every singer must learn to drop vocal weight on ascending pitches in order to enter and sustain the high range. Of course the released larynx is a pre-requisite in learning to accomplish this skill of adding and dropping vocal weight.

The "ah" /ɑ/ vowel automatically tends to add vocal weight as one moves downward in pitch. The /o/ and /u/ vowels tend to drop vocal weight when one ascends in pitch. If a singer has difficulty in adding vocal weight when moving downward in pitch, most likely the larynx is rising. This can be solved by adding more "uh" /ʌ/ at the base of the larynx, which will encourage more fullness of sound. Make sure to sustain the "ng" /ŋ/ tongue position in order to keep the ring factor stable, especially when moving downward in pitch.

Adding Head Resonance to Chest Register

To add head resonance to the chest mechanism, the singer learns to employ higher overtones by keeping the tongue arched and the palate position wide and lifted slightly. Maintaining this position while moving downward in pitch allows the singer to sustain higher overtones.

Adding Chest Resonance to Lower Head Register

Adding vocal weight involves the use of more chest resonance when *descending* in pitch, which is directly connected to the singer's ability to connect the voice more deeply into the body. Adding body vibration employs more vocal fold mass and may be accessed by employing the Italian *appoggio,* or forward sternum stretch. This type of body connection allows the singer to sustain a slightly lower larynx position when descending in pitch. It is not to be confused with a depressed larynx, which involves depression of the larynx with the tongue-root.

You can add chest resonance within the lower head voice range without employing chest mechanism—what some would call "crossing the break." This is accomplished by sustaining a healthy body connection, or *appoggio*, while descending in pitch. The function allows the singer to add vocal weight (fullness of tone) when descending in pitch, without breaking into the chest mechanism.

When a baritone or mezzo goes lower in the head voice range, the listener expects to hear them add chest resonance in order to expand the fullness of tone in the lower middle register. This requires the engagement of more sympathetic vibration on the sternum bone and careful use of breath management, often requiring less breath pressure in order to sustain balance in registration. Adding vocal weight when going downward in pitch must be accomplished without loss of the ng /ŋ/ tongue position or higher overtones.

Exercise 6.2

u___ o___ a___ o___ u___ o___ a

Exercise 6.3

u   o___   a   o___   u   o___   a

Exercise 6.4

da me ni po tu_____ la

Exercise 6.5

i   e   a   o   u   o   a   e   i

Exercise 6.6 Caruso Scale

a___ o_____ u_____ o_____ a_____

Chapter 6 | Achieving Balance in Registration

Jaw-Larynx Function and the Effects on Registration

Any tension in the jaw, larynx, or tongue can result in the employment of too much vocal weight, making access to the upper range challenging at best. Virginia Botkin called this "breath weight," meaning that the thicker vocal cord mass engages when too much breath pressure, or compressed breath, is forced through the larynx. The resulting over-blowing of the vocal folds creates major problems in registration balance.

During consonant-vowel relationship in text, the jaw must wrap gently back and slightly downward at each vowel, directly after each consonant. The larynx must also drop slightly in response to the back jaw motion. In the middle and low registers, the emphasis must be more on the back motion of the jaw rather than on the downward motion.[1] In the high range, the jaw must unhinge and open more. Lindquest's tool for releasing the tongue and jaw was through the use of the gentle chewing motion. This motion (straight up and down, not side to side) allows for a slight dropping of the larynx after each consonant. Lindquest often encouraged me to chew several times and then sing. The result was always more vocal freedom and more resulting overtones.

This gentle chewing motion of the jaw is a trained skill that does not occur naturally in speaking. I recommend that teachers and singers use a slow, careful study of the Italian syllables *da me ni po tu* in a five-tone scale, monitoring the back release of the jaw after each consonant. If the jaw does not release, then monitor the jaw muscles carefully with the fingertips.

It may also be helpful to study videos of singers who have achieved the back jaw motion at vowel function. Observe videos of great singers and especially pay attention to profile shots. Olga Borodina and Placido

---

[1] Many singers need to close the mouth slightly to sustain higher overtones.

Domingo are two singers who have achieved this jaw release. Observing them carefully can be helpful.

Exercise 6.7 Careful Supervision of the Jaw-Larynx Function

Connecting this jaw function to actual singing is critical to the correct execution of this exercise. You will most likely find that the jaw is reasonably relaxed for the speaking part of the exercise, but it might pressurize or tense more during the function of singing. Repeat the process carefully until you have released the jaw slightly back and down for singing as well as speaking. Perform this exercise using two mirrors, ideally placed at a 90-degree angle in order to see the profile.

1. Facing the mirror, take the forefingers of each hand and rest them on the cheeks, just behind the back teeth, on the large jaw muscles located just behind the back teeth. Start by speaking the Italian syllables *da me ni po tu,* while wrapping the jaw gently back after each consonant. Remember to use the flipped and dentalized Italian consonants while pronouncing these syllables. This requires independence of the jaw and tongue; the tongue-tip should come up behind the upper teeth when pronouncing /d/, /t/, /l/, or /n/.
2. Notice the pressure in the muscles just behind the back teeth. Place a small amount of pressure on these muscles (not too much) and speak the syllables again. It is necessary to educate these muscles so that they do not push or thrust the jaw forward.
3. At first, the jaw will very likely thrust forward. Use the fingertips to monitor the jaw muscles, encouraging the back motion of the jaw at the vowels. This exercise demands slow practice, but will result in more balanced registration. The vocal folds will also close more efficiently, resulting in more resonance.
4. After speaking the syllables, add singing tone on a single pitch. Then sing a five-tone ascending scale while monitoring the jaw function.

da me ni po tu   da me ni po tu____

Exercise 6.8 The Floor Exercise

The basic form of this exercise was described in Chapter 2. Here it is applied to the study of the correct jaw motion in pronunciation of text. This is an important study in learning to pronounce the text without neck tension.

1. Lie facing upward on the floor, with the knees bent (to protect your lower back).
2. Using the Italian syllables *da me ni po tu* sing a five-tone scale.

da me ni po tu____

3. Allow the jaw to fall back with gravity for each vowel.
4. Observe the motion of the jaw as it falls down and back. Notice that the larynx also releases at each vowel.
5. Work slowly, sometimes speaking instead of singing, and then add more speed and vocal tone.

Registration Problems: Extremes of "Placement"

Finding the balance between space and ring plays an especially important role in achieving registration balance. Not only does it allow for the development of more vocal freedom, but it also gives the singer a fuller understanding of what defines healthy resonance. It is important to learn how to vocalize in balance, not in extremes. If you have studied a school of training that works in one extreme or the other, realize that you will probably have to go through a certain period of realignment in order to find your healthy vocal balance.

The "Dark" Sound: Over-Spacing

If a singer produces an overly dark sound, it is an indicator that the tongue is retracting or pulling back into the pharynx. Not only does it tend to create an over-engagement of the chest (heavy) mechanism, but also distorts the ring-factor in the voice. Any retraction of the tongue not only mutes resonance, but it also results in pressure at the vocal folds, a pressure that distorts registration.

One of the most common causes of tongue retraction is over-stretching the outer laryngeal muscles, or the side walls of the larynx. I call this over-spacing of the throat the "heave reflex", or the full vomit reflex. Over-spacing engages the gag reflex at the root of the tongue, which blocks the singer's ability to use the small controlled air stream on which to pronounce. It also distorts the singer's ability to employ the laryngeal tilt in the middle register, a must for preparing the healthy head voice transition.

Another problem with engagement of the gag reflex at the tongue-root is the resulting engagement of the thicker vocal fold mass. In employing the thicker vocal fold mass, the singer's ability to transition easily into the head voice, or light mechanism, is extremely compromised. Hyperextension of the outer laryngeal muscles tends to lock the laryngeal area, requiring that the singer employ too much breath pressure for phonation.

"Mask" Resonance—Working Too Much Frontal Vibration

Working too frontally, with what some call "mask resonance" can be as detrimental to register balance as over-spacing. It can create both a high larynx (resulting in a closed throat), and tongue tension, as a result of attempting to intensify frontal sensations. Both factors contribute to distorting registration. Healthy "mask resonance" is the *result* of an open pharynx with a forward tongue position—the sensation in the "mask" is not the origin of sound.

Lindquest once said, "One of the worst things a teacher can say to a singer is to place the voice forward!" An extreme forward placement technique usually closes the throat, which compromises the high range and increases the development of register breaks in the voice. as a direct result of the high larynx position.

Should We Study Ring to Space, or Space to Ring?

The determining factor of whether to vocalize space to ring or ring to space depends solely upon a singer's vocal history. Many singers achieve positive results exercising the voice from space to the ring, especially when the throat has been closed over a long period of time. Singers who have historically sung with a closed throat must learn to create a pharyngeal vowel stretch, including employment of the laryngeal tilt in the upper middle register.

Other singers find more vocal balance by working from the ring to the space, especially if they have had a history of over-spacing, or using a retracted tongue position. Finding balance between the space *and* the ring is crucial in the process of blending the registers. It requires that the singer achieve the balance of the open throat (pharynx), the forward arched tongue position (middle tongue arch), and the high and wide soft palate. Remember that an open pharynx not only involves a low larynx but also includes a widening at the base of the larynx, the root of the tongue, and the soft palate.

Singing in the low range requires less acoustical space in order to keep the ring factor consistent. However, the singer must increase the acoustical space when ascending higher in pitch toward the upper *passaggio* and high range.

Some exercises work to achieve space and ring simultaneously. This way of working with the voice achieves the Italian *chiaroscuro*, both brightness and darkness in tonal production.

Exercise 6.9 Working Space and Ring Simultaneously

- Place the tongue between the lips.

- Sing a descending staccato five-tone scale on a body-connected hum.

- At each note, make sure you feel a stretch of vowel space directly behind the root of the tongue. If you look in a mirror, you will observe that the lower laryngeal muscles stretch slightly in an east-west direction automatically.

- Then sing the five Italian vowels /a/ /e/ /i/ /o/ /u/, keeping the same stretch of the acoustical space behind the tongue-root. Think of this space as the origin of each vowel form.

- Keeping the tongue arched and forward in the mouth space, notice that the voice begins to ring as a result of the open pharynx.

m m m m m   i e a o u

The forward tongue position and open vowel space (behind the tongue-root) allows the ring and space to work simultaneously to form a healthy balance.

Exercise 6.10 Kiu-ex

This is an exercise designed to open the acoustical space (pharynx) and release the jaw while the tongue moves forward out of the pharynx. It is also an exceptional exercise for achieving acoustical balance in the /e/ vowel.

- Using the syllables /kju/ /ɛks/ for each note, sing an ascending and descending major triad. Notice that the /k/ implodes the palate upward and wide.

kiu ex kiu ex kiu ex kiu ex kiu ex
/kju/ /ɛks/

- As the jaw releases, the larynx drops slightly which opens the acoustical space. Then the tongue moves forward to make the "ex" sound, bringing in the ring factor.
- Work this exercise slowly in order to study the physical results carefully.

Exercise 6.11 Working Ring to Space

The result of correctly employing this exercise will be a balance of ring and space functioning simultaneously without tongue pressure.

- First release the jaw slightly downward and back.

- Using a single pitch in the middle register, start a tone with the French "ain" /ɛ̃/, then slowly move to an open /a/ or /o/ vowel. Notice the frontal vibration that results from the use of the French /ɛ̃/ and how it tends to reflexively vibrate under the cheekbone area. Keep a thread of this function as you move to the open vowel. Make the transition from ring (/ɛ̃/) to space (/a/ or /o/) slowly, observing the subtle frontal vibration under the cheekbone area as you open to the vowel.

- Work slowly on this exercise without over-spacing or pulling the tongue backward. Over-spacing on the vowel function will result in a retracted tongue position that is never healthy in searching for registration balance in singing.

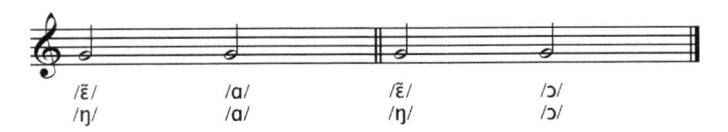

/ɛ̃/   /a/   /ɛ̃/   /ɔ/
/ŋ/   /a/   /ŋ/   /ɔ/

- **Variation:** You may also use the "ng" and then transition to an open (/a/ or /o/) vowel. Allow the soft palate to lift away from the tongue-root when opening to the vowel.

Daily Exercise Routine for Register Balance

It is important to exercise the voice carefully on a daily basis, using a healthy routine of reflexive vocal exercises, exercises that employ vowel sequences that drop vocal weight and encourage register balance. Each exercise in the following sequence has been developed to fulfill a specific purpose, e.g., release of the diaphragm, the lowering of the larynx, etc. In Old World training, every exercise has a physical purpose, encouraging proper responses in the body, working toward promoting healthy vocalism.[2]

The following series of exercises is designed to assist the singer in achieving register balance.

One-Octave Cuperto

a_____ u_____

Open Throat Exercise

m m m m m   i e a o u

Laryngeal Pivot

i_____

Arpeggio with Vowel Sequence

i e a o u o a e i

---

[2] A healthy daily vocal routine may be found on my CD, *"An Introductory Lesson with David Jones: A Resource for Teachers and Singers"* available at www.cdbaby.com.

Chapter 6 | Achieving Balance in Registration

Alleluia

A - le — lu - ia

Bellisario

bel - li - saw — rrio
/ɔ/ —— /rjɔ/

The Caruso Scale

a — o — u — o — a —

Caruso Scale (advanced)

a — aw — uh — aw — a —
/ɑ/ /ɔ/ /ʌ/ /ɔ/ //

Dentale

a. b.
de — nta — le   de — nta — le

Da me ni po tu

da me ni po tu —

Nye ri tu mi kya nya be la

nie ri tu mi kia nia be - la
/nje/ /ri/ /tu/ /mi/ /kjɑ/ /njɑ/ /bɛ/ /lɑ/

Sieber Vocalises

Ferdinand Sieber: *Eight-Measure Vocalises* for Soprano (op. 92), Mezzo-soprano (op. 93), Alto (op.94), Tenor (op. 95), Baritone (op.96), Bass (op. 97). Be sure to use the set of exercises appropriate for your vocal type.

CHAPTER 7

Understanding and Solving Middle Register Problems

Undiagnosed vocal issues in the middle register are quite common in both male and female singers. These vocal problems can become worse with time, negatively affecting access to the upper *passaggio* and consequently the high range. Many singers who experience difficulty in freeing the high range may not realize that the key issue originates in the lack of proper middle register coordination. This can stem from several sources: inadequate or incomplete instruction, confusion about how to produce healthy tone (which is usually unattractive in the inner hearing), or physical tension. This chapter will outline typical problems that occur in young singers who are working toward balance in registration.

Lack of Voce Cuperto

Lack of the *voce cuperto* function in the mid-range can create major issues for both male and female singers. As I have defined previously, the *voce cuperto* that Allan Lindquest taught me is based on what I call the *small Italian /u/ vowel*, which, along with the open pharyngeal cavity, results in an acoustical release that simultaneously expands resonance and warms tone. In the middle range the singer must use a more rounded vowel, often adopting a more closed mouth position, without tensing the lips. Rather, if the rounding of the /u/ vowel originates in the sinking and forward stretch of the cheek muscles between the upper and lower teeth (as in the sucking function), it encourages the expansion of the pharyngeal space. This process must be executed slowly and carefully in order to balance the open pharynx as well as the resulting ring. At first this approach to the *cuperto* must be executed with a smaller mouth opening in order to begin the process of stretching the interior space. Later in vocal development, the singer may open more, without spreading the *embouchure* (mouth opening). Note: I find that many singers tense the front of the tongue and the tongue-root on this particular vowel. The tongue must be free from retraction and bunching or narrowing.

Addressing the Laryngeal Position

Laryngeal position is frequently overlooked in the middle register, even though it plays a critically important role not only in balance in registration, but also in proper vocal fold stretch and vocal fold approximation (closure). Many singers who were trained decades ago reflect on how their teachers focused on laryngeal function in the middle register. These instructors knew that they were helping the singer to establish a foundation for healthy vocalism. The following sections will discuss laryngeal function and how to avoid extreme or incorrect application of the basic concept.

Depressed Larynx

Singers sometimes attempt to force a fuller, darker sound in the middle register by depressing the larynx. A depressed larynx occurs when the singer tenses the tongue-root and pushes downward on the larynx. When tongue depression is employed, the singer must then resort to forcing breath pressure through the larynx, a common irritant to the vocal folds. Over-darkening in the middle register frequently results in tongue retraction (pulling back of the tongue), which reduces the singer's high overtones and compromises the upper *passaggio* and high range. While the depressed larynx may produce a large, impressive vocal sound, the negative result is employment of too much thick cord mass too high in pitch, resulting is loss of high range. This kind of vocal production can be released by employing the /ng/ tongue position, which discourages tongue depression, and staccato exercises to thin the cords.

High Larynx Position

There are several causes of a high larynx position in the middle register including (1) the lifting of the larynx in the middle register in an attempt to "lighten" the voice; (2) inadequate laryngeal release or opening of the throat at inhalation; (3) lack of laryngeal tilt in middle register; and (4) insufficient lower body connection (support) at the onset, which holds back and regulates air pressure much as in the laugh reflex.

Singing with a high larynx position in the middle register can be a persistent habit that is sometimes difficult to pinpoint. The resulting tone may be somewhat acceptable and the singer may not typically sound throaty. But the tonal quality will be less full in resonance and warmth. It can be a major cause of weakness in vocal fold adduction. The inability to find sufficient laryngeal release in this register can be a contributing factor to breathiness and lack of resonance in the middle register, especially for the female singer. It can also lead to intonation problems, breath management issues (due to tension in the tongue-root), the inability to find sufficient resonance and tone in the middle register; and it often leads to frustration and a more muscular approach to singing in the lower middle range.

As indicated earlier, some young singers are encouraged to sing with a high larynx position because it is incorrectly perceived as a way of lightening the voice, and making a "lighter" tone. This is where the instructor must train his/her ear to hear when the larynx is not fully released. "Lightening" the voice this way is a dangerous practice that often results in vocal problems stemming from insufficient laryngeal tilt in the middle register, a vocal fault that can take a singer years to correct. While some schools of vocal training are obsessed with the "high, light, bright, forward" concept of singing, it is important for every instructor to understand that true and authentic head voice has warmth and color that results from the appropriate amount of laryngeal release.

Because a high larynx position is such a common middle register issue, I recommend that instructors frequently check a singer's laryngeal position in this range. In addition, many singers who suffer from a high larynx position also suffer from tongue-root tension, I recommend singers/teachers also check the area under the chin with the thumb, to be sure tongue root is not pushing down on the larynx. That area may descend as the larynx moves slightly downward, but the texture of the tongue-root should remain somewhat soft in sensation. If the laryngeal tilt is present in the middle register, the laryngeal muscles and the tongue-root release simultaneously.

Deception of the Inner Hearing

The acoustical deception of the inner hearing is a major problem for every singer, whether student or professional. Male singers tend to lose volume in their inner hearing as they move toward the upper *passaggio*, while female singers tend to lose their inner sound toward the lower *passaggio* transition. Because of the frustration of not being able to "hear" their own sound, singers are tempted to employ too much breath pressure, driving the larynx upward and inhibiting full resonance.

The characteristics of a truly beautiful, resonant sound are usually *not* enjoyed by the singer him/herself. The inner hearing distorts sound and many performers will tell that you their inside sound is quite different from what the audience experiences. Unfortunately, there are some singers and teachers who confuse shrillness with resonance. In truth, fully realized resonance reflects both high and low overtones, marrying both ring and warmth or color. I often quote Birgit Nilsson, who said, "I get my big released sound from my tiny released sound!" She was referring to singing with what felt like a small sound inside her head, yet to the listener it was huge because the overtones were concentrated. The foundation of achieving full overtone in the upper range stem from the proper vocalization of the middle register.

Singers must learn to embrace an inner sound (inside the head) that can be sometimes slightly noisy, ugly, and more distant in the inner hearing. Some singers report a "noisy rattle" in front of the face, which is a result of an open acoustical space, not the origin of sound. Every singer must learn to guide his/her voice through sensations instead of sound. Over-listening can be exacerbated when singing in an acoustically dry or dead room or theater—this is why it is a good idea to practice in a dry/dead acoustic.

Insufficient Vocal Cord Closure

Some professional singers who are well into their careers develop insufficient vocal fold closure in the middle register. Both male and female professionals can suffer from this problem, although it is more common in the female singer. It is somewhat related to a habit of opening and re-adducting the vocal folds at pitch changes, rather than employing a gradual stretch of the vocal folds for pitch change. If left unaddressed, this problem leads to a laryngeal "bobble" (too much adjustment of laryngeal muscles for pitch change). Learning to sing from pitch to pitch while sustaining the perfect adduction of the vocal folds is key to resolving this issue, and it allows the singer to develop pure legato line.

This issue of opening and re-adducting the cords for pitch change can be resolved by a gentle employment of Garcia's *coup de glotte*—the healthy closure of the vocal folds after inhalation. It must be a gentle *touch* of the glottis. Lindquest used the two English words *"every orange"* to help the singer find this slight sensation. To feel movement between pitches without a sudden adjustment at the vocal folds or any laryngeal movement, the "ng" is an excellent tool. Singing with a lower larynx position and a strong pharyngeal /u/ vowel will encourage better vocal fold adduction as well.

Laryngeal Release in Text

I consistently hear singers report that they can vocalize beautifully, but then they have difficulty applying technique to repertoire. For the middle register, the key to application of technique to repertoire is to allow the larynx to drop for each vowel in text. At the same time, the jaw must be trained to gently wrap back for each vowel. This expands the vocal sound through acoustical release, and helps to accomplish legato line in singing. It is critically important that the mouth *not* be too open in the middle register, as this causes the tongue to retract and the voice to be "belted" as in mouthy vowels. The acoustical space closes when the jaw is hyper-extended too open, and laryngeal movement and release are dramatically diminished. When the jaw is gently relaxed back at each vowel in text, it teaches the interior space of the pharynx to open more. As a result, this more closed mouth position in middle voice also helps to achieve more ring in the voice.

Another laryngeal release technique is the concept of vocal fold "clicking." It is a way of releasing the lower laryngeal muscles while accomplishing a healthy closure of the vocal folds. Caruso used what he called a tiny "silent cough" function, without blowing breath pressure through the folds. Allan Lindquest learned this from him in 1914 during his vocal sessions, and later used it in his teaching as a way to not only close the cords, but to release the larynx.

Case Study: Dramatic Tenor

Several years ago I taught a dramatic tenor who could produce a large impressive sound, but had lost easy access to his high range. It took little time to diagnose his major problems: he tended to breathe with his jaw thrusting forward instead of allowing it to fall slightly back. Because of this habit, he could only force his voice, pushing too much breath pressure through the larynx. Many dramatic tenors suffer from over-breathing and over-compression of breath. Then they must push too much sound and therefore too much air pressure. Because this singer had developed a strong push reflex, he had little or no dynamic control.

Through slow and consistent, supervised body work and vocal work, he learned a slightly downward-and-back jaw motion at inhalation, which began the process of releasing the vocal weight throughout the middle register. We also did staccato exercises in the middle register (employing the laugh reflex) to thin the cords. As he began to sing with less breath pressure, his larynx began to release, making it possible for him to gain more vocal control throughout the different registers of his voice. After mastering the staccato exercises to thin the cords, it became easier for him to sing a variety of dynamic levels. We then worked on the laryngeal tilt exercise, using an ascending major 3rd. Feeling the vowel deeply dropping (down and back) behind the tongue-root miraculously accomplished the slight down and forward tilt of the larynx.

Most dramatic tenors who come into my studio have one major question: "How do I open my upper register?" The answer to this question lies in proper vocalization of the middle register, including achieving the laryngeal tilt (down and forward movement of the thyroid cartilage as described in William Vennard's book), learning correct posture and flexible inhalation, and by learning to engage the body elastically at the onset, which inspires the larynx to drop slightly more at the onset or attack.

Exercises for the Middle Register

Exercise 7.1 Preparatory Breath

The concept of laryngeal release is important for the proper training of the middle register, and it needs to be trained as a correct habit during the preparatory breath. I often use the image of breathing the larynx wide as to discourage pushing it down with the tongue-root.

1. Breathe the larynx slightly downward, widening the lower laryngeal muscles during the preparatory breath. This can be achieved by monitoring the lower laryngeal muscles with the

fingertips, observing whether or not they slightly descend and widen at inhalation. It is related to the laugh reflex. Often staccato helps a singer to achieve this.

2. When training the preparatory breath, monitor the root of the tongue to be certain that it is wide and that the tongue assumes the /ŋ/ position or an arched posture. The tongue-root will relax slightly down and forward, to create more space between the tongue-root and the back wall of the pharynx.

Exercise 7.2 "Vacuum Cleaner" or "Snore" Preparatory Breath

To accomplish a slightly lowered larynx position, Lindquest used what he called the "vacuum cleaner" or "snore" breath. The benefit of this kind of preparatory breath is that it brings the larynx slightly downward without depressing it with the tongue-root. This concept serves to open the acoustical space in the throat, encouraging a healthier adduction of the vocal folds.

- Inhale through the nose with the lips closed as the tongue sustains the "ng" /ŋ/ position (as in "*singing*"). The larynx will move about halfway down at inhalation. Repeat this until the laryngeal muscles release with the breath response.

Exercise 7.3 The Laryngeal Tilt

Careful employment of the laryngeal tilt will result in a freer and more resonant middle register, making it easier to access higher pitches. The laryngeal tilt is important for all voices, accessing more low and high overtones in the middle register. It is also an especially useful tool to help the beginning male singer to find his upper register without a high larynx. You will find that the head voice (light mechanism) will transition naturally with this exercise.

1. Using the Italian /u/ vowel, vocalize on an ascending major third (do-mi-do).
2. Allow the front half of the tongue to be arched ("ng" position) and the tongue-root wide and relaxed. It is very important not to bunch the tongue-root or depress the larynx with the tongue-root

when working with this exercise. The tongue root should remain soft and wide.

3. Think of a slight rocking motion of the larynx downward and forward as you ascend toward the upper pitch. The laryngeal tilt is only a slight movement, and it may take time and repetition to feel this transition smoothly. It is related to deepening the vowel space while ascending in pitch.

4. As the larynx tilts down and forward, feel the vowel drop deeper. Concentrate on feeling the vowel deeply, as though it originates below the vocal cords.

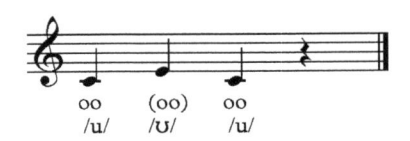

oo   (oo)   oo
/u/   /ʊ/   /u/

5. Notice that the vowel will alter slightly and the singer will have the sensation of dropping it deeper when ascending in pitch. The /u/ vowel will alter on the upper pitch toward /ʊ/ (as in "book").

6. Take this exercise up gradually by semitones through the middle register.

7. Repeat this exercise with a wide east-west stretch at the lower laryngeal muscles, soft palate, and root of tongue. Maintaining the image of a wide east-west stretch discourages depression of the larynx with the tongue-root.

Exercise 7.4: Using "Primal Sound"

What is often called "primal sound" requires a healthy stretch of the pharynx when making the altered vowel sound /ʊ/, as in the English word "*book*." This vowel encourages the expansion of the Italian /u/ vowel, making it deeper in the pharynx, encouraging the pharyngeal wall to open. This allows for a fuller release of the larynx in the middle register, which then in turn allows more resonant tone.

1. ***Female singers***: Make the /ʊ/ sound (as in "book") several times, using chest voice (heavy mechanism). ***Male singers:*** Make the /ʊ/ sound (as in "book") several times, using the sound of the speaking voice.

/ʊ/ /ʊ/ /ʊ/   /y/_____
               (i)_____

2. Then sing a five-tone descending scale in the head register (light mechanism), using a rounded /i/ vowel and keeping a feeling of vowel-strength under the vocal folds.

Exercise 7.5 Coordinating Jaw Release and Correct Laryngeal Function

Proper function of the jaw during language production will help establish the proper laryngeal release in singing text in repertoire.

1. Sing the Italian syllables, *da me ni po tu la,* in the middle register on a single repeated pitch.

2. Imagine that after each consonant that the larynx descends slightly. Imagine that at each vowel the jaw wraps straight back and slightly down. This must be accomplished without placing too much pressure on the larynx with the jaw, so it must be a relaxed jaw function.

This exercise is based on the syllables used by Ferdinand Sieber in his sets of *Vocalises*. Allan Lindquest strongly advocated using the Sieber *Vocalises* as the perfect bridge between vocalizing and singing repertoire, and I recommend them to students and teachers as supplemental exercises.

Exercise 7.6 Breathing Correct Jaw Position

This exercise is designed to help discover the appropriate down-and-back jaw position on inhalation.

1. Place a forefinger over the lips (as if you are signaling someone to be quiet).
2. Inhale through the mouth feeling resistance at the lips. As you do this, notice that the jaw assumes a more back position. There will also be a resulting relaxation in the jaw muscles with this exercise. Practice this inhalation several times.

a e i o u____

3. Keeping the forefinger over the lips, vocalize a five-tone scale on the five Italian vowels (a e i o u) without the jaw moving or thrusting forward. You will find a gentle back motion of the jaw without pressure on the larynx. You will also notice that the larynx will slightly descend for each vowel.

Exercise 7.7 Staccato for Thinning the Cords

Many singers employ too much vocal weight (using too much of the thick vocal fold mass too high in pitch). To counteract this tendency, staccato exercises (in conjunction with the idea of thinning the folds, or touching only the thin edges of the folds) can be useful. This exercise is an example of how the mind can stimulate a physical function, and it works beautifully toward releasing vocal weight in the middle register, making the upper range easier to access.

1. Choose a middle-voice pitch and sing it staccato on the vowel /i/, using the idea of touching just the thin edges (fine points) of the vocal folds.

/i/ /i/ /i/ /i/ /i/____

2. Directly following the repeated staccato notes, sing a five-tone scale. As you ascend the scale, vibrate lower on the sternum to insure a more complete vocal protection. You will find the scale

to be much freer and easier to produce. Use the image of vibrating the vowel sound on the sternum. This is an image that can help diminish the reach reflex.

Final Thoughts

> Joan Sutherland often spoke of the importance of vocalizing the middle register correctly. She understood the value of aligning the middle register in order for the high voice to achieve freedom. In a television interview that can be found on YouTube, Dame Joan and Richard Bonynge discuss the importance of the middle register. The discussion takes place toward the end of the video clip.[1]

---

[1] "Joan Sutherland talks about high notes" http://www.youtube.com/watch?v=XMWiQG2RuoY

CHAPTER 8

Balancing the Upper Passaggio

Frequently vocal professionals describe the upper *passaggio* as the range from approximately E-flat to F-sharp at the top of the treble staff for female singers, and one octave lower for male singers. Allan Lindquest regarded the entire head voice from approximately B-flat to F-sharp at the top of the treble staff (one octave lower for male singers)—as an upper *passaggio*. He described each half step in the upper *passaggio* as "another shade of ring and color," referring to the slight difference in resonance for each half step while ascending in pitch.

Approximate Head Voice Transitions

The entry pitch into head voice varies depending upon voice type. For example, baritones and mezzos move into head register at A-flat instead of the soprano and tenor B-flat. Contraltos and basses can transition as low as F-natural. Heldentenors, depending upon whether the singer is a tenoral heldentenor or a baritonal heldentenor, can transition at the baritone A-flat or the tenoral B-flat, and sometimes the A-natural. Realize that there are variables within each vocal category, depending upon the physical structure of the vocal folds: length and thickness determines into which vocal *fach* a voice might fall. The laryngeal tilt in the middle register is key to discovering the exact head voice transitional pitch, at which point there will be a sudden release of higher overtones. The laryngeal tilt cannot be realized until laryngeal muscles are fully released, including the sternocleidomastoid muscles.

The Middle Voice Is Key to Upper Passaggio Alignment

Lindquest was a proponent of the theory that the middle register serves as the foundation of the upper *passaggio*. He also said that waiting until the upper *passaggio* pitches to adjust or alter vowel formation is too late. Some schools of singing advise the singer to wait until E-flat at the top of the treble staff before making any laryngeal adjustment; this approach requires an extreme adjustment of the laryngeal muscles at the upper *passaggio*. A sudden adjustment at the high E-flat is contrary to the goal of achieving a unified vocal sound—laryngeal adjustment must be employed gradually (beginning at the head voice entry pitch) in the upper middle register before moving upward toward the upper passaggio. It is vital to blended registration.

Appropriate Acoustical Space. Developing the ability to sing freely in the upper *passaggio* requires that the appropriate acoustical adjustment be achieved in the upper middle register. This adjustment consists of stretching the pharyngeal wall, which is achieved partly at inhalation and partly by realizing the laryngeal tilt (the down and forward motion of the larynx) in the upper middle register. While the tilt is often achieved by thinking the vowel deeper when ascending in pitch, it may sometimes require a more direct approach in the form of laryngeal massage, especially on the sternocleidomastoid muscles.

Cuperto. The use of an open-throated small Italian /u/ vowel in the pharynx, allows for the gradual increase in vowel space toward the upper *passaggio*. Healthy singing never mirrors a forward vowel that is produced directly out of the mouth cavity. It must be enhanced by the *cupo* space. This *cupo* or *cuperto* function enhances the singer's ability to achieve a more polished and professional tonal quality. The *cupo* space is somewhat present in the middle and low registers, and increases at the upper *passaggio*.

The laryngeal tilt plays a direct role in rounding vowels without over-tensing the lips, making it easier to ascend without laryngeal tension. This is because it helps to achieve a lower and wider release of the laryngeal muscles. The laryngeal tilt is also a factor in helping the singer to find the neutral *schwa* vowel (/ə/ or /ʌ/), a primary factor in finding full-throat release in the upper passaggio.[1]

Rounded Vowels. Navigating this range always requires the use of rounder, somewhat altered vowels. It is important to remember that the rounded vowels must be altered in the pharynx without retracting or narrowing the tongue. The embouchure is slightly rounded, avoiding over-tensing the lips. Lindquest once said, "Tight lips tie up the throat!" He was referring to the reflexive tension in the tongue-root and laryngeal muscles that is often triggered by too much lip tension, especially "trumpeted" lips. It is necessary to learn to round the lips without protruding them forward. Evelyn Reynolds uses the image of

---

[1] I specifically instruct the singer to form the neutral *schwa* in the wide soft palate, never at the tongue-root, as this invites the gag reflex.

covering a yawn in public to accomplish this, which triggers all of the correct muscular reflexes.

Sinking Cheek Muscles. Achieving rounder vowels is directly related to the sinking of the cheek muscles located at the back teeth. These "sucking muscles" can play a huge role in opening the back wall of the pharynx, which in return assists in registration balance toward the upper *passaggio*. They must move inward and forward in direction.

Jaw Release Down and Back. In order for the pharynx to remain open, the jaw must release slightly down and relaxed back when moving higher in pitch. The pillars of fauces must achieve a wide or east-west stretch in order to alter vowels without engaging the gag reflex at the tongue-root. The gag reflex must be avoided at all times, because the resulting pressure at the glottis will block healthy airflow. Think of the cords as a valve: if over-squeezed, the healthy flow of air stops. If a hum is employed with the lips closed and jaw unhinged, the singer will achieve both jaw release and perfect air flow.

The Value of Kinesthetic Sensations

Employment of a vocal protection (open throat) and the resulting feeling of sympathetic vibrations allows a singer to go higher in pitch more easily. The vibrations also act as a form of register navigation. When the throat is open (with a forward, arched tongue position), the resulting kinesthetic sensation can be similar to that of the "*ng*" /ŋ/. The sensation of frontal vibration is a result of coordinating the open acoustical space, a slightly rounded or oval mouth shape, an arched "*ng*" tongue position, a somewhat back jaw position, a released laryngeal tilt, a high and wide soft palate and a wide tongue-root. While producing healthy tone, the sensations are subtle, especially in the middle voice and in approaching the lower part of the upper *passaggio* range. Realize that the frontal vibration is a *result* of an open acoustical space, not the origin of sound.

I refuse to use the term "forward placement", as I would never instruct any singer to "place their voice forward"—world-renowned voice scientist Dr. Johan Sundberg has shown that sound cannot be "placed."

The concept of "placement" invites the singer to close the pharynx and/or squeeze the throat in order to intensify frontal sensations, making easy access to the upper *passaggio* impossible. This is a common mistake and can lead a singer toward a closed throated production. It can take up to three years to release the laryngeal muscles of a singer who has employed a "placement" technique. Navigating one's singing on sound, rather than on healthy sensations and an open acoustical space, always results in a push reflex. Lindquest would repeatedly say in my lessons, "Feel, and try not to listen."

Correct vocal sensations are a *result* of a proper vocal coordination. They are not the *origin* of sound, but a healthy result. When achieved, the singer can then use them as a guide to transition from pitch to pitch and from register to register without muscular interference. Some have called this "threading on the ring." You may observe that a singer who uses sensations as a guide sings more easily and consistently, without forcing a large amount of breath pressure, and with access to legato line.

"Narrowing" the Passaggio

The term *"narrowing"* is sometimes used to encourage laryngeal release or pivot in order to accomplish registration balance from the upper middle range into the upper *passaggio*. I use the term *narrowing* rarely and judiciously, because often a singer will attempt to achieve the narrow ring by narrowing and constricting the back of the throat, which also results in tension at the tongue-root. It is important to clarify that narrowing, in the healthy sense of the term, is an acoustical phenomenon that takes the form of the sensation of a narrow ring.

The narrow ring sensation comes about as a result of an open, north-south (vertical) *and* east-west (horizontal) pharyngeal stretch. Contributing to this open acoustical space are wide soft palate stretch; the "*ng*" /ŋ/ tongue position formed by using the middle of the tongue not the back of the tongue; slightly down and back jaw position; rounded or oval *embouchure*; and low and wide stretch at the base of larynx. This must be achieved without tongue depression. Thus, the narrow ring is actually a result of opening the back wall of the pharynx while releasing the tongue forward toward the "*ng*" position.[2]

The Wide-Open or Spread Passaggio

A wide (open) *passaggio* is often the result of the singer spreading the *embouchure* and raising the laryngeal position. This approach to the high range is usually accompanied by a forward thrust of the jaw and the employment of too much breath pressure. A wide or spread *passaggio* is sometimes an attempt to "lighten" the voice. Some singers adopt this kind of vocal production to seem "authentic" in certain styles of music, employing a light sound with minimal vibrato (classical singers are not immune to such vocal imbalances). The problem for mature singers who employ this approach is that it leads to squeezed laryngeal muscles, a high larynx, and frequent vibrato problems.

The wide, open, and spread approach to the upper *passaggio* can also be an attempt to produce what some consider a more "natural" sound. This is a destructive technique over time, and a singer can never achieve a free upper *passaggio* using this approach. When a high larynx is employed, the singer's only way to crescendo is to push too much breath pressure through the larynx and vocal folds. Often when you hear a healthy early music singer, it is because he/she has studied proper laryngeal release (laryngeal tilt) in the middle register. When one hears a healthy sound in a pop singer, he/she has often studied classically. I compare it to jazz, modern, or Broadway dancers who study ballet as a foundation. This foundation assists in freeing other styles, and protects the throat if employed carefully.

A spread upper *passaggio* often results in chronic hoarseness. This is related to the employment of too much breath pressure, which can result in such damage as polyps, hemorrhages, or nodules. Realize that a spread upper *passaggio* is usually accompanied by a high larynx position, tongue pressure in the form of a depressed tongue or bunched tongue-root, a forward thrust of the jaw, and the use of too much breath pressure through a closed acoustical space.

[2] The "ng" must be produced with the middle and front of the tongue, never the back of the tongue.

Because this type of *passaggio* production lacks proper register alignment, the singer experiences a lot of sound (internal feedback) inside his/her head. But listening to the voice with the "inner hearing" gives a false sense of color and volume. If a singer is producing the upper *passaggio* correctly, the internal feedback will not be that of big sound, but often of a distant tone. Then the audience gets the polished, professional sound.

The "Hooked Over" Passaggio, or False Tongue Cover

I never like to use the term "*cover*," especially in dealing with the upper *passaggio*. Why? Because it encourages a dramatic throat adjustment when approaching the upper *passaggio* range, taking the form of unnecessary and abrupt muscular laryngeal adjustment. This approach is destructive to healthy registration in the voice and creates a great deal of tension at the vocal folds. Some schools of singing teach this dangerous *passaggio* training technique, sometimes calling it the "hook," or "hooked over" sound.

The danger of this method is that it engages the gag reflex at the root of the tongue, blocking healthy airflow and free upper *passaggio* resonance. Due to the direct pressure on the vocal folds, it also encourages a heave reflex of the outer laryngeal muscles. Hyperextension of the lower laryngeal muscles (to the point of the heave reflex) is usually accompanied by a flat or retracted tongue. This tongue position depresses the larynx and diminishes one's access to the high range. Some male singers experience an upper *passaggio* adjustment, but this is merely a register change.

This technique can lead to thickening of the vocal cords, which requires that the singer push too much air pressure in order to go higher in pitch. Once the gag reflex is engaged, the singer can only produce an unrefined. throaty sound—one that is loud inside the singer's head, but is smaller and unfocused to the audience. Tongue retraction mutes resonance. Over time, employment of the "hook" in the upper *passaggio* results in the development of the *vocal wobble* (wide vibrato), mainly due to the engagement of the thicker mass of the vocal folds. And over time, the singer may also develop intonation problems, a sporadic vibrato rate and as described before, could experience vocal damage such as nodules or polyps.

The Acoustically Balanced Passaggio: Chiaroscuro

The most desirable type of vocal production in the upper *passaggio* is an acoustical balance based on what the Italians call the *chiaroscuro* (bright-dark tone). In this approach, each pitch finds its own appropriate color and weight. The correctly produced upper *passaggio* is a result of an open acoustical space, directly influenced by the proper laryngeal pivot in the middle register, and careful, minor alteration of the vowel. When the laryngeal tilt is accomplished correctly in the upper middle register, the singer benefits by accessing the thin-edge function of the vocal folds, a contributing factor in balanced registration, and easy access to the upper *passaggio*.

Singing should never feel as though the tone or vowel is being pushed out the mouth. The small breath-stream should feel as though it travels through the open acoustical space, especially in the area back and upward beyond the wide soft palate. This results in a more protected tone in the entire voice.

A gradual adjustment through the upper passaggio is in direct contrast to a sudden adjustment, which often involves tongue tension and muscular adjustment.

In producing correct sound, the singer will experience a low and wide laryngeal position, which allows the cords to thin, thus assisting in dropping vocal weight while ascending in pitch. The expansion of the Italian pharyngeal /u/ vowel also plays a vital role in balancing the upper *passaggio* range.

Singers who master this type of upper *passaggio* production enjoy vocal longevity because of the absence of breath pressure (and/or tongue pressure) on the larynx and vocal folds.[3] Those who have achieved this balance are either fortunate enough to sing this way naturally early in their study, or they have found an excellent vocal instructor who helped them achieve this balance through proper vocalization and training. Upper *passaggio* release is simply an acoustical result of properly formed vowels.

Training the Upper Passaggio Correctly

When a mature singer is experiencing vocal difficulties in the upper *passaggio*, it is very often due to confusion about the correct application of the vocal protection. The upper passaggio difficulty is directly related to the loss of laryngeal tilt in the middle register, loss of pharyngeal stretch, and loss of freedom in the tongue-root.

Knowing the *cause* of tension and its solution are key in finding vocal freedom. Singers usually are very aware of tension when they experience it in a specific range. It is usually felt in the tongue and the laryngeal muscles. While I was making the transition from tenor to baritone, I would sometimes feel a choking sensation on the E-flat at the top of the staff. I listened carefully to recordings of excellent professional baritones to try to learn how they achieved their vocal freedom in the upper *passaggio* range.

With the help of Dr. Evelyn Reynolds, I learned that the choking feeling I was experiencing was connected to the gag reflex at the tongue-root. This reflex was engaging because the middle register was not functioning with the proper laryngeal pivot or tilt. The vowels had not achieved enough depth in lower pitches. It is important to know that tongue freedom can only be realized when laryngeal pivot is correctly employed in the middle register.

In order for the upper passaggio to balance, the sub-glottal breath pressure must be managed carefully. The total body "hook-up" should reflect a forward stretch of the sternum, wide pectoral stretch, slightly back jaw position, aligned head posture, an east-west stretch of the solar plexus, a slight, forward and upward pull of the lower abdominals, and an opening of the lower lumbar region.

---

3   Sir Thomas Allen is one such singer who has enjoyed a long and healthy career, greatly due to a balanced upper *passaggio*.

As with any vocal issue, a symptom may show up in a seemingly unrelated part of the body. Look at the problem of singing with a high laryngeal position—the actual problem could be caused by the inability to regulate the sub-glottal breath pressure. The resulting tongue tension can block the regulation of the healthy small air stream, or budgeted outflow. The high-larynx could also be caused by a forward jaw position. This is an example of why vocal instructors must always be diligent in researching every possibility in problem-solving and diagnostics. If we simply treat the symptom instead of the cause, then vocal progress will be impeded.

Upper Passaggio: Problems and Solutions

The approach to teaching balance in the upper *passaggio* is quite similar for both male and female singers, using exercises designed to equalize this range of the voice. A balanced upper *passaggio* leads to free and polished singing in the upper range, offering the singer vocal health and longevity.

Weakness in the pharyngeal wall: Weak ("mouthy") vowels, or lack of stretch in the acoustical space (especially in the upper middle voice), leading to lack of laryngeal pivot. Insufficient acoustical space can also cause breathy tone.

Solution: Work pharyngeal vowel exercises, keeping the strength of the vowel both at the glottis and within the pharyngeal wall. Use a 5-tone descending scale on staccato function. First sing the scale on a hum function (with the tongue between the lips), imagining a vowel stretch behind the tongue-root. Then sing the five Italian vowels: i, e, a, o, u, again on staccato function. As you sing the vowels, keep the back of the throat stretched. You will experience an open neck while keeping the integrity of the spinal curve. *See exercise 3.17.*

Breath pressure—too much loose, uncontrolled air forced through the larynx without proper subglottic compression: The primary cause of this problem is a lack of resistance in the lower body muscles. This requires coordination of an east-west solar plexus stretch, open tall feeling in the intercostal muscles, open and wide lumbar muscles in the lower back, and engaged lower abdominal muscles. Another common cause of this disconnect from the body can be related to a forward jaw position, a high larynx position and/or tongue pressure or gag reflex at the tongue root. It can also simply be a direct outgrowth of improper posture.

Solution: Work with the chair exercises in Chapter 2 (especially Exercise 2.8) using a straight chair, to feel the upper and lower back open at inhalation. Then produce a slow sustained hiss to feel the lower body resistance and balance the healthy tiny air stream.

Spread mouth position and forward jaw: The upper *passaggio* cannot balance nor can the larynx be fully released when the jaw is thrusting forward or if the mouth shape is too spread. Keep in mind that an oval mouth position does not involve tight lips and/or protruded lips, as this tightens the tongue.

Solution: Work with a mirror to round the *embouchure* toward a (vertical) oval shape, without tensing the lips forward. You can achieve this by imagining you are covering a yawn in public.[4] Additionally, use two mirrors (placed at a 90-degree angle) to view the profile. This way you can check to see if the jaw is thrusting forward and then make the appropriate correction.

Be sure that the jaw is gently wrapping back after each consonant in the middle and low registers. It is important to never use muscular force to jam the jaw back. You can find a released back jaw position by looking toward a ceiling and allowing the jaw to hang down and back with gravity. Bring the head back to singing position with the jaw in this relaxed down and back position, and sing the Italian syllables: *da me ni po tu*, wrapping the jaw gently back after every consonant.

Forward head, neck, and jaw posture: This posture encourages the larynx to rise, by shortening the muscles in the front of the larynx. This problem may begin with tension in the back of the neck and in the sternocleidomastoids.

---

4   This is an idea that Evelyn Reynolds gave me during my study with her.

Solution: Use two mirrors to help solve this problem. Place them at a 90-degree angle and make sure that you look at your profile. Align the ears approximately over the shoulder area and release the jaw, gently moving it back and slightly down. Begin by doing this exercise without singing, using an up and down chewing motion.

Then gradually begin singing small scales without using much vocal or body intensity. As you begin to add more sound, does your head thrust forward? If so, begin again and repeat this exercise until the neck, jaw, and tongue stay free as you add more sound. In addition, I recommend study of the Alexander Technique to help resolve this problem.

Listening to the inner sound, instead of using sensations. Men experience a loss of volume in the inner hearing when they sing in the upper *passaggio* properly. Women also experience this loss of inner sound, but more so in the lower *passaggio*.

Solution: Begin the realignment process by learning to feel instead of listen. This can be a psychological challenge that can take time to accomplish.

1. Sitting in a straight chair, vocalize starting with exercises based on the "*ng*", making sure that the throat is open. Observe the release of the lower body muscles at inhalation. Discourage over-breathing by taking less air under the rib cage and by thinking inhalation in a north/south direction.
2. Now close your ears completely with your fingers and vocalize in the middle register. Do one exercise with the ears open, and one with the ears closed. Alternate back and forth.
3. Memorize the sensation when the sound is vibrating freely. Encourage your body to remember these sensations instead of listening. Do this exercise repeatedly.
4. Additionally, in the range where you are tempted to push, try singing more softly. If you find that your throat tends to close

when singing softly, intensify the forward sternum stretch so that the tone remains fully body-connected. This encourages a lower larynx position.

Shaking diaphragm. The shaking diaphragm is actually a result of a shaking solar plexus area. This shaking motion thrusts fluctuating levels of air pressure through the larynx, which destabilizes the vocal line and over-blows the vocal cords.

Solution: Learn to balance a slow and consistent support line, or what I like to call the "legato moan" function.

1. Sit in a straight chair and inhale with the feeling of the hip sockets opening and the lower abdominal muscles relaxing downward as the lower back or lower lumbar area expands.
2. Now speak a strong, voiced /v/ on any pitch. Feel the resistance in the lower body. Make the sound pulsate and then move toward a sustained, equalized sound.
3. Now place the hands directly below the lower rib cage on each side. As you inhale, feel the solar plexus area expand *slightly* wide. This movement must be slight or you will hyper-extend the front ribs.[5] You will feel resistance under the outer sides of the solar plexus as you speak or sing. There will be an east-west stretch of the solar plexus area as a result of the voiced /v/. This stabilizes the solar plexus so that there is a consistent resistance, or even breath-flow. Memorizing this sensation will correct the shaking diaphragmatic response when singing. Next, experiment with scales, using vowels. Then add consonants, without the body bouncing or thrusting air pressure at the consonants—they must flow on the same breath stream as the vowels. There should be no difference, otherwise you have the resultant "barking" of consonants that disturbs legato singing.

---

5   Note that it is important to never thrust the solar plexus forward beyond the line of the lower front ribs.

Vowel Sequence for Upper Passaggio Alignment

When moving from the open /a/ to the rounder vowels, make certain that the tongue-root remains wide and that the pillars of fauces sustain a wide stretch. Otherwise this can cut high overtones when moving toward the rounder vowel formation.

Exercise 8.1

a o u o a

Exercise 8.2

a____ o____ u____ o____ a

Exercise 8.3

a e i o u o a e i

Exercise 8.4

be - lli - sa - rio
/bɛ/ /li/ /sɔ/ /rjɔ/

Exercise 8.5

Allan Lindquest was given this series during his study with Enrico Caruso in 1914.

Variation

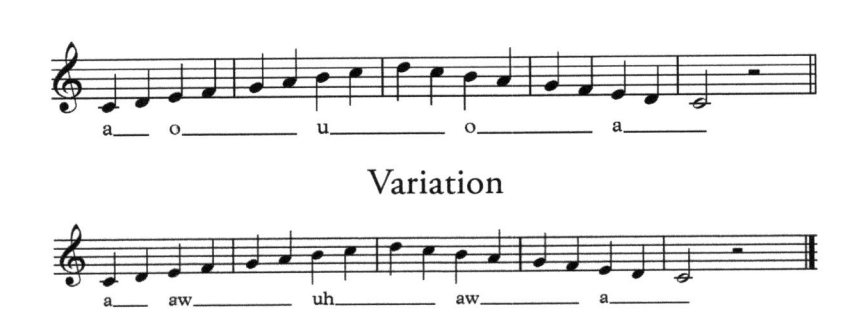

Final Words

> "*A free high range is almost completely dependent upon a properly produced middle and upper passaggio range.*"
>
> - Allan R. Lindquest

CHAPTER 9

Healthy Training of the Female Lower Passaggio

Navigating the lower passaggio range is frequently one of the more challenging technical issues for female singers. They are often faced with a large transitional break between light mechanism (head voice) and heavy mechanism (chest voice), and may experience an abrupt shift in registration. Balance can be found by developing a fuller understanding of how to approach the lower passaggio through the use of better options in vocalization; specific exercises can assist in creating more vocal balance. This new-found balance offers the singer a more dependable instrument, one that can transition easily between registers, allowing for the development of a more professional, polished sound.

Navigating the Lower Passaggio Register Transition

Many female singers suffer from a lack of higher overtones in the chest register and a lack of lower overtones in the lower head voice range.

Female singers need to integrate a healthy amount of body-connected lyrical tone into the chest register. It is a necessary factor in more easily matching the timbre of chest register and the lower head voice.

In "lightening" the voice there is sometimes a tendency to disconnect from the sternum and lower body, weakening the vocal fold adduction in the lower head register. Instructing a singer to "lighten the voice" without explaining how to accomplish it correctly can encourage their body to disconnect, which can create a myriad of other issues, in a domino effect—higher larynx position, lack of vocal fold adduction, breath issues or inability to sing longer phrases, registration problems, a forward thrusting jaw, and neck tension.

Accomplishing body-connected lightness in the chest voice requires working with the thin-edge function of the vocal folds along with the proper tongue-root release. It must be coordinated with an open acoustical space, but without tongue retraction. Allan Lindquest once said in a lesson with a female student, "*We must learn to diminish the muscular weight (thicker cord mass) out of the chest register, and fill in the lower head voice range with proper laryngeal release, allowing for lower overtones to be released. This is achieved by thinning the cords in the chest register, and by opening the lower laryngeal muscles in the low head voice.*" This is a process of major importance for the female singer in balancing the lower passaggio.

Descending Phrases

Maintaining higher overtones in heavy mechanism can be challenging when singing descending phrases. But it can be accomplished by (1) sustaining a forward arch of the tongue, as in the "*ng*" position; (2) lifting and widening the soft palate; and (3) thinning the vocal folds using staccato exercises. It is critically important that the "*ng*" be formed with the middle/front of the tongue. Avoid forming it with the back of the tongue as this inspires a gag reflex at the tongue-root, which tends to close the acoustical space. Remember that the tongue-root must remain wide, relaxed slightly downward and forward, and free of any narrowing or bunching. But continue to check that the front of the tongue remains forward and arched in position.

Outlining Common Technical Problems and Health Issues

Vocal difficulties in the lower passaggio can be frequent and can stem from multiple sources—each unique voice mirrors individual issues that are related to specific technical problems. But these technical issues can also be related to physical health issues.

Technical Issues

Use of too much vocal fold mass in the chest register. Many female singers have an over-development of the chest register, which can weaken the lower head voice (light mechanism), frequently resulting in a breathy tone in the lower head voice register. An over-developed chest register can also play a major role in the development of a wide, slow vibrato, or what many call the vocal wobble.

Solution: Instruct the singer to use staccato exercises in the chest register on both open and closed vowels. This thins the cords and reduces the amount of vocal weight employed. After working with staccato exercises, then move toward a legato 3-tone scale while remembering the sensation of the staccato 3-tone scale.

Lack of healthy body connection. Loss of full body connection (support) can be due to a fear of the lower passaggio transition. It can result in weakness of tone and/or breathiness in the low head voice range. Weakness in the light mechanism is directly related to a lack of chest resonance in the lower head voice range. This is caused by a narrowing of the lower laryngeal muscles or a lifting of the larynx position in the low head voice range.

Solution: Use the laryngeal tilt on the "ü" /y/, allowing the laryngeal position to tilt down and forward while ascending on a major third.

Also vocalize tongue/lip trills from the lower head voice range into the chest register.

Relying too much on "inner hearing." In navigating the lower *passaggio* area, many singers are enticed by their inner hearing, a trap that invites the singer to push for too much sound in the lower head voice range. This often results in forcing too much air through the vocal folds. The resulting issues include a high laryngeal position and a resulting weakness in vocal fold adduction in the lower head voice range.

Solution: To work toward using sensation rather than sound to navigate the voice, use an earplug in one ear while vocalizing. This minimizes the internal auditory feedback, forcing the body to use more sensation as a guide. Work with the idea of going for less sound inside the head, at least at first.

Pushing too much air through the vocal folds at the onset in the lower head voice. This is usually a direct result of the singer "over-listening" and working toward too much sound at the lower *passaggio* pitches. The female singer experiences much less volume in the lower middle register (low head voice), which can invite her to push for more sound.

Solution: Learn to vocalize blocking both ears. Earplugs may be used to accomplish this. Then use one earplug so that internal sound feedback is lessened, yet there is some internal sound. Also work on lower body support in the lower head voice range.

Compressing the rib cage at the lower passaggio register transition. Pulling down the rib cage can feel like support, but it contributes to over-locking the vocal folds by over-compressing the breath, at which point the tongue-root is also invited to lock. Then the singer must push large expulsions of breath through the vocal folds in order to force phonation.

Solution: Work with a good Alexander teacher to reverse the downward pull of the ribcage. The ribs under the arms must be taught to elongate and become taller when moving through the transitional area of the voice.

Spread embouchure or spread vowels. Spreading the embouchure and/or vowels encourages a higher larynx position, diminishing the pharyngeal space and results in a lack of healthy closure of the vocal folds.

Solution: Work with a mirror to achieve a rounder embouchure (mouth opening). Also work on the ü (/y/) in the mid-range, sinking the cheeks inward and forward at the molars. Use fingertips to accomplish this. The singer will experience more acoustical space. This opening assists in a healthy closure of the cords.

Any forward thrust of the jaw raises the larynx position and disturbs proper adduction of the vocal folds. It especially compromises phonation in the lower head voice range. A singer is tempted to develop this habit because she will receive more internal sound; however, the audience will get less volume due to the lack of vocal fold adduction.

Solution: Work with Lindquest's gentle chewing exercise, chewing only up and down, not side to side. This teaches a slight back-and-down movement of the jaw. Make certain that the motion is small and the jaw muscles are working in a slow elastic motion. ***Note:*** *The forward thrust of the jaw can be a result of a high larynx position.*

Work on breathing a wider stretch at the lower laryngeal muscles at inhalation. Also place fingers slightly behind the ear-line and stretch downward on the sternocleidomastoid muscles as you sing upward. This will release any tendency for the larynx to rise.

Improper head position. Misalignment of the head or a forward head posture can contribute to the closing of the pharyngeal space. This in turn lifts the laryngeal position. A tucked and overly lowered head position should also be avoided, as this depresses the larynx with the jaw and tongue-root.

Solution: Work with two mirrors, or a wall mirror and a hand mirror. Watch the profile while vocalizing and look for the ears to be somewhat over the shoulder area. Another tool is to place fingertips behind the ears and stretch straight upward, which assists in releasing the sternocleidomastoid muscles in the neck.

Tensing the tongue-root and jaw at the lower passaggio transition: This issue results from a fear of the "lower break." The tongue/jaw tension can be confused with muscular support, but it works against the process of proper register blend.

Solution: Vocalize through the lower transition on the tongue/lip trill. Also vocalize placing the tongue-tip on the hard palate in an upward direction. Many singers may feel a release at the root of the tongue; however, this does not work for everyone.

Bunching, narrowing, or retracting the tongue-root. This is often an unconscious attempt to force a clean adduction of the vocal folds when breathiness is present in the lower head voice.

Solution: Vocalize with a chopstick under the tongue, with the tongue-tip tucked behind the lower teeth. This stretches the tongue-root and allows it to take a wider shape. If the tongue is shorter, place the chopstick on top of the tongue, which will help resist any tongue retraction.

Creating a false color. Many tongue problems are caused from the singer's attempt to create a false internal color by pulling the tongue back or depressing the tongue-root. The resulting tongue pressure disturbs the healthy adduction of the vocal folds.

Solution: Use the chopstick idea once again, placing it under the tongue and tucking the tongue-tip behind the lower teeth. If the tongue is shorter, simply roll the tongue forward slightly out of the mouth and place the chopstick on top of the tongue to detect any tongue retraction. Also realize that you must memorize the resulting balanced sound and what that offers the inner hearing. I often tell my students, "I go for the slightly far-away slightly unattractive sound in my inner hearing. The resulting ring can sound like a noisy rattle inside the head!"

Dealing with Specific Health Issues

In addition to technical vocal factors, some health issues can also contribute to problems with the female lower *passaggio*. The following segment is designed to offer an outline of these issues and solutions that help to solve them.

Allergies (nasal drainage, etc.) can cause slight vocal cord swelling or edema. This makes the lower *passaggio* register transition more difficult to negotiate.

Solution: I advise that a singer go to a good ENT (Ear, Nose and Throat doctor) or laryngologist, preferably one who works with singers. Get some advice on both alternative treatment and standard treatment. [1]

Acid reflux, parasites, or candida can cause swelling of the vocal folds, slight hoarseness and/or breathiness of tone and inconsistency in phonation from day-to-day.

Solution: Find a good doctor who deals with both Western and alternative solutions. If you have been on antibiotics repeatedly, you may need a round of anti-candida medication, which will reduce drainage and therefore any residual edema. If you have acid reflux, check your diet and find a good practitioner who works regularly with this condition.

Coughing, due to an infection or other illness can cause breathiness of tone, due to edema and/or a slight bowing of the vocal cords.

Solution: Vocal rest until a full recovery is reached. Also if your cough is persistent, check with your doctor, preferably an ENT. Apply

---

[1] Dr. Benjamin Asher in New York works with alternative and Western modalities. His website is www.benjaminashermd.com.

exercise 9.1 to reintroduce a healthy vocal fold adduction once you have recovered.

Hormonal Shifts: As singers become more mature, hormone imbalances can occur. Many singers investigate bio-identical hormone replacement to assist in bringing the voice back to more balance. Some are not candidates for such treatment. In such cases, I have an article on my website.[2] There are also helpful exercises on my instructional CD.[3]

Frequently Asked Questions About the Female Lower Passaggio

On what pitch should the singer transition into chest register?

This question pertains to the transition pitch from the middle register (lower head voice or light mechanism) downward into the chest register (heavy mechanism). A number of factors must be considered in addressing this question. The following list of questions and answers should clarify any questions.

Is the passage to be sung on an open or closed vowel? Open vowels tend to encourage a higher pitch transition into the chest register, as opposed to closed vowels. Singers tend to achieve a better adduction on the closed vowels, making it easier to mix head voice mechanism lower in pitch.

Where does the note occur in the musical phrase? If a transitional note occurs toward the end of the breath line (when the singer is running out of breath), then she may go into chest register higher in pitch. Moving into chest higher in pitch frequently occurs when the singer is running out of breath.

---

2 "Vocalizing Through Menopause: Regaining Lost Vocal Function" www.voiceteacher.com/menopause. This article also applies to andropause.
3 "An Introductory Lesson with David Jones: A Resource for Singers and Teachers", available at www.cdbaby.com/david.

What is the intervallic relationship being navigated? The larger the leap downward, the more likely the singer will transition into chest register on the lower note (also depending upon vowel, pitch, and whether the note is at the beginning or the end of a phrase).

What is the singer's vocal fach? Contraltos often go into and sustain chest register higher in pitch, while sopranos and lyric mezzos usually delay the chest register transition until lower in pitch. For example, a contralto might take a chest mix all the way up to F, but the lyric mezzo might not go above E-natural or E-flat in chest. The lyric soprano may not be comfortable taking the chest register above the E-flat. This can also change depending upon the emotional intensity of the phrase and the singer's temperament or personal choice.

The level of dramatic intensity. Dramatic music often invites using chest register a little higher in pitch. This must be carefully managed in order to be safe for the voice, and the chest register must be produced with a healthy amount of high overtones and thin edge function of the vocal folds. This requires an arched tongue position and a high, wide tongue position with a released tongue-root.

The dynamic level indicated by the composer. If a tone sits right at the lower passaggio and the composer wants a *forte*, then the singer is more likely to use chest register, especially if it is an isolated single pitch. Phrases that move downward with closer intervallic relationships must judicially be orchestrated into comfortable registration.

The vocal energy of the singer on a particular day. Fatigue can invite going into chest register higher in pitch. At such times, the singer may have to concentrate more on sustaining lower body resistance (support) in order to mix head register further downward in pitch. I recommend some type of physical exercise to awaken the vocal energy. Panting is also a wonderful way to awaken the body.

Personal choice. Because voices are highly individual in function, there is also the aspect of personal choice. However, in the interest of a vocal longevity, I discourage utilization of heavy chest singing. The personal choice in deciding how transitional pitches are to be navigated can also reflect the choice of a conductor.

Why are certain vowels more difficult to navigate on transitional pitches?

The increased level of difficulty for the production of certain vowels depends upon vocal fold function. Open sounds, such as /a/ or /ɔ/, are more difficult to maintain in the head voice function than closed vowels, such as /i/ or /e/. This is because the vocal folds approximate slightly further apart on open vowels than on closed ones.

Exercises that move from closed vowels to open ones are frequently found in Old World training. Their purpose is to match the vocal fold approximation of the closed vowel to the open vowel function. Moving slowly between the two types of vowels, making as little adjustment as possible, can help the singer find acoustical balance between open and closed vowel sounds. When approaching this concept, I recommend that you begin with the closed vowel such as /i/ or /e/. ***Note:*** If the larynx rises on the open vowel, correct vocal fold adduction will be disturbed. For open vowels it is important to use the depth of the schwa "uh" (Λ) vowel at the base of the larynx in order to assist vocal fold approximation for those vowels.

What will help the singer balance the thickness of the chest voice register and middle register?

When a singer suffers from an overly heavy chest register, the lower register transition (break) is more obvious and difficult to manage. This is partly due to the fact that the singer has not trained the thin edge function of the vocal folds in the chest register. The transition can be minimized and disguised by combining the thin edge function with learning not to blow too much breath pressure at transitional pitches (***Note:*** the singer may always *feel* a slight break in the lower *passaggio*).

The balance between chest and head mechanism can be enhanced by using more chest resonance within the lower head voice mechanism, what some call "picking up vocal weight." The goal is to add vocal weight or fullness in the lower head voice range and drop vocal weight in the chest register, which assists in mixing these two registers. Staccato exercises in the chest register can be helpful in achieving this goal. Vocalizing in the lower head register with wide lower laryngeal muscles can be helpful in filling out the lower head voice range.

What role does posture play in blending the lower head voice and the chest voice?

A slight low and forward pull on the sternum, often referred to as the Italian *appoggio,* or leaning of the body, assists in controlling the small stream of breath on which to pronounce. This is accomplished by expansion of the lower back. The resulting breath control makes it possible for the singer to achieve and sustain a lower larynx position.

If the singer's posture is incorrect, she will often pull the chest mechanism too high, making it difficult to increase chest resonance when descending into the lower head voice. This is quite limiting, especially for lower-voiced singers. Mezzos and contraltos particularly need to internalize the concept of healthy open posture, making it a daily part of healthy vocalization.

Why does my lower middle voice seem so small to me?

You are listening with your inner hearing. There is an acoustical deception for women, especially when singing in the lower head voice. This deception makes them believe that little sound is being produced. In the lower middle voice, female singers only hear about one-third of the volume that the audience hears. We all know that hearing our voice played back on a recording is a totally different experience from what we hear internally. Therefore, it is critical that singers learn *not* to listen, but to allow sensations to be their guide. This way the resulting resonance can expand the sound.

Why are certain styles of music easier for negotiating the lower passaggio than others?

Singing a slow, legato line makes it easier to accomplish the proper balance between lower head voice and the chest register, mainly because there is time to concentrate on kinesthetic sensations that assist in navigating the lower *passaggio* correctly.

Some styles of music may invite a fuller, more robust sound that encourages a more open acoustical space. This open space can make it easier to transition down into the chest register, because it encourages more laryngeal pivot, allowing a more complete approximation of the vocal folds. An open acoustical space, without over-spacing (hyperextension of the lower laryngeal muscles and/or tongue retraction), is a major factor in smoothing the lower *passaggio* transition. Remember that the tongue must be arched and forward in the mouth space in order for ring to be sustained in the lower head voice register.

Why do some female singers have a minimum amount of register break, while others have a large break between registers?

Everyone has different length and thickness of vocal fold structure. Some singers rarely need to transition downward into full chest because they have enough sound without down-shifting. Most singers, however, do need to develop the ability to shift smoothly into the chest register without evidencing an abrupt break.

Minimizing breath pressure at the transitional point, and sustaining the wide, high soft palate can be quite useful. In addition, the laryngeal position must be stabilized. If the larynx rises in the lower head voice range, then the transition into chest register will be more abrupt.

Why are rounded vowels important in the lower passaggio?

The primary reason for rounding the embouchure in the lower *passaggio* (feeling the sensation of a narrow ring) is that it maintains the elongation of the vocal tract, which assists in achieving a low larynx, and high, wide soft palate. This produces more resonance in the lower head voice range, thereby resulting in more sound and an easier transition into the chest register.

What is the most efficient way for me to vocalize on my own, without pushing too much sound or without under-singing?

Using the tongue-lip trill through the lower *passaggio* transition is an easy way to vocalize through the break or transition point between the lower middle register and the chest register. The tongue-lip trill teaches the body an evenness of breath flow, which is a major factor in avoiding either the over-blowing or under-fueling of the vocal folds. Too much breath pressure at this transition point causes a bigger break. The goal for the singer is to find balance in the flow of air, using neither too much breath nor too little. The tongue-lip trill can be performed on musical phrases, as well as with scales and arpeggios.

How do I add vocal weight in the lower head register, employing the Italian appoggio?

This is a fundamental question. As stated earlier, the *appoggio* is a crucially important tool to assist the singer in holding back breath pressure, because it invites engagement of both the lower lumbar muscles and the upper and lower abdominal muscles. Lean slightly forward and down with the sternum while vocalizing, without losing the open chest posture. Vocalize, using the image that you are vibrating lower and lower on the sternum, perhaps beyond the sternum, all the way down to the solar plexus area. This will fill out the lower head voice without pushing too much breath pressure.

Exercises

Exercise 9.1

This exercise helps close the cords. It should be used from about F sharp 3 to B flat 3.

1. Using the vowel /ae/ (as in "cat"), sing a three-note scale in chest voice.
2. Take a breath. Then, using head voice on the vowel /u/, sing a descending octave scale, keeping the feeling of the /u/ vowel deep under the cords.

Exercise 9.2 Increasing Vocal Weight when Descending[4]

In this exercise, the singer must feel a low and deep vibration on the lower sternum when descending the scale toward the open vowel sound. This will yield more chest resonance in the lower head voice mechanism and can be achieved by using a slight forward, open, and downward pull at the sternum. (*Note:* If the chest is too high or hyperextended, it will be impossible to acquire more vocal weight on the descent).

Sing a descending-ascending-descending five-tone scale, picking up chest resonance when descending toward the /a/ vowel.

---

[4] This exercise may also be used in the training of male voices, especially when the singer has difficulty in finding more chest resonance when descending in pitch. It is an especially necessary study for lower male voices—basses, baritones, and bass-baritones.

[musical notation: u_ o_ a_ o_ u_ o_ a]

Exercise 9.3

This exercise helps close the vocal folds and release the tongue root.

- Placing the tongue over the lower lip, and starting as low as comfortable, allow head voice to come in with a feeling of the vowel deep under the glottis.

[musical notation: /æ/_____]

Exercise 9.4

This exercise helps to sustain a lower larynx on descending passages.

- Sing the scale using the French /œ/ vowel[5] (as in "coeur").

[musical notation: /œ/_____]

Exercise 9.5

[musical notation: a u a u a u a]

1. First, sing the above pattern, yodeling between chest and head register.

[musical notation: /œ/_____]

---

5   Shape the mouth for /ɔ/ (aw) and pronounce an /ɛ/ (eh).

2. Then, using the French vowel /œ/ (as in "*coeur*"), sing a descending scale, mixing into a stronger chest resonance as the scale descends.

a u a u a u a /œ/

Exercise 9.6

This exercise helps balance the thickness of chest register and middle register. Use a rounded /i/.

i i i i i i i i

Exercise 9.7

Tongue-lip trills on descending octave scales, and on descending arpeggios.

tongue-lip trill

The tongue-lip trill is accomplished by placing the tongue over the lower lip in a relaxed way, and then by blowing. Anything that vibrates is fine. The goal is to make the sound of a "slow motorboat."

CHAPTER 10

Understanding the Physical Function Required for Legato Singing

The term *legato* is used to describe a smooth, uninterrupted vocal line, whether sung with or without text. Achieving legato singing is essential for not only for vocal health, but also for artistic development. Legato singing is achieved when the singer is able to produce a connected line of sound without sudden interruptions, which are often a result of abrupt changes in sub-glottic breath pressure. These sudden shifts can be a result of the use of too much breath pressure at the consonants, or when there are large leaps in pitch. Naturally it is more of a challenge when language or large intervallic leaps are involved in a musical phrase.

Achieving Breath Regulation in Legato Line

It is quite simply not enough to request that a singer sing legato without explaining *how* to achieve it. Imagery alone will not suffice—singers need to learn the technical, physical factors involved in achieving legato singing, in vocalization as well as repertoire. This chapter discusses the physical causes of non-legato, expulsive singing, and offers corrections to help solve these issues, allowing the singer to accomplish a legato line.

Inhalation and Balanced Posture

When balanced posture is achieved, a singer can simply release the lower body and the intercostal muscles, and a new breath will respond automatically. A tense inhalation will simply lock the body, causing difficulties for the singer. The truth is that singers who over-breathe, over-sing.

Breathing Low in the Body

Allan Lindquest believed in taking in less air, with the feeling of inhalation low in the body. Since we cannot anatomically breathe below the line of the lungs, the feeling of a low breath simply means dropping the internal organs at inhalation so that a complete breath can be realized. Lindquest instructed singers to breathe into the lower curve of the back (the lumbar area), while keeping the lower abdominal muscles rather flat (to encourage expansion in the back). The lower breath also releases the hip sockets so that they feel wider as breath is taken. The Alexander Technique's "monkey" position is a good tool for helping a singer to feel lower body release. It also assists in realizing flexibility in the back ribcage, a must for flexible breathing.

Breath Usage: Maintaining a Small, Even Breath Stream

A small even breath stream is necessary to produce a legato line. This small, controlled stream of air is the fuel for pronouncing text without pushing the voice, balancing the elements of holding back breath pressure, while fueling a small air stream on which to pronounce. It must be produced with a flexible ribcage and a flexible body.

Exercise 10.1 Hissing Breath

Use a strong hiss function, employing quite a lot of resistance at the tongue and teeth. This will offer the singer the feeling of holding back the breath pressure (support) with the lower body resistance, while allowing a small, controlled breath stream to come through the larynx. A similar effect can be achieved by blowing strongly through a small straw; you will immediately achieve the feeling of body resistance.

Exercise 10.2 Tongue/Lip Trill

tongue-lip trill _____ ah _____

The tongue/lip trill is a good tool for regulating breath flow. Dr. Evelyn Reynolds uses the five-tone scale, moving from the lip/tongue trill to a vowel in the scale.

Exercise 10.3 Using /z/ and /v/

A singer can use the voiced consonants such as /z/ or /v/ to encourage legato line in music. Sing through phrases using /z/ or /v/ and notice the feeling of maintaining constant breath compression.

Avoiding Over-Breathing

Legato singing requires balancing the outflow of breath, and key to achieving a balanced outflow is to avoid over-breathing—including taking a large amount of breath in the upper chest area, and/or hyperextending the ribcage too wide. Over-breathing, including hyper-extending the ribcage, tends to encourage over-blowing the vocal folds, especially at consonants. Taking less air efficiently invites budgeted outflow of breath, a goal in legato singing.

I like to describe the sensation of inhalation as *deep and narrow*, and the sensation of support as a *wider* feeling. Evelyn Reynolds taught the sensation of breathing low in the body by having singers place a fingertip over the lips to create resistance, then having the singer inhale quickly, while keeping the resistance. This inspires the sensation of breathing lower in the body.

The tendency to push can be minimized by using Caruso's image of producing the consonants and vowels under the vocal folds or at the base of the larynx. Caruso's image is somewhat related to what the Italians call *"inhalare la voce"* or *"drinking in the voice,"* which encourages a sensation of vacuuming the breath below the vocal folds. Even though there is a small air flow using this idea, these images help the singer achieve a lower larynx position and can lead to a more balanced vowel alignment.

Negotiating Wider Intervals

Regulating an even outflow of breath to achieve a legato line can be especially challenging when large intervals must be navigated, especially from middle register to the upper *passaggio* or higher. Lindquest often used the terms *"legato grunt"* or *"moan,"* using the leaning of the body (*appoggio*) to assist in regulating the outflow. The *"deep moan"* resembles a deep hum, which comes from a coordination of the lumbar muscles (lower back) gently stretching wide as the tone is being produced. The lower abdominal muscles react first by resisting slightly outward, then by lifting upward as the singer moves through the musical line.

Exercise 10.4 The Deep Body Moan

Leaning slightly forward from the waist while making a deep moaning sound will help the singer to feel the proper sensation of legato breath support. When performing this exercise, the body weight should be on the front pads (balls) of the feet. This flexibly engages the upper gluteal and lower abdominal muscles.

Jaw Function in Legato Singing

Many singers open their mouths too much, either by locking the mouth open, or by thrusting the jaw downward abruptly at consonants ("barking"). Both of these behaviors distort legato singing. Thrusting the jaw forward when singing causes leakage of the vocal folds, loss of resonance, and invites a higher laryngeal position, distorting legato line. The forced, downward thrust of the jaw must be avoided completely, as this results in a gag reflex at the tongue-root, which disturbs legato line.

In the middle and lower registers, try to avoid opening the jaw too much. When the jaw is thrust open too far in the lower range of the voice, the resulting gag reflex at the tongue-root forces the singer to use too much breath pressure in order to force phonation.

The gentle chewing motion of the jaw is a wonderful tool for releasing jaw and tongue tension, which in turn encourages legato singing.[1] For unvoiced consonants, the gentle chewing motion between vowel and consonant function enables a smoother line of sound, because of the release of the jaw, neck, and laryngeal muscles. The resulting *"uh"* /ʌ/ vowel at the base of the larynx creates more purity of line, increasing the vibration-time of the vowels and minimizing the time spent on the consonants.

Tongue Function in Legato Singing

Legato line is dependent upon the gentle chewing motion of the jaw in combination with the independent use of the tongue. I tell singers to pronounce 90% with the tongue and only 10% with the gentle jaw motion (gentle chew).

The *"ng"* /ŋ/ sound can play a major role in assisting the development of legato singing. Kirsten Flagstad said, "The /ŋ/ is the silver thread that is the soul of my voice and the basis of pure artistic legato singing."

---

[1] In employing this concept, the jaw should only chew gently up and down, not side to side, within a small range of motion. Allan Lindquest often instructed me to chew gently before going to the next vocal exercise. He emphasized that the proper position of the jaw for singing is hanging slightly down and back, much as the jaw would hang down and back if lying face up on a bed or sofa.

Flagstad used exercises that involved a quick movement from the "ng" to /a/ or /o/ vowel; she also used it reflexively with the /e/ vowel. Mme. Haldis Ingebjard Isene, one of Flagstad's teachers with whom Lindquest studied in 1939, used the *"ng"* as a basic exercise to achieve legato line. Lindquest often encouraged the use of the /ŋ/ position of the tongue as home position for the tongue. This encourages a forward arched front half of the tongue, as the tongue-root relaxes slightly down and forward.

Moving from the /ŋ/ to a vowel encourages the soft palate to elevate slightly and to widen reflexively without over-stretching or over-spacing. Over-stretching the soft palate can encourage depression of the larynx with the tongue-root, which in turn encourages tongue retraction. Threading the /ŋ/ over each vowel, while also avoiding nasality[2], assists in learning the proper sensations that guide legato singing.

Important considerations for using "ng": First, in order for the singer to benefit from the use of *"ng"*, the jaw must be hanging loose and the /ŋ/ must be produced with the middle of the tongue, never at the tongue-root. Second, the /ŋ/ often does *not* work for a singer who suffers from a great deal of laryngeal tension or a history of high larynx singing. The study of *"ng"* may need to be delayed for any singer who has not first achieved the open pharyngeal space.

Exercise 10.5 "Ng" with a Pre-Sneeze Feeling

Use the /ŋ/ sound and gradually open to an open vowel such as /o/ or /a/. Keep a slight amount of the /ŋ/ sensation as you open to the vowel. There should be a resistance at the cartilages by the nostrils, as in a slight pre-sneeze feeling. The pre-sneeze feeling helps to lift the soft palate while opening from the /ŋ/ to the vowel. The result will be a vowel that contains ring, which will assist in achieving legato line. If performed properly with a free tongue root, there will be no nasality in the tone.

---

2   Nasality is a result of closing the pharynx, tensing at the tongue-root, dropping the soft palate, or forcing too much breath through the nasal port. It should be avoided.

Language Factors in Legato Singing

Beyond simply achieving a smooth flow of sound between pitch change and vowel change, there is the additional challenge of coordinating the consonant-vowel relationships in text. Pronunciation in singing differs dramatically from pronunciation in speaking. In singing, the pharynx is absolutely more open; the jaw becomes less active, while the tongue becomes more active, increasing the ability to articulate clearly.

Jaw-Tongue Independence

Independence of jaw and tongue is fundamental to efficient diction in singing. Jaw-tongue independence encourages a more sustainable pharyngeal space throughout a given musical line. William Vennard encouraged singers to pronounce all languages using an Italianate approach, which encourages the independent use of tongue and jaw on flipped and dentalized consonants.

Flipped and Dentalized Consonants

Producing the consonants such as /d/, /t/, /n/, or /l/ with only the action of the tongue tip flipping up to the hard palate behind the upper teeth allows the jaw to stay slightly open, allowing for more acoustical space. The goal is to pronounce mostly by flipping the tongue. I tell singers to pronounce 90% with the tongue and 10% with the jaw. This idea diminishes the extreme thrusting of the jaw in pronunciation of text.

I often ask singers to vocalize on Italian syllables on a repeated note, using the syllables *da me ni po tu*. When sung properly, this particular group of syllables requires little or no motion of the jaw.

Exercise 10.6

Study the Italian word *dentale* (with jaw slightly open) and you will find a healthy separation of the tongue and jaw. The jaw is slightly open for the pronunciation of the dentalized /d/. The /nt/ of *dentale* is produced with only one flip of the tongue-tip toward the hard palate. The /l/ is also flipped and voiced, and it should be voiced under the cheekbones as in the /ŋ/. This exercise is only effective using a slightly open (down-and-back) jaw position.

On Consonants

Certain consonants must be pronounced with the jaw slightly released down and back. When an /m/ is pronounced with the jaw slightly open, the result is more space in the back of the pharynx and more flow of air. I instruct singers to only brush the /m/ on the same breath flow as the surrounding vowels, as this avoids squeezing the throat on this consonant. This approach can also be adopted in considering consonants such as /b/ or /p/, using the idea of producing them only with the compressed air in the mouth cavity. If /b/ and /p/ are produced with the jaw slightly open, there is less tendency to over-blow them with breath pressure. This image can have very positive results with a singer who has been coached incorrectly to over-pronounce in repertoire, exploding the consonants and over-blowing the vocal folds.

Consonants that Require Closing the Jaw

Any consonant or group of consonants in English that involve /s/, /z/, /f/, /v/, /j/, /r/, /tʃ/, or /dʒ/ sounds requires a quick closing and reopening of the jaw. This motion must be negotiated quickly in order to avoid disturbing legato line. I instruct singers to brush these consonants on the same breath flow as the vowels, never allowing them a sudden expulsion of air. In order for a legato line to be achieved and sustained, this motion must be performed without changing breath pressure. To minimize over-blowing at the consonants, Lindquest used the image of forming the consonants in the soft palate. His use of the "gentle chew" to accomplish a free jaw in pronouncing these sounds was instrumental in developing legato line for his students.

Exercise 10.7 Hanging, Relaxed Jaw with Gentle Chewing

Use gentle chewing exercises, chewing only up and down, not side to side. Vocalize from closed vowels to open vowels. This could be /ioio/, or /eaea/, etc. Use five-tone and 9-tone scales.

Work these exercises with a mirror to ensure that the jaw is making slow and gradual movements rather than a fast, thrusting motion. Remember that the gentle chew not only releases the jaw, but it also assists in releasing the root of the tongue. The gentle chew is basic for eliminating jaw tension, which distorts legato singing.

Exercise 10.8 Drinking from a Large Glass

Sing the Italian syllables, *da me ni po tu la be*. Use the hanging jaw as proper position to pronounce these sounds. This can best be found by using the position of "drinking out of a large glass." There should be only about a fingertip's width between the teeth. Allow the tongue to do all of the vowel change. This will release the jaw, and the result will be a more open pharynx. *Note:* If there is a slight lift of the cheek muscles under the eyes, the relaxed hanging jaw will be much easier to establish.

Do this exercise only up to middle C for men, one octave higher for women. Above this, pronunciation must be accomplished with the jaw unhinged and the tongue doing most all the work.

Exercise 10.9 Legato and the Neutral Schwa Vowel /ʌ/

uh da   uh me   uh ni   uh po   uh tu

The Italian school used the concept of an *"uh"* /ʌ/ under each vowel, which elongates vowels (by elongating the vocal tract) when pronouncing text, and helps the singer achieve a more open pharynx when pronouncing voiced consonants. Use of the neutral /ʌ/ sound is the critical foundation of establishing an open throat in legato singing. Using a neutral *"uh"* sound immediately before each consonant assists in legato singing by releasing the larynx, adding fluidity to the legato line.

Over-Pronunciation

Over the course of their studies and performing career most singers will be invited by well-meaning coaches and conductors to over-pronounce. Over-pronouncing disturbs legato singing, as there is too much air pressure forced through the consonants. Firm articulation, using equalized breath flow can be useful for the singer to achieve both clear diction and legato line.

Checklist: Characteristics of Healthy Legato Singing

In observing professional singers who have mastered a pure legato line, it is interesting to note the specific physical behaviors that help them achieve it—from posture, to jaw function, to tongue position, to breath usage, etc.

- **Release of the jaw slightly down and back** after each consonant in middle and low registers.
- **Use of the /ŋ/ tongue position** as home position after each consonant. This encourages the development of higher overtones. Note that this is only an approximate position, designed to encourage the healthy arch of the tongue. The tongue should never be frozen in position.
- **Use of the *appoggio*** (slight forward leaning of the body weight), focusing on the straight forward stretch of the sternum. (This also engages the lower body resistance, and assists in regulating the airflow for legato singing.)
- **Smooth and even flow of breath** between vowel function, consonant function, and at larger intervallic leaps. This encourages the larynx to drop slightly for each vowel in singing text, a must when applying technique to repertoire.
- **Consistent pharyngeal vowel formation** (open throat), which elongates the vowels and diminishes time spent on consonants.
- **Correct facial posture**, which assists in acoustical vowel alignment. This includes a gentle, wide stretch of the muscles under the outer cheekbone area (widening the soft palate), and sunken cheeks at the back teeth to open the pharynx (this requires a slightly unhinged jaw).
- **Careful matching of breath flow and resonance**.
- **Separation of jaw and tongue function** for dentalized and

flipped consonants (the tongue tip flips upward behind the upper teeth in this tongue motion).

- **Use of the gentle chew** in pronunciation of text (the jaw should never thrust downward abruptly).

- **Use of the lower body** to engage the "deep cry" of the Italian School. This is accomplished using resistance in the lower body muscles. Remember that the rib cage must always sustain a tall posture while keeping the intercostal muscles flexible, as taught in the Alexander Technique.

- **Use of the *"uh"* /ʌ/ vowel** directly before each consonant. This sustains a lower larynx in text.

Checklist: Physical Factors that Distort Legato Line

The following conditions can block the development of legato singing:

- **Crunching of the head into the neck at consonants**. This closes the back wall of the pharynx at each consonant, inhibiting resonance. Careful study with a good teacher of the Alexander Technique can solve this issue.

- **Thrusting the jaw forward at consonants and/or vowels**, resulting in a high larynx position, which diminishes resonance.

- **Sudden expulsion of breath pressure at consonants**, which disturbs consistent healthy phonation.

- **Irregular lower body resistance** or pulsations in the lower body muscles, which can include shaking in the abdominal area. This distorts balance in airflow, often resulting in the over-blowing of the vocal folds.

- **Lack of vowel alignment** (each vowel functioning in a dramatically different acoustical space), which encourages imbalance in registration.

- **Lack of consistent ring in the voice**, which leads to the use of differing amounts of air pressure in order to force phonation.
- **Thrusting the jaw downward** in an abrupt motion at consonants. This can be a trap for singers who become dramatically involved in the music in an incorrect way. Intensity must come from body connection, never from downward jaw thrust.
- **Percussive approach to singing larger intervals**, often a result of fear of higher pitches. This results in sudden change in subglottic breath pressure.
- **Lack of low larynx under the consonant function**. The larynx should not rise significantly for consonants, especially voiced consonants.

CHAPTER 11

Applying Vocal Technique to Repertoire

In my experience, I find there are two types of singers: (1) those who sing repertoire more easily than they vocalize, because they are inspired energetically by the music; and (2) those who vocalize more freely than they sing repertoire, but who find it somewhat difficult to merge the technique efficiently into musical expression. Most singers fall into the second category. Even if a singer has a history of excellent training, he/she may still find it a daunting task to integrate healthy vocal technique into the music. Kirsten Flagstad described this process as "orchestrating the voice into the music, or the music into the voice, however one wishes to consider it!" Studying how world-class performers have approached this technique-to-repertoire bridge can be extremely helpful. Each singer discussed in this chapter exemplifies a slightly different approach to fine-tuning and orchestrating the music into the voice.

Security in Performance: The Role of Vocal Technique

Feeling nervous before a performance—sometimes wondering if the voice will perform properly—can be disconcerting. A recurring technical issue can trigger a high level of emotional anxiety and vocal insecurity. The goal of studying vocal technique is to achieve technical balance so that the artistic expression can be spontaneous, singing more on instinct than thought. But one can safely sing on instinct only after technique has been fully integrated into the singing response.

During one of her master classes in New York, Birgit Nilsson remarked, "In my entire career, I had only about 50 days when I awoke feeling balanced spiritually, physically, and vocally. In all those 50 days, I had only two performances." In other words, every singer must learn to find vocal consistency on a daily basis, even though the voice and the body may feel slightly different from day to day.

When a singer is in the process of vocal realignment, he/she must think of technique to some degree. Later, when the correct muscular-vocal response is connected to the singing instinct, the singer can be more spontaneous. Several years ago, I taught a soprano who is still enjoying an international career. After we had worked for about a year, she said to me one day, "I am still having 'off' performances!" I asked, "Well, are you thinking of your technique even 10 percent?" Her answer was, "No, should I be?" I encouraged her to think about technique at least 10-15 percent until she reached a more complete vocal balance, or until the singing response was consistently free.

Healthy vocalization is the absolute foundation of consistent performing. When a singer is in the midst a busy career, it is necessary to have problem-solving tools that work quickly and efficiently. Many years ago, I taught mezzo-soprano Sandra Warfield, widow of James McCracken. She once said that her professional colleagues typically used a small number of vocal exercises that worked efficiently for their individual voice. It kept their warm-ups simple, concrete and effective, while accessing the total voice. She related that McCracken favored a 5-tone scale using the nonsense syllables "*frrima, frrema, frrama, frroma, frruma*" using a rolled "r" to release the tongue-root. He jokingly called this exercise "The Five Sisters"!

Creating Resting Spots

Many composers provide little time to breathe between phrases, and it is up to the singer to learn the craft of creating time. In 1994 I had the privilege of teaching Ms. Shirley Verrett in preparation for her performances of *Carousel* at Lincoln Center. Directly following that production, she presented a master class for the Marilyn Horne Foundation. Ms. Verrett was masterful in helping singers understand breath management, especially in instructing the singers to "cheat," or shorten notes at the end of a phrase, to allow more time to breathe for the next musical phrase. She called this "creating resting spots" within the music, so that the body could release between phrases. Relaxing the body between phrases is critical to singing freely through an entire aria or song.

Singing the Words: Healthy Diction

Applying healthy vocal function to the jaw, larynx, and tongue plays a crucial role in transitioning between efficient vocalization and singing repertoire. Many singers pronounce with the tongue and jaw engaged together, as one function. However, this practice breaks the legato line and closes the acoustical space (pharynx) in the upper *passaggio* and high range.

Vennard's Italianate Approach to Consonants

William Vennard recommended an Italianate approach to consonants (in all languages), utilizing flipped and dentalized consonants produced without the throat or jaw closing. When the jaw closes and the teeth come together, the pharynx (acoustical space) also closes, encouraging a lifted larynx. A raised larynx position encourages the gag reflex at the tongue root, which places pressure at the glottis and blocks airflow, resulting in a throaty tonal quality. Basically, no one can sing well in text until he/she achieves independent use of the jaw and tongue.

Equalized Airflow Through Vowel-Consonant Relationship

Equalization of airflow through vowel-consonant relationship is vital to professional-level singing. In other words, singers must learn to pronounce with a loose, unhinged jaw, brushing the consonants on the same airflow as the vowels. The direction of the airflow should be imagined as traveling up and beyond the soft palate area, spinning the breath flow upward beyond the uvula, never out the mouth (Lamperti was a proponent of this approach). This assists the singer in achieving a protected tone.

Middle and Lower Range Considerations

In the middle and lower range, some singers may achieve optimum ring with a more open or a more closed mouth, depending upon their physical structure. For those singers who find greater ring by using a more closed mouth position in the middle and low registers, the jaw must remain loose and relaxed, with a small space between the teeth. Lindquest encouraged a slight unhinging of the jaw, feeling the small indentation just in front of the ear at the tragus, or the small lobe beside the ear canal.

Jaw Motion Between Vowels and Consonants

To sustain an open acoustical space and an elongation of vowel function, the jaw must move slightly back after each consonant in the middle and low registers. A slight up-and-down chewing motion allows the larynx to drop after each consonant, encouraging a healthy down and forward tilt of the larynx. Laryngeal tilt is especially important in transitioning from middle voice to head voice (light mechanism). Gently wrapping the jaw slightly back at vowel function is a vital skill in sustaining resonance through a purer legato line, a major key in applying technique to text. The gentle back motion of the jaw must be practiced slowly. This can be realized by chewing in an up-and-down motion with the lips sealed. The jaw should never be allowed to thrust forward, as this results in a high larynx position and too much leaking of air through the vocal folds.

The Sieber Vocalises

Lindquest recommended studying the Sieber *Vocalises* as a component in bridging the gap between vocalization and singing repertoire.[1] Ferdinand Sieber (1864-1942) was an Italian-trained voice teacher who knew the importance of vowel alteration and vowel sequencing and their role in establishing and sustaining balance in registration. His *Thirty-Six Eight-Measure Vocalises* are melodies with lyrics based on the Italian syllables *da me ni po tu la be*. The exercises assist in balancing registration and encouraging freedom in pronunciation of text. The vowel sequences are also designed to naturally drop vocal weight when ascending in pitch, accomplishing fullness of tone while ascending.

Another goal of the Sieber *Vocalises* is to establish acoustical balance between open and closed vowels, encouraging the space of the open vowels to integrate into the closed vowels, and the ring and brilliance of the closed vowels to integrate into the open vowels. Lindquest called this the "acoustical vowel line-up," meaning that all the vowels function in a similar acoustical release. When studied slowly and correctly, this type of vocalization can help the singer move toward efficiency in vowel-consonant relationship.

Sieber wrote a different set of exercises for each voice type: tenor, baritone, bass, soprano, mezzo, and alto. Each set of vocalises was written with special attention to the register transitions of each specific voice type. Each singer should use the appropriate book for his/her vocal *fach*; however, if the singer is experiencing a high larynx position when singing, it is acceptable for a higher-voiced singer to work with the mezzo or baritone vocalises first and transition upward later in vocal development.

---

[1] Sieber, *Thirty-Six Eight-Measure Vocalises for Soprano, Op. 92 (Mezzo-Soprano, Op. 93; Alto, Op. 94; Tenor, Op. 95; Baritone, Op. 96; Bass, Op. 97)*. G. Schirmer.

In addition to the *Thirty-Six Eight-Measure Vocalises*, Sieber wrote advanced vocalises for every voice type, to be used as the singer gains more experience[2]. The advanced vocalises present more vocal challenges found in operatic arias. They assist the singer in increasing vocal stamina as the voice grows in resonance and strength. These exercises should not be attempted too early in vocal development. The advanced exercises may be out of print, so finding a copy may be challenging; however, it is worth the effort to find them.

The Flagstad "ng"

Another tool that has long been employed by both the Italian and the Swedish-Italian Schools is the "ng" /ŋ/, as in the English words "singing" or "hanging". Lindquest called it the "Flagstad /ŋ/". In a 1938 interview Kirsten Flagstad said, "I vocalize phrases of arias on the /ŋ/ to establish the sensation of threading each phrase on maximum resonance and registration balance. I affectionately call the /ŋ/ the silver thread that is the soul of my voice."

As a tool for register alignment, the *"ng"* is tremendously effective in working phrases that move from the upper *passaggio* downward. You will note that healthy register changes occur naturally. Careful employment of the *"ng"* /ŋ/ can be especially effective for larger-voiced singers who tend to carry too much vocal weight too high in pitch. Dramatic singers also tend to push too much breath pressure through the larynx, something that is less likely to occur when employing the *"ng"*.

Two Important Considerations about "ng"

First, it must be stressed that the proper formation of the /ŋ/ is with the middle of the tongue, never the back of the tongue. Forming the /ŋ/ with the back of the tongue engages the gag reflex and places direct pressure on the vocal folds. Second, some singers experience tension when taking the /ŋ/ higher in pitch, so I encourage that it be used only within the pitch range that is free. In general, I avoid the use of the *"ng"* beyond the

---

[2] Sieber, *Ten Easy Vocalises and Solfeggios for Soprano, op. 44 (Mezzo-Soprano, Op. 45; Alto, Op. 46; Tenor, Op. 47; Baritone, Op. 48; Bass, Op.49)*. G. Schirmer, Kalmus.

upper *passaggio*, except for some lighter, higher-voiced singers, who find it helpful.

Use of the French [ɛ̃] (as in "plein" or "fin")

Over time, some singers can tend to develop tongue tension, which blocks the free release of upper overtones and makes access to the upper range more challenging. In the lower and middle registers, the /ŋ/, when employed with consistent breath flow, assists in releasing the root of the tongue. However, when approaching the upper range, the French [ɛ̃] (as in, *fin*, *main*, *plein*) can sometimes be a more useful tool in finding freedom in the tongue, releasing it up and out of the pharynx. It also helps the singer to release a small and even flow of air through the larynx on which to pronounce healthily.

In applying this technique to repertoire, I often request that the singer start the first note of the phrase, or sometimes sing an entire phrase, on the French [ɛ̃] or another French nasal, to release the tongue. This technique works especially well for tenors and sopranos in learning to sustain a higher tessitura.[3]

Voce Cuperto: Use of the Tiny /u/

The tiny Italian /u/ plays a crucial role in teaching the *vocal protection* (what some call "cover"). Lindquest frequently called this small vowel the "sweet spot", and when first finding it singers often have the same reaction. "It feels so very small and as though I am doing nothing!" The voice becomes more concentrated acoustically with the use of a smaller, oval-shaped mouth position, accompanied by the pre-sneeze feel at the muscles directly by the nostrils. The pre-sneeze widens the soft palate and closes the cords. The resulting tone travels as concentrated sound, rather than a frayed, spread tone that dissipates in the opera house or concert hall. Lindquest strongly recommended the use of this concept during my study with him as a way of balancing the voice when singing repertoire.

---

[3] I learned a great deal about the use of the French nasals in my work with Dr. Suzanne Hickman.

In an interview, Luciano Pavarotti spoke of using this approach when working on an aria. First, he vocalized every phrase of the aria on what he called the "small Italian /u/ vowel". Next, he would sing the aria on the vowels, keeping the strength (shape) of the /u/ in the pharyngeal stretch. Finally, he added the consonants without interrupting the vocal line and/or breath stream, and without disturbing the stretch of the pharyngeal wall.[4] It is interesting to observe the acoustical results of Pavarotti's approach in his recordings. Study of the recordings of Joseph Hislop and Jussi Björling reveals a similar use of the pharyngeal /u/ vowel in the upper *passaggio* as a basis for all vowels.

Emotion in Singing: The Psycho-Emotional Response

Maintaining technical accuracy while expressing emotional content in the music is vital for every performer. Sometimes we hear emotional singers with little technique, or technical singers with little emotion. How does a singer find balance between these extremes, to be able to express intense emotion without sacrificing good technique and vocal health? The techniques discussed below can help to create balance for both types of singers.

Lindquest once said, "While touring and performing concerts, I often sang eight times per day, seven days per week, sometimes feeling exhausted or ill. But when I saw the faces of the people in the audience, I became so inspired that an internal energy carried me through these numerous performances." He later wrote of the "psycho-emotional response" in singing; something that inspires the singer's voice/spirit connection. When I studied with Lindquest in 1979, I observed him use several emotional reflexes or triggers as a catalyst in establishing the balance between technique and interpretation. He had learned this approach from several teachers, and especially during his study in Stockholm with Joseph Hislop and Haldis Ingebjard-Isene.

---

4   It is important to note that the /u/ vowel must be employed with a wide tongue-root and wide pillars of the fauces—this in turn creates a wider sensation in the soft palate.

The Joyful Surprise Preparatory Breath

One of the first psycho-emotional responses that I heard Allan Lindquest teach was the "joyful surprise" preparatory breath—the breath directly inspiring the physical reflexes of a high and wide soft palate; slightly low and wide larynx; open, tall, and suspended body posture; and a loose jaw. The term "joyful surprise" was common in his voice studio, offering the singer the opportunity to open the acoustical space at the preparatory breath.

The Feeling of Inner Peace

In addition to the joyful surprise breath, Lindquest also asked singers to envision a feeling of inner peace, which was designed to release the entire body at inhalation. He would often say, "Take your breath with a sense of joy *and* peace!" The concept of inner peace can lead the singer toward a deeper internal feeling and a calmer general approach in breathing, singing, grounding, or anchoring the voice. This concept discourages the push reflex, a problem with which many singers continually struggle. While the emotions of joy and peace do not replace technical concepts, they do inspire physical responses in the body that help achieve vocal balance. Of course, the instructor must consistently monitor the singer's physical body responses.

Employing Contrasting Emotional Responses/ Accomplishing Different Vocal Colors

Another powerful tool I learned from Allan R. Lindquest was training the singer in contrasting emotional responses. Teachers of the Swedish-Italian School employed contrasting emotions arising directly from the desire to communicate. This was intended to inspire the body energetically and create contrasting colors in the voice. It was accomplished first in vocalises by singing the same vocalise with a variety of emotions (often in the same key), to evoke a variety of colors in the voice while encouraging complete body-voice coordination. This practice solidifies the vocal technique so that emotional content does not disrupt the voice-body connection. Later this technique was incorporated into the artistry of expression in repertoire.

The primary contrasting emotions Lindquest used in my lessons were anger, sadness, joy, surprise, and grief. I tend to use the three contrasting emotions of joy, sadness, and anger in early training. It is interesting to observe the body-voice response: some singers close their throat when thinking of sadness, or they blow tremendous breath pressure when concentrating on the emotion of anger. Once all the emotions are connected with a similar body response, the singer is on the way to gaining control of the vocal instrument, even in the most dramatic or the most serene moments.

"Emotional" Singers: Pushing and Over-Blowing

In addition to psycho-emotional responses, there are several other technical approaches that can aid the singer in healthily expressing the intense emotions encountered in operatic and song repertoire.

Posture

It goes without saying that when singing with emotion, healthy body posture must be maintained. Drastic changes in posture while singing create drastic changes in the subglottic breath pressure. This is a big contributing factor in the push reflex. Working on a tall, yet grounded, posture while singing can minimize this problem.

Speaking Vowels Below the Cords

"Emotional" singers can tend to push too much breath pressure through the larynx, resulting in loss of vocal control in text. The resulting body energy is too "upward"—disconnected from the body—and does not allow for a low feeling in the body at inhalation. To deal with this issue, Lindquest employed Caruso's approach of speaking the vowels under the vocal cords, which grounds the voice without too much breath pressure. Once the voice feels grounded, then the singer can allow for more emotional interpretation without disconnection from the body. Also, when the ribcage remains flexible in breathing, a more grounded feeling is possible.

Engaging/Resisting at Vowels, Not Consonants

Dr. Evelyn Reynolds taught that to sing text with intensity of emotion, the singer must engage (resist) at the lumbar and lower abdominal muscles. Resistance happens on the vowels, not the consonants. This type of body connection helps the singer express intensity of emotion without over-blowing the vocal folds.

Over-pronunciation/"Barking" at Consonants

Over-pronouncing consonants with expulsions of air pressure distorts the legato line, and can be injurious to the singer's technique and vocal health. I recommend that classical singers find a professional coach who encourages legato singing and fine musicianship. Remember, text reveals itself through legato singing, equalizing breath flow between vowel and consonant function.

In her book, *Nail Your Next Audition, The Ultimate 30-Day Guide for Singers,* Janet Williams discusses emotions and how to express them in audition preparation. I strongly recommend this book as a valuable resource for singers and teachers.[5]

The Björling-Flagstad Connection: The Swedish-Italian School

Jussi Björling and Kirsten Flagstad, two great singers of the twentieth century, exemplify the vocal concepts of the Swedish-Italian school of training. Both Flagstad and Björling reflect the strength of the pharyngeal Italian /u/ in their singing, and both artists were able to successfully transition from vocalization to performing repertoire.

---

5   Janet Williams, *Nail Your Next Audition, The Ultimate 30-Day Guide for Singers,* Performance Enhancement by Design: 2006. ISBN 0-9787521-0-4.

Several years ago, I wrote an article on the artistry of Jussi Björling, in which I analyzed in detail his performance in a video of a 1950 *Voice of Firestone* television program.[6] It is easy to observe how he employs a rounded embouchure, and opens carefully when he goes into the higher range above the staff. He depends upon more internal space to accommodate pitches in the middle voice and upper *passaggio* range. When singing higher pitches, he opens the mouth by lifting the cheek muscles and moving the skull slightly upward, rather than spreading the mouth position. As a result, his sound is consistently balanced, warm, and evenly produced. He carefully employs the Italian /u/ and he never abandons what the Italians call the *cupo* or the *voce cuperto* (the use of an expanded /u/ in the pharynx) while singing.

An interesting example of Kirsten Flagstad's technique may be seen in the video of 1938 Hollywood movie, "The Big Broadcast of 1938."[7] In that film, Flagstad made her Hollywood debut singing Brünnhilde's war cry. Even though the sound is dubbed, you can see how Flagstad forms her embouchure in an oval position until the very highest notes. Flagstad's oval mouth position and understanding of back-breathing—a basic concept of the Swedish-Italian School—are greatly responsible for the beautiful, dark, and resonant quality that she sustained throughout her long career. It is unfortunate that there are so few recordings of Flagstad that capture the full ring and color of her voice. I recommend viewing the documentary of Flagstad's life produced by the Flagstad Museum in 1995.[8] There is a rehearsal clip of her singing at the Mermaid Theater in London (1950) that exemplifies both her fullness of resonance and her vocal color.

---

6   The article can be found on my website: *A Visual and Audio Study of the Artistry of Jussi Björling*. http://www.voiceteacher.com/bjoerling.html (based on *Voice of Firestone: Jussi Björling: In Opera and Song)*

7   *The Big Broadcast of 1938* (1937)/*College Swing* (1938). DVD. Turner Classic Movies SKU ID #310692

8   Voice of the Century: The Enthralling Documentary of Kirsten Flagstad's Life. (http://www.kirsten-flagstad.no/Webshop/tabid/4689/ProductID/813/CategoryID/196/List/1/Level/a/Default.aspx?SortField=ProductName,ProductName)

There is a reason that the Italians used the term *chiaroscuro* (bright-dark tone): for singers to find vocal balance, they must achieve both color and ring. It is not surprising that the videos and recordings of these old artists reflect a color and resonance that is special, and specific. These videos paint a clear picture of how they applied healthy vocal concepts in performance and rehearsal settings.

Checklist: Applying Technique to Repertoire

1. Train the voice using psycho-emotional response triggers to achieve holistic singing, including the joyful surprise breath, and the feeling of peace when breathing.
2. In vocalizing, train the voice using contrasting emotional responses on the same vocalise in the same key, to train appropriate emotional expression in repertoire.
3. Recognize the difference between spoken pronunciation and sung pronunciation, which requires more equalized air flow.
4. Work to achieve healthy independence of jaw and tongue function.
5. Use the Italian approach of flipped and dentalized consonants when pronouncing text, even while singing languages other than Italian. This requires independence of tongue and jaw. The jaw should be slightly unhinged for these consonants.
6. Learn to pronounce with a loose unhinged jaw, brushing the consonants on the same airflow as the vowels.
7. Visualize directing the breath-flow to spin up the soft palate, not directly out the mouth. This avoids operatic belting.
8. In the low and middle registers, and in the transition from middle to head voice, let the jaw release down-and-back in a gentle up-and-down chewing motion that allows the larynx to drop for each vowel.
9. Incorporate the Sieber *Vocalises* into your study as a transition between vocalization and singing repertoire to assist in balancing registration.

10. Vocalize difficult phrases on /ŋ/, forming the /ŋ/ with the middle of the tongue, and feeling the root of the tongue released wide.
11. When approaching the upper range, use the French /ɛ̃/ or other French nasal vowel to help find freedom in the tongue. This promotes the release of a small and even airflow.
12. Use a tiny Italian /u/ vowel to vocalize difficult passages, especially those passages in the *passaggio* that tend to carry up too much vocal weight into the upper register. Be sure to employ the arched and wide tongue position, thinking the arch in the middle of the tongue.
13. Sing ascending arpeggios on the tiny Italian /u/ (*cuperto*), allowing the voice to find the proper register changes (flip points) without vocal weight. Relax the lower lip flat against the lower teeth with a fingertip. This relaxes the jaw.
14. Observe yourself in a mirror and make sure that you round the *embouchure* as you sing consonants and vowels. This will line up the vowels in a similar acoustical release. **Note:** Lindquest once said, "If you spread your consonants, you will spread your vowels."
15. Study the great singers, past and present. Make use of audio recordings and videos (and live performances, where possible).
16. Psychologically, it is a good idea to find ways to create fun in practice. Use practice time as an opportunity to develop self-awareness and make friends with your voice. Vocalize in 20-minute segments, several times a day if your schedule permits.

Final Words . . .

"You study technique until it is reflexive. Then you can forget about it and concentrate on the performance."

- Allan R. Lindquest

CHAPTER 12

Achieving Acoustical Balance in Singing Onstage

With time and experience, an aware singer learns to sing efficiently in various acoustical environments. The process of developing the finest professional-level sound for the audience requires understanding how his/her voice works in the theater. To accomplish this, each singer must embrace an acoustical self-analysis, a consistent vocalization routine, and professional guidance from a high-level diagnostic instructor, preferably one with a foundation in Old World time-proven vocal principles. Finding balance in vocal acoustics can challenge the singer to find fullness of color and volume; volume that expands from a release of unimpeded resonance, rather than the push of breath pressure.

The Acoustical Deception of the Inner Hearing

Achieving maximum resonance leads to the development of the acoustical phenomenon often called *focus*, or *blade* in the voice, a sound that will travel well in the theater. But how does one healthily achieve this kind of tonal quality? This *cut,* or *ring-factor,* is amplified when the pharynx (primary resonator) is fully opened. Soft tissue, such as the tongue, the pillars of fauces, and soft palate must be adjusted out of the way; and the vocal folds must approximate gently and efficiently. A spread or diffused sound, which involves a spread embouchure, never carries well in a performance. Even though it may sound somewhat large in the singer's inner hearing, it defrays and dissipates in a larger space. In a theater or concert hall a larger-voiced singer lacking focus will carry much less well than a smaller-voiced singer who has accomplished intensity of ring. Many know that the primary navigational tool for the voice is that of sensations, learning the feel of the sound and learning the accompanying (often unpleasant) sound inside the head.

Since we cannot hear the true sound of our own voice, we must adopt an internal sound that is often harsh. Embracing an internal sound that is unattractive can be psychologically challenging, but the process offers greater acoustical benefit. When the tongue is fully released, concentrated high overtones result, giving the singer the internal feedback of a more unattractive sound. But a tone that is beautiful inside the head is usually quite ugly to the listener and vice versa.

In Paris several years ago I taught a long master class, and I recorded it from the back of the theater. During this class, I focused a great deal on French nasal sounds while keeping the back of the pharynx open. When I demonstrated, I remember experiencing my internal sound as small and shrill. But when I heard the recording played back, it was a warm, dark, ringing baritone sound. It has taken years to train my inner hearing to approve of a tone that is unattractive in my inner hearing, yet attractive to the listener. My brain now translates the unattractive inner sound to the polished tone that the listener hears.

This most critically important process I call "translating the inner sound". This approach moves the singer closer to guiding the voice through internal sensations rather than through auditory or tonal feedback. Embracing the internal "ugly" sound is a way to free the voice, but it must be accompanied with memorization of correct internal sensations. This is why during my study with Allan Lindquest, he constantly reminded me to "feel and not listen." Sensations are the only authentic dependable tool with which to navigate the voice.

Exercise 12.1 Embracing Internal Noise

ü_____
/y/_____

I often use an exercise that involves what I call "listening to the ugly frequencies." I instruct the singer to close his/her ears with fingertips and sing a 5-tone ascending scale on a rounded "ee" vowel, which opens more acoustical space while keeping the tongue forward and arched. The internal sound will be filled with many overtones and a sense of noise, which is sound conduction through the hard structures of the lower laryngeal area. Some singers report feeling vibration as low as in the tracheal area behind the sternum.

Then I request that the singer open the ears and sing the scale again, this time listening for the same noisy sensation as when the ears were closed. The positive outcome is that the singer releases any muscular reach reflex while ascending in pitch. In order to sustain the myriad of vibrations, he/she must release any internal laryngeal tension.

Embouchure: Its Effect on Ring

Both Evelyn Reynolds and Allan Lindquest regarded an oval embouchure to be fundamental to healthy facial posture. When accompanied by a free, wide tongue-root, and wide soft palate, an oval embouchure assists in intensifying the ring factor. Intensity of overtones is the result of an open resonator (pharynx), which is enhanced by using an oval or rounded embouchure (mouth opening). It does so by lengthening the vocal tract. Other physical factors that assist in maximizing overtones are the back jaw position, which opens more acoustical space; efficient control of breath compression; which is directly influenced by a healthy closure of the vocal folds; and a forward tongue release, disengaging tongue-root. You may observe in your study of a variety performers that an oval or rounded embouchure produces more concentration of sound, while encouraging more warmth and color simultaneously. The opposite shape—a spread embouchure (smile technique)—usually produces shrillness or harshness of tone, a high larynx position, intonation problems, and imbalance in registration.

I advise voice teachers to educate their ears in telling the difference between shrill tone and authentic resonant sound. Train your ear to hunger for the *dark ring!* Lindquest once said to me, "David, you find the color in your voice from the freedom of the ring and the released breath-flow. It is an outgrowth of total laryngeal freedom."

Exercise 12.2 Working in Opposites

In the Feldenkrais Method, the student is often instructed to move in a variety of ways, even some that may seem to be the "wrong" way. Then the body immediately wants to adjust back to balance. You will find a similar response in using this concept in singing.

First, sing a tone with a very spread, "smiling" position, and a closed jaw, paying close attention to your sensations. You will find that the tone is bright, but with little throat space. The larynx will rise immediately and you will find little resonance. Then do the opposite: round the embouchure (mouth shape), release the jaw gently back and down, and sink the cheek muscles between the side teeth. In doing this you will feel the sucking muscles stretch inward and forward. Notice that the larynx immediately finds a lower and more expanded stretch, and the entire throat begins to expand. In working with a rounded embouchure, make certain that the lips are rounded but not protruded forward. You can achieve this by pretending to cover a yawn in public, a concept I learned from Evelyn Reynolds.

Master Class: An Acoustical Experiment

The previous exercise has prepared you to understand the following experiment. Several years ago I presented a master class entitled "Vocal Acoustics in the Theater" at Lincoln Center in New York. In this experiment, I first requested that each singer deliberately spread his/her embouchure to make a bright and unprotected tone (as in the "smile" technique). The resulting tone was an edgy sound with little warmth or color, that sounded pretty good to the singer; however, it did not carry in the theater and sounded quite thin and shrill to the audience. Then came the part of the acoustical experiment that surprised the audience. I instructed each singer to round the embouchure, sink the cheeks at the molars using a forward stretch of the sucking muscles, and to release the jaw slightly down and back. The result was stunning! Every voice grew to almost twice its previous size. The experiment elicited an enormous reaction from the audience. I then worked with each singer on the rounded embouchure in conjunction with the /ŋ/ tongue position and the wide, lifted soft palate to ensure the ring. This produced a warm, resonant tone that was balanced in the theater.

Often, when the tongue is fully arched and forward, the singer will ask, "Doesn't it sound shrill and terrible?" This is a common question even from professional singers; however, in a concert hall or theater it takes on more warmth and color. But do realize that you will not get a warm sound while recording in a small room. I have been privileged to work in rehearsals at the Metropolitan Opera and I have heard these acoustical principles in assisting the singer to carry over a large orchestra in a 4,000-seat-plus opera house. This experience offered me an invaluable apprenticeship and has educated my ear to know what works in the studio and how it translates to the opera house. Training the ear to translate tone from studio to stage is critically important ear training for voice teachers. It is a fundamental tool for helping singers to apply technique to proper vocal acoustics in the theater.

Vowel Alteration: Its Effect on Ring

Most voice scientists know that vowels must be altered through the use of the pharyngeal stretch in order to accomplish the singer's formant. It is an Old World concept that elongates the vocal tract and widens the pharyngeal chamber, resulting in a tone that carries efficiently in the theater. However, vowel alteration must be accomplished without narrowing, bunching, or retracting the tongue. I have done many master classes for universities and conservatories. I remember that I once said, in a class for Dr. Barbara Mathis at Lamar University, "We alter the vowels with the pharyngeal stretch as we speak the integrity of the vowel using the appropriate tongue position." Dr. Mathis then said, "Mr. Jones, will you say that about three times for our vocal pedagogy majors?" Her question elicited laughter from the audience.

When I studied with Lindquest, he would tell me to "round and darken the vowels" toward the upper *passaggio*. Today many consider the idea of 'darkening' a negative, yet it is a part of Old World training. When taught judiciously with a released tongue, it is a tool that can help to accomplish a fully protected tone through expanding a fuller opening of the pharynx. Lindquest was also trying to correct my tendency to spread my embouchure, which helped me to move toward a more rounded shape. This in turn encouraged a lower laryngeal position. Lindquest would often say, "Over the beautiful dark sound, there is a tiny thread of the '*ng*'!" This is the *chiaroscuro*—a balanced tone that includes both ring and color (bright and dark)—the opposite of a closed-throated "placement" technique, which leads to throaty high-larynx singing.

Considering the Importance of Vocal Sensations

Allan Lindquest was a proponent of using sensations to guide the voice. He once said, "Feel your correct, healthy vocal sensations, but try not to listen to yourself, because the inner ear distorts the true sound." In other words, develop your concentrated tone using physical sensations as your guide, almost imagining them in your mind during the preparatory breath. We have established that a beautiful sound inside the singer's head is often unattractive to the audience, and what is beautiful to the audience often sounds ugly in the singer's inner hearing. The idea of using sensations instead of sound is a major factor in developing a professional sound.

There are a number of professional singers who have spoken about guiding their voice through sensations rather than sound. Mezzo-soprano Sandra Warfield (widow of James McCracken) once said to me during her study in my studio, "On the days I could find that feeling of a noisy rattle in front of my face (with an open throat), I knew that I would have a great performance. On the days I could not find it easily, I had to work much harder!" Ms. Warfield was utilizing the ring factor and sensations rather than over-listening. Flagstad's use of the "ng" /ŋ/ sensation is another example of a professional singer using sensations as a guide. Birgit Nilsson, in a master class she conducted at the Manhattan School of Music in New York, said, "My big relaxed sound originates from my tiny concentrated relaxed sound, which is not so beautiful in my inner ear!" All of these accounts are important for the young developing singer to consider.

Inner Hearing—Is Louder to You Really Louder?

Some singers may not understand that a massive sound in a smaller space (usually reflective of a tone that is pushed out of the mouth rather than circulating through the soft palate) does not carry well in a theater. If a voice sounds large in a studio space, the singer is often pushing or over-blowing the voice. Some call this "operatic barking" or "classical belting." This over-blowing is a result of the use of too much breath pressure through the larynx, which is usually accompanied by a higher larynx position and a tight jaw. While it will sound loud to the singer, this kind of vocal production disturbs any ability to establish an acoustical protection, a factor that is vital to sustaining vocal health. A vocal production that uses mouth resonance than pharyngeal resonance will never develop a large tone. Also, the resulting closed pharynx makes intensity of true ring impossible to accomplish.

We have established that it is impossible to hear the true color and timbre of our "outside" sound from inside the head. For balanced acoustical singing we must change the aesthetic of our inner hearing to one of less beauty. Every singer must go through this process of changing the "approved" inner sound. Learning this discipline can take time and supervision and eventually the singer must 'translate' the inner sound to what they hear on recordings. When a singer records their voice repeatedly over a longer period of time, he/she can then learn to translate the inner sound to the outer sound. It is a challenging process to bridge the gap between the two extremely different sounds, and it can take a psychological adjustment as well as a vocal one.

Vocal Acoustics in the Theater

When a singer walks into a large performance space, he or she tends to think that it must be filled with a big sound. This is a misleading perception, because when we sing on the ring efficiently with a rounded embouchure, open throat, and a forward tongue position, the sound can be trusted to carry in the theater. In a 1938 interview with Lindquest, Kirsten Flagstad stated, "I study every acoustical response in every performance space in which I perform, and I embrace each performing space as my primary resonator, thinking of it as a 'voice enhancer.' This way I look at the performing space as part of my resonating space, or an acoustical friend."

I have had experience with vocal acoustics in many theaters, hearing students perform in such theaters as the Metropolitan Opera, the Berlin Staatsoper, Philharmonie Hall in Berlin, the San Francisco Opera, Avery Fisher Hall at Lincoln Center, Alice Tully Hall at Lincoln Center, and other smaller concert halls and opera houses. In Berlin in 1989, just days after the Berlin Wall came down, eleven of my students sang at the Berliner Philharmonie; after the concert the conductor of the Hanover Opera House asked, "Which were the large-voiced singers and which were the smaller-voiced singers? They all carry equally well!" He was interested in the special ring and warmth in each singer's voice. This is a characteristic of singers trained in the Swedish-Italian School.

Each singer from my studio produced his or her sound with both space and ring, maintaining the individual voice quality. No two singers should ever have the same quality of tone. Individuality of vocal timbre reflects healthy vocal production, mirroring the unique timbre of one's speaking tone. If the speaking timbre is not present, then the technique is contrived or artificial.

Every professional singer must embrace the study of vocal acoustics in the theater. It is the only safeguard against pushing (or over-blowing) in large concert halls and theaters, and it forms a healthy understanding of how to approach public performing. For this reason, it is better to study singing in a dry or dead acoustic, because it forces the singer to feel instead of listen.

Why the "Push Factor" Distorts Vocal Acoustics

Pushing or over-blowing tends to be a common problem for some singers. Teachers often comment, "You are pushing your voice." But it is important to clarify what "pushing the voice" really means. I reflect on what Caruso said to Lindquest in 1914: "I use the same amount of breath to sing as I do to have a casual conversation with a friend." In other words, a singer does not have to produce tone by pushing a large amount of breath through the vocal folds. Nellie Melba said: "You only need use enough breath to set the cords vibrating."

We know that high overtones are achieved by concentrating the tone (using the Flagstad "*ng*," the pre-sneeze sensation, and sustaining the open pharynx). Flagstad said, "I can sing as loudly as my back muscles are strong, and no louder." She meant that she could only sing to a certain level of volume before her voice would be pushed with too much breath pressure, which would result in a high larynx position and the over-blowing the vocal cords. In one of her New York master classes, Birgit Nilsson said, "I only give 90% of my voice when having to produce the loudest phrases. I always save 10% for myself. This saves my voice."

Case Study: Bass Singer

Several years ago, when I was guest teaching, a professional bass requested lessons. The first lesson was difficult for my ears because his vocal production was spread and over-blown, with little or no vocal protection (or /u/ function) in the pharynx. He had been singing in a large opera house of nearly 3,800 seats, and his concept of filling the space was the reverse of what it should have been. His mouth was open too much, and he was pushing his sound directly out the mouth instead of having it circulate through the open pharyngeal chambers and the soft palate. I gave him a couple of the Flagstad exercises; in particular, the small /u/ (*cuperto*) and the "ng" /ŋ/. I could tell he was not happy with the result.

The next time I traveled to that city, this singer booked lessons again. I was actually dreading the experience of teaching him because of his loud, unprotected sound. It is hard on the ears to listen to this kind of unprotected sound and teachers must be careful in order not to develop tinnitus. When he walked into the room, he said, "To me, my voice keeps getting smaller and smaller, but I keep getting bigger and bigger jobs. I am now being cast opposite international opera stars!" When he opened his mouth in that session, it was one of the most beautiful bass sounds that I had ever heard, acoustically efficient, protected, and balanced. He had worked on the *cuperto* (small Italian /u/) and "ng" /ŋ/ exercises, and he had practiced them diligently. Not only did his voice change dramatically in size and color, but he had also dealt with the psychological challenge of giving up the previous big sound in his inner hearing. He worked toward developing the ability to work more through sensations than sound. This was a tremendous change for this singer, and I congratulated him repeatedly for his accomplishment.

He accepted the fact that he had been pushing his voice most of his career and he committed to changing that behavior, allowing his voice to develop a more beautiful sound that was larger in volume through the resulting acoustical efficiency. One evening I attended one of his performances, deliberately sitting in one of the worst seats. His voice soared over the orchestra.

Pitfalls for Larger-Voiced Singers

Many larger-voiced singers can sound impressive (especially in a smaller room) by employing a large, driven sound. But, as stated earlier, the voices of singers who adopt a pushed production—usually pushing the sound out of the mouth rather than spinning it into the soft palate—do not carry in the theater. I cannot stress this enough. In addition, these singers compromise their long-range vocal health and longevity. When such a singer then begins to develop vocal problems, they usually resort to pushing even more breath pressure, the opposite of what is needed to solve the problem.

A friend of mine, Elizabeth Howell, sang with Kirsten Flagstad in 1939 at the Cincinnati May Festival. At one point during a rehearsal, Flagstad tapped her on the shoulder and said, "Remember, dear, we big-voiced singers tend to sing loud all the time, and *we* are the ones who do *not* have to sing so loudly."

Another issue to consider is that when larger-voiced singers are told they have a big voice, they tend to try to fulfill that role, which is a psychological trap. Because they end up pushing their voices with the use of too much breath pressure, they often develop severe vocal problems later. To avoid this, I use the idea of *inhalare la voce* (inhale, or drink in the voice). Lindquest used this concept over and over in his teaching, derived directly from the concepts of the Old Italian and Swedish-Italian Schools. Dixie Neill used the concept of 'vacuuming the sound' under the vocal folds. Of course some air was moving, but not large expulsions of breath pressure. Use of the tiny air stream keeps a voice healthy and allows for the possibility of legato singing.

Audition Spaces

It would be very helpful if vocal acoustics were considered in choosing audition spaces. It is critically important to audition singers in a space that is acoustically neither too live (bright) nor dead (dry). Flagstad, in speaking of her first audition for the Metropolitan Opera, said that when she first auditioned in 1935, she sang in a small room that had dry, dead acoustics—it was full of sound-absorbing furniture and had heavy fabric curtains. This tempted her to push too hard on the breath. The room was so dead that her voice was not heard properly and the auditioners were unimpressed—it was questionable as to whether or not she would be hired. It was not until she was given an on-stage audition that the staff could hear the actual beauty of her voice, along with its impressive size and resonance. The story goes that even the cleaning staff, which was accustomed to hearing a good deal of great singing, came in with their mops and brooms and sat and listened to her.

Alice Tully, who funded Alice Tully Hall at Lincoln Center in New York, once commented, "Two voices that could never be recorded properly were Flagstad and Caruso, both of whom I have heard in live performance." My personal feeling, agreeing with the opinion of Ms. Tully, is that it was difficult to record Flagstad's voice, especially considering the limitations in recording equipment of that time. We do not experience the true resonance of her voice on most recordings. There is one exceptional recording called *Ein Liederabend*, recorded at a live performance in a room constructed with a great deal of wood.[1] I also recommend the video from the Flagstad Museum on her life story, to hear the 30-second film clip of a rehearsal at the Mermaid Theater in London. It was recorded in 1950 and the listener can hear the true, full resonance of her voice.

In Summary: Vocal Acoustics in the Theater

Every vocal instructor needs to understand vocal acoustics in a theater. A knowledgeable teacher with a good diagnostic ear can hear and identify problems and then offer effective corrective tools. There are three main factors contributing to the vocal problems that often develop when singing in larger spaces:

- The singer's subconscious desire to hear his or her own voice through listening (which is impossible).

---

1   Kirsten Flagstad: *Ein Liederabend*. Acanta CD B000KBZJM8

- The body's tendency to push breath pressure in a large space.
- The tendency for the singer to spread the embouchure (mouth opening), causing the voice to be bright and louder inside the head (inner hearing). This makes the voice much smaller acoustically to the listener.

All three of these tendencies are traps that can easily distort good vocal sound. Even the seasoned professional singer must be aware of these challenges and must work diligently to correct them.

In considering the correct coordination that establishes an acoustical balance in singing several elements must be considered. They include:

- Correct body posture
- Correct tongue posture
- Correct facial posture
- Jaw position
- Proper vocal fold closure
- The opening of all three pharyngeal spaces
- The laryngeal tilt
- A healthy coordination of breath and breath management.

CHAPTER 13

Thinking Critically About Vocal Technique

Although the voice itself is only one part of the total package of a singing career, most voice teachers, coaches, and conductors agree that structuring a competitive instrument is a fundamental preparation for the profession. Learning how to recognize and employ healthy vocal concepts opens the opportunity for each singer to learn to protect his/her voice, progress at a faster rate, and establish a solid, healthy vocal technique that can serve them for years. A solid technical base builds confidence that comes from a dependable vocal technique that inspires repeated success.

The Importance of Self-Awareness and Self-Monitoring

Even though we all need outside ears from time to time, career-oriented singers must eventually learn how to work vocally on their own, establishing a certain level of independence. Developing self-diagnostic skills—defining and applying healthy vocal concepts to one's own voice—should be fundamental to voice training, enabling the singer to become more self-reliant. The ability to self-monitor one's practice sessions efficiently requires adopting a healthy, daily vocal practice routine. The process of self-exploration regarding one's voice can be exciting and informative, paving the way toward developing a dependable vocal instrument. It is important for every instructor to mirror the exact concepts and skills that inspire healthy coordination in the student's unique instrument.

Developing Awareness of Unhealthy Vocal Techniques

While self-awareness and self-monitoring are critical, perhaps even more important is learning to recognize unhealthy vocal concepts and how to avoid them. The employment of unhealthy techniques can be injurious to the voice, can shorten or cost a singer his/her career, and in extreme cases can lead to vocal damage. Unfortunately, many younger singers know little about what defines an injurious approach to singing. Confusion—due to many varying opinions and approaches in the teaching of singing, along with inexperience—can lead young singers to make unhealthy choices. It is important to note that many of these unhealthy choices may not be deliberately taught as part of a technique. Problems result from vocal imbalances, which can result from an incorrect concept, or from taking a good concept to the extreme, or simply misinterpreting what the instructor is saying.

Harmful Vocal Techniques and Their Consequences

In my early study I was taught a number of incorrect concepts, and I was placed in the wrong voice category *(fach)*. By the age of 22, I had developed quite severe vocal problems, which led to my long quest for vocal concepts that would resolve these issues. As a result of my early experience, I have a personal concern regarding how young singers approach their study and whether the principles within their study are safe, or are dangerous and should be avoided.

With the help of several excellent and dedicated vocal technicians over the years, including Allan Lindquest, Virginia Botkin, Dr. Barbara Mathis, Dixie Neill, Dr. Suzanne Hickman, and Dr. Evelyn Reynolds, I recovered my vocal health. Even though my vocal recovery was a challenging and long journey, it served as an apprenticeship for learning about the process of safely structuring the voice, and is responsible for expanding my vocal pedagogical knowledge-base. I made this journey back to healthy vocalism using principles specific to Old World training, including concepts of both the Swedish-Italian and Italian singing schools. Some of these concepts have been adopted in the practices of voice therapists whom I have taught over the years and have proven to have therapeutic qualities. These therapeutic qualities were first proven in the research of Dr. Barbara Mathis, using fiber optic research.

This chapter offers an overview of the kind of instruction and vocal habits to avoid, including explanations as to why a concept could have a negative effect, and case studies of singers who have suffered vocal problems due to the employment of injurious vocal concepts.

Negative Effects of a Flat, Depressed, or Retracted Tongue

Many students become confused regarding the healthy position of the tongue in singing—there are certainly varying opinions on the subject of tongue position and whether it should be arched and forward, or flat. I have worked directly with singers who have studied a flat tongue position (often using tongue depressors) and they usually suffer tongue retraction as a result, frequently experiencing intonation problems, loss of resonance, breath control issues, imbalance in registration, and inefficient phonation at various register transitions. The flat tongue position can be one of the more difficult vocal problems to correct. This is due to the fact that the singer's inner hearing becomes attuned to the internal color, even though the color is false and usually dampens resonance. Since I have repeatedly witnessed extreme vocal problems resulting from the flat tongue position, I advise singers to avoid this concept altogether. My advice to singers is to question whether or not a concept or exercise feels good or fatiguing.

Even though most vocal professionals have abandoned the concept of the flat tongue in favor of a healthier approach, some private studios and schools of training are still basing instruction on this injurious technique. When the tongue is depressed, pressure is placed directly at the vocal folds. While the flat tongue technique is basically a misguided attempt to find more acoustical space in the throat, in fact it closes the acoustical space, filling the oropharynx with tongue mass. When the oropharynx is filled with tongue mass, it is impossible to access full resonance, and range will also be compromised. I often compare it to singing with a pillow in the back of the throat. Soft tissue that creates blockage also mutes tone.

Resonant singing can only be possible if soft tissue is managed so that the primary resonator (the pharynx) can do its work. Retraining a singer who has been instructed in a flat tongue approach can be challenging, sometimes taking years to correct. It is an approach that also tends to block healthy nasal resonance. Healthy nasal resonance can assist in releasing tension at the tongue root, allowing for more efficient vocal fold approximation and enhancing freedom of range.

Note: There are rare circumstances where an individual might need to relax the tongue-root with a feeling of dropping it downward and forward, but this must be taught with an arched and forward front half of the tongue.

In 1983, when I first met and worked with Dixie Neill (an early instructor of Ben Hepner), my tongue would retract, flatten, dip like a spoon and shake nervously. As a result, not only was my voice nasal, but my high range was also compromised. Many of my vocal issues were caused by tongue-root tension placing pressure directly at the glottis. It was through the employment of both particular tongue and laryngeal exercises that Ms. Neill helped me to overcome this vocal issue.

Lindquest once told me, "David, you get the true color of your voice through the free-functioning ring in the voice! But this results from a free released tongue and an open throat." It took some time for me to understand what he meant by this, but I finally realized that when true freedom of ring is realized, that the tongue must be free along with freedom in the laryngeal muscles.

Flat Tongue and Registration Problems

Establishing the ability to find an easy transition from register to register is basic to vocal health and to a uniform sound. However, in employing a flat-tongued technique, the singer compromises much of his/her ability to navigate these register transitions healthily. This is because depressing the root of the tongue directly interferes with the laryngeal tilt, the flexible down-and-forward motion of the larynx that is vital to the head voice transition and healthy vocal fold stretch. Female singers who employ a flat or retracted tongue position will experience difficulty transitioning through the lower passaggio—going from lower light mechanism (head voice) into heavy mechanism (chest register)—as it will make the break much larger.

Male singers will find it difficult to align the upper passaggio when the flat tongue posture is employed. The resulting gag reflex creates a false sense of "cover" for the male singer, leading to difficulty with higher pitches. Another negative side effect (for both male and female voices) is that the tongue-root tension can negatively impact healthy phonation, encouraging the development of a vocal wobble (wide and/or slow vibrato). It is also a primary cause in the inability to employ the "fine edges" of the vocal folds. Finding the fine-edge function is critical in achieving the shimmering balance in the vibrato speed and in releasing high overtones.

When the gag reflex is engaged at the tongue-root, the singer must then use too much breath pressure to force phonation. In extreme cases, the duality of a flat tongue position and the use of air pressure can play a role in causing such vocal damage as hemorrhages, nodules and/or polyps. It is what I call the "lock and push" reflex. The vocal folds are over-squeezed and then the singer must force breath pressure to force phonation. This injurious practice may work for a short time, but in the end the singer will suffer severe problems.

Flat Tongue: Using Tongue Depressors

The ultimate in vocal abuse is the use of tongue depressors. I have worked with singers who have been taught to use tongue depressors, and the resulting vocal problems are difficult to correct. Confusion about using such a technique lies in the fact that some teachers believe the front of the tongue to be in the way; the tongue appears to be filling the mouth space. They think that flattening it will create more space. In fact, it is the exact opposite! Flattening the tongue fills the pharynx (back wall of the throat) with tongue mass (root of the tongue). Singers who train in this way often sound as though they are "gargling marbles", or they develop a hooty, dark, false resonance. It can also cause such problems as dysphonia.

Lamperti said, "The singer's vowel origin for pronunciation is in the pharynx, located beyond the root of the tongue, not in the mouth." When the tongue is relaxed and arched healthily in the /ŋ/ position (Lindquest's home position for the tongue), then the singer can pronounce the vowels clearly and experience the resulting ring in the voice. If the pharynx is filled with tongue mass, neither clarity of resonance nor clear vowels is possible.

Flat Tongue and the Big Wrong Sound

Another source of confusion for many singers is that the use of a flat tongue position (and a depressed larynx) can make a huge, forced sound that sounds large in a smaller room, but does not carry in the theater or concert hall because of its lack of high overtones. A vocal sound that is dominated by lower laryngeal resonance and a dropped tongue position lacks the high overtones that assist in developing the intensity of ring. The intensity of ring, or what some call *blade* or *cut* in the voice, is what offers the singer more carrying power in the theater without pushing too much breath pressure through the larynx and vocal folds. A flat tongue position, with the tongue root tense, blocks this function in the voice. A large sound that is dominated by low overtones never produces appropriate acoustical balance.

Belting Breath Pressure: Over-Developing the Chest Register

When breath pressure is forced through the larynx, it results in engaging the thicker vocal fold mass rather than the thin-edge function of the folds. If a singer pushes too much loose, uncompressed air through the larynx, the result is often a high larynx position, a flat/retracted tongue position, a forward thrust of the jaw, lack of the laryngeal tilt in the middle register, and general intonation problems. This chain of events makes accessing the head register an impossibility.

This is a perfect example of how the coordination of singing involves different inter-related elements—if the jaw is forward, the larynx will rise; if the larynx rises from forcing too much breath pressure, then the vocal folds will separate, encouraging the singer to push harder and harder to achieve more sound. So the idea of pushing breath pressure may not be a conscious one, but rather a side effect of one or more aspects of the singing coordination becoming out of alignment.

Over-Compression of Breath (Locked Upper Abdominal Wall)

Many young singers are taught the incorrect technique of pushing out at the solar plexus (thrusting it forward below the sternum) in order to produce a big vocal sound. Often the teacher puts his/her fist in the singer's solar plexus area and then the singer is instructed to "push out" with a substantial amount of force or pressure. The result is a loud, pushed sound that has little or no acoustical balance.

This *perceived* big sound, popular in some schools of training, is manufactured by pumping a tremendous amount of breath pressure through the larynx. I call this the over-compression of the breath. It inspires too much grunt reflex, accompanied by a forced-down rib cage. Due to the downward pull of the ribcage, the root of the tongue becomes locked. The gag reflex locks the tongue-root, placing pressure directly at the vocal folds. The result is insufficient breath-flow through the vocal folds, or over-locking the glottis. Usually these types of singers develop an overly chested technique with little or no possibility for authentic head voice development. The singer then has difficulty in singing high notes, and exhibits a larger and larger imbalance in registration, often producing a large, hooty, overly-darkened sound. Vocal freedom is compromised with such an overly-pressurized approach to supported tone. I call this the *over-compression* of breath.

Understandably, some might believe that a singer must have a big sound in order to compete in the singing profession. It is true that a large amount of ring in the voice is desirable, but ring is not achieved by pumping a big sound-mass out of the mouth space, accompanied by the use of too much breath pressure. Healthy resonance is created with the help of nasal resonance, which plays a major role in reducing the pressure or tension at the tongue-root. In healthy singing, the solar plexus gradually widens and turns freely as the singer slowly fuels a small stream of breath through the larynx. The lower abdominals stretch slightly forward, wide, and upward. (Recall that Caruso said he needed no more breath to sing than to have a casual conversation with a friend).

Case Study: French Mezzo-Soprano

I once taught a French mezzo-soprano who had been accepted into a very exclusive conservatory where she studied with a teacher who used the "fist in the stomach" technique. By the end of her study there, she could no longer phonate in the high range, and as a consequence was not allowed to perform her graduation recital. I wrote a letter to the Dean and she was finally allowed to study with me outside the school for credit for one year.

The "fist in the stomach" technique had created a gag reflex at the root of her tongue. Once this extreme reflex is taught to the body, it can take a long time to correct. It took one and a half years to rehabilitate her voice, which allowed her to recover her high range. After concentrated hard work at recovering from this damaging approach, she graduated and is now a successful voice teacher and singer. She was indeed a victim of a damaging technique taught by someone who was ignorant about the vocal consequences. This singer paid a large sum of money to attend a conservatory that not only did not serve her needs, but also compromised her voice through bad teaching. My message to every young singer, "Avoid this kind of study at all cost!"

Pulling In on the Abdominal Wall at the Onset

Pulling in on the lower abdominal wall to begin a sound or phrase is a problematic approach because it drives too much air through the larynx and vocal folds. I was taught this concept when I was an undergraduate student and the results were catastrophic. It caused me to over-blow the cords from the beginning of every musical phrase, and I had no chance of attaining a healthy closure of the vocal folds or to achieve an un-pushed tonal production. I developed consistent hoarseness, the inability to sing in tune (due to the resulting high larynx position), and my high range was compromised. I realized later in my study that achieving the laryngeal tilt at the head voice transition was also impossible due to the over-use of breath pressure, so transitioning into head voice properly was impossible. When the vocal folds are overblown at the onset, the singer has no chance of regaining control.

Singers should avoid the use of this concept at all cost, as over-blowing the voice can result in various types of vocal damage, which begins with a high larynx position and squeezed laryngeal muscles. Kirsten Flagstad once said, "If my cords are not closed properly on the first note of a phrase, I have no way to redeem my control until I breathe for the next phrase."

Case Study: Professional Soprano

A few years ago I taught a European soprano who had been singing professionally for about 10 years. By the time she got to my studio, she could no longer sing in tune. Most notes were under the pitch. We worked on resisting the outflow of air by using the laugh reflex. This engaged the antagonistic pull between the wide solar plexus and the slight forward and upward pull of the lower abdominal muscles. The result was a healthy closure of the vocal folds at the onset. We worked for almost two months and by the end of the eight-week period, she had achieved a perfect onset (attack). Lindquest frequently spoke of the "perfect attack" in his teaching, emphasizing its critical importance to sustaining vocal health. As this soprano learned body resistance, the vocal folds pulled gently together, allowing her a clear tone at the onset. Her stamina improved and she could sing in tune once again. She went on to have a larger-scale career.

Confusing the Heave Reflex with Open Throat

The throat heave is sometimes touted as a way of opening the throat, but when taken too far this concept can engage the gag reflex, weight the voice, and place tremendous pressure at the glottis. Healthy phonation is compromised because the vocal folds often become overly-locked or overly-adducted. It is one of the more destructive vocal habits and it absolutely can destroy the vocal health of the singer. The primary reason that it is so dangerous is that it does not allow a healthy flow of air through the vocal folds.

When a singer feels this gag reflex, he/she then has no choice but to push a tremendous amount of breath pressure through the larynx in order to force phonation. Larger voices can get away with this type of vocal production for a period of time, but eventually they end up losing access to the high range, often developing a vocal wobble (wide vibrato), shortness of breath, inability to access pure head voice, and loss of the ability to sing softly.

In my teaching I see the benefit of the "pre-vomit" reflex at the base of the neck as a way of opening the lower laryngeal muscles and the pharynx, but never the full vomit, or "heave" reflex, as in lifting heavy weights. The full vomit reflex engages muscular pressure at the outer walls of the larynx and actually closes the interior space of the pharynx. Some schools teach this dangerous concept based on the full vomit reflex. It can be extremely injurious to the voice over time if left uncorrected. This is an example of taking the concept of open throat too far, to the point that it not only compromises healthy vocalism, but it can be injurious to the voice.

The Danger of Teaching the Throat Heave as "Cover"

The throat heave is sometimes taught to male voices as a way to "cover" in the upper *passaggio*. There is no such thing as a "hook" to get over the upper *passaggio*, only laryngeal release. Either the voice is open-throated and rounded enough to change registration naturally, or the production is wrong. I warn singers to never develop a "hooked over" concept for the upper *passaggio*, as it disturbs balance in registration, making the voice thick, heavy, and often developing a wide vibrato. When the heave reflex is employed, the upper *passaggio* will always suffer from a hollow sound that has little or no ring. In teaching registration alignment, the singer should never make a sudden muscular adjustment at the upper *passaggio* transition. Once the heave reflex is established, it can take years to correct, and some singers never recover from it. Upper *passaggio* transition is nothing more than a shifting in registration.

Over-Development of the Neck Muscles

In a vocal world where more and more emphasis is placed on physical appearance, many singers are working out at the gym. While exercise is to be encouraged as a part of healthy singing, I want to warn singers that lifting heavy weights can be injurious to healthy phonation if the neck muscles are built up too much. Singers who lift heavy weights tend to lose their ability to achieve freedom in the neck muscles, a requisite for achieving the laryngeal pivot in the upper middle voice and freedom in the tongue. When weights are lifted incorrectly, the gag reflex is engaged, making a healthy transition into head voice (laryngeal tilt) virtually impossible to accomplish.

Case Study: Heavy Weight Training

Several years ago, a singer contacted me for lessons. He first sent me a recording of a recital he had sung almost four years earlier. His voice on the recording was attractive and expressive, exemplifying beauty of tone, lyricism, body connection and freedom. This made me curious as to why this young man was so concerned about his singing and why he urgently wanted lessons, even though he had to travel from Europe to my New York studio. I later found out that he had been working out in a gym almost four hours per day.

When he arrived, I heard a completely different voice, one that had become throaty, tense, pushed, and out of tune. The vocal cords would not approximate in the upper range without the gag reflex, forcing him to push tremendous amounts of breath pressure on any pitch above C sharp. For the baritone, this note is usually a healthy acoustical release. The gag reflex at the root of the tongue, plus the heave reflex with the external laryngeal muscles had become the support system for his voice.

Attempting to have this singer release the throat pressure was a psychological game as much as a physical one, because he had become attached to the large internal sound. Yet this internal sound did not travel in the theater. He had done a lot of performing in operas and concert, but he was being hired less and less. I understood why when he arrived in my studio. The sound was frightening to hear, as though phonation took a tremendous amount of effort, making the listener feel that the voice was 'on the edge'.

With proper vocal exercises, he began to sing better and more freely. But when the gag reflex finally released, he became fearful because he no longer felt anything in his throat and he could not hear his own voice. Even though the Lindquest exercises were bringing back his free sound, he felt emotionally lost without his throat engagement. I witnessed an Alexander session where he released the heave reflex, but he felt totally out of control and frightened. Because he had identified his effortful, throaty sound as being large and resonant, he felt his voice was being taken away. When he finally divorced his inner ear from being too attached to the large internal sound, he began to have success. But his neck muscles were too overly developed for his laryngeal tilt to be fully released. In this case, this singer's limited success was related to his over-development of the neck muscles.

Training in the Wrong Vocal Category or 'Vocal Fach'

A few years ago, I had the opportunity to work with a young professional bass-baritone. At 23, he was experiencing hoarseness after each rehearsal or performance. There were two main culprits that interfered with his healthy vocal production: tremendous breath pressure, and a flat-tongued technique. Because he thought he was a bass-baritone, this young singer was consistently depressing his tongue to create the false vocal color he associated with the bass-baritone sound. There were four negative results: (1) absence of healthy nasal resonance (higher overtones); (2) inability to achieve ring in the voice due to lack of space in the pharynx; (3) chronic hoarseness from a flat tongue position that created pressure directly at the vocal folds; and (4) absence of an easy transition into the upper *passaggio* and high range, which involved carrying up too much vocal weight or cord mass.

I began to analyze the singer's tongue position and realized that in his attempt to manufacture a bass-baritone color in the voice, his tongue was not only completely flat and depressed, but it was dipping and making a spoon shape. After working with this singer for a period of about ten minutes, and hearing the absence of true resonance in the voice, I decided to vocalize him higher. Lindquest's exercises invite balance in the upper *passaggio*, and this singer could quite quickly go up to the high C and even to the high D without difficulty. After listening to a recording of his first lesson, he described his own voice as sounding simply like "a tenor who was trying to make a baritone sound."

By the third lesson, this singer was singing the tenor solos in Handel's *Messiah* with great beauty of tone and great musicianship. It was evident that he had been trained to sing in the wrong vocal category or *fach*. The flat tongue position was only one of the negative results of singing in the incorrect voice category. His past hoarseness was only one warning sign, as he had also suffered small hemorrhages after long rehearsals and after performances. This is yet another case of a young singer who was on the road to vocal damage because the instructor at school was absolutely determined to make him a bass-baritone. There was no denying the truth that he was a high tenor, vocalizing to the E flat above high C. This young singer then trained as a tenor, and in two years' time was singing professionally again.

The Danger of the Jaw-Forward Technique

Some vocal instructors teach that the jaw position should be "relaxed forward." I remember the first time I taught a singer who had been instructed to "relax" the jaw forward and it was not a good result. The singer's tonal quality was like that of a small child—breathy, with a high larynx position and lacking authentic resonance. Because the throat was closed, the vocal cords would not approximate fully, so his voice lacked both color and ring. Having experienced continuous vocal fatigue, he found that he had little stamina.

There are several negative results when the jaw is forward, including: (1) healthy vocal fold adduction or closure is compromised; (2) the tongue retracts back into the pharynx, filling the primary resonator with tongue mass; (3) the larynx position is high, allowing only a thin, immature tonal quality to be produced; (4) the soft palate assumes a lower and narrower position, often resulting in a nasal or thin tone; (5) legato line is disturbed, due to tongue tension and jaw position, blocking healthy separation of the jaw and tongue function in pronunciation of text; (6) breath flow is blocked because of tension at the tongue root; (7) musical phrasing is compromised because of the inability to realize healthy breath flow; and (8) the vowels become distorted due to tongue tension. Since a thrust-forward jaw position creates numerous vocal issues and challenges, the singer cannot realize his/her full vocal potential. My friend Dr. Barbara

Mathis proved years ago in her fiber optic research that if the jaw is forward, the cords are apart. Avoid this kind of instruction at all cost, because the voice will never develop to its full potential.

Note: Realize that the jaw must hang slightly down and back, as in chewing up and down with the lips closed. This trains the jaw to fall like a trap door on a hinge. The jaw motion will then relate to a slow movement of the elastic jaw muscles. This is the most efficient way to find a fully released jaw.

Negative Side Effects of Straight Tone Singing

Many wonder why straight-tone singing can be harmful to healthy vocalism, especially because it seems so light and easy on the voice. The answer to this question is simple. When a healthy tone is produced, the result is a taut and shimmering vibrato, resulting from the healthy oscillation of the vocal folds. The voice is designed to vibrate naturally, and when this function is inhibited by holding too much tension at the glottis (vocal folds), the singer's vocal health suffers.

Many singers of early music adopt the straight-tone style. Straight-tone singing often has long-term negative effects on vocal health. Some of my favorite music is from the Baroque period; Bach and Handel are two of my favorite composers. But this music need not be sung with straight tone, as a great deal of the beauty is compromised. Arlene Auger is an example of an exceptional singer who sang Baroque music beautifully without straight tone.

It is understandable that choral conductors want an excellent blend in their choral groups, but straight-tone singing is not the answer. Straight-tone singing actually cuts out many of the higher overtones in vocal production, making choral blend more difficult. If a singer is required to sing a straight tone for a choral director or teacher, the singer has to squeeze the vocal folds too tightly and close the throat in order to stop the vocal cords from fully vibrating. This does not allow a healthy amount of air through the vocal folds. Over a longer time period, holding tension in the throat can create negative results such as a closed acoustical space (pharynx), nodules, and polyps. Choral directors would achieve a great deal more efficiency in blend using a combination of the /u/ vowel plus the /ng/ sound in training choral groups. A shimmering vibrato tunes a choir beautifully.

Some teachers and singers try to employ a straight tone to correct an over-wide vibrato (wobble). Certainly, singers should always have a shimmering vibrato without a vocal wobble, but attempting to solve the vocal wobble with straight-tone singing often makes the problem worse instead of better.

Most straight-tone singers find it extremely difficult to make a healthy transition into authentic head voice, often singing with what I call a "white, belted sound". The straight-tone sound is often so thin and light (with a high larynx) that it disguises chest voice as head voice. This kind of singer is actually unaware that he or she is belting from the lower register upward, and whitening the sound with a high larynx to try to create a "boy choir" sound.

Case Study: Straight Tone Singing

A few years ago a professional singer came to me from abroad. She was having a major career in the Baroque classical world, yet she sang almost every performance on cortisone shots, due to constant swelling of the vocal folds from high-larynx singing. This singer was a great interpreter of Baroque music and she was exciting to hear. However, her vocal production was too spread (*voce aperta*) and the larynx was too high. Her tongue-shape was narrow and bunched in the back (another negative side effect of straight-tone singing). It took just over two years to help this singer find her true voice and allow it to vibrate properly. She had suffered from recurring vocal nodules for fifteen years. Amazingly, with healthy vocalization, including the laryngeal tilt, these nodules disappeared and she enjoyed heathy vocal production from that time on.

Incorrect Facial Postures

Facial posture, including the mouth shape, the position of the jaw, and the cheek muscles, can affect the internal acoustical space. Consequently, facial posture has a dramatic effect on vocal acoustics. It is important to study correct facial posture in order to achieve a professional acoustical release, balancing both upper and lower overtones.

The "Smile" Technique

Although it produces an often shrill and unattractive sound, the so-called "smile technique" is still a popular concept in some schools of singing. Many teachers and singers think that it is important to smile at the mouth opening to achieve "bright" vowels. Unfortunately, this is destructive to the healthy coordination and protection of the voice. The smile technique is taught because of widespread confusion regarding healthy laryngeal function and healthy tonal production. The Italian School teaches the *inner smile*, which is actually a high and wide soft palate, slightly lifted cheeks at the outer cheekbone area, sunken cheeks at the back teeth (which creates more acoustical space in the pharynx), with a somewhat oval or rounded mouth shape. The smile of the Italian School is actually in the eyes, never the mouth. It is impossible to sing with a low larynx when employing the smile technique. An east-west stretch of the mouth corners results in a high larynx; drops the soft palate; invites the jaw to move forward; creates a thin tonal quality; and encourages a flat tongue position, making tuning difficult.

Although there are some excellent early music singers, the smile technique is unfortunately quite popular among many in that musical genre. Many early music singers are obsessed with pitch, but over time they cannot sustain healthy pitch using a straight tone and/or closed throated approach. Those who use this concept seeking "authenticity" will suffer the consequences over time.

Use of the smile technique can also represent an attempt at making a mature voice sound very young. Many singers are taught the smile technique in an attempt to brighten the tonal quality of the voice. Instead of using the smile technique, a singer can attain brilliance of tone by bringing the tongue more forward and arched, out of the throat.

The Smile Technique: Soprano Case Studies

I once taught a well-known singer who had so identified with the smile technique that she could not give it up psychologically—it had become her vocal identity. But by age 43, her voice was maturing, a process that demands sound to be produced with a more open throat. She kept squeezing her voice to make it light and bright. By age 48 she could not sing any two consecutive pitches in tune in the middle voice because the vocal cords would no longer approximate. Every pitch was flat and out of tune.

Voices change timbre and quality with maturity; if they are not allowed to mature properly, the results can be frustrating and can cost a person their vocal health. I worked with another well-known singer whose early career was identified with very light repertoire. She was attempting to keep that young sound as she grew older, which resulted in multiple vocal problems. Eventually she just gave up her career.

When I first moved to New York many years ago, there was a young soprano who was getting a lot of attention. She was a great interpreter of Baroque music, and she was still young enough to sustain accurate intonation with a spread-mouthed and high-larynx singing production. I remember hearing her in a Handel opera, and I commented to a friend, "This singer will not last with this kind of vocal production!" In just a few years, her career came to an end. She suffered so much laryngeal tension from this spread smile technique that she had to stop singing. Sadly, she is now a university instructor and is teaching this destructive concept.

Pulled Down Facial Posture

Because of its direct influence on the interior posture of the throat, a singer's facial posture directly affects acoustical release, which dramatically affects tonal quality. If the facial posture is pulled downward (with a forced low or hyperextended position of the jaw), then the singer cannot find acoustical balance in tonal production—it becomes a physical impossibility.

I have witnessed many singers who pull down on the facial posture, forcing the jaw downward too far, and covering the upper teeth completely with the upper lip. They also pull down on the upper cheek muscles, which in turn pulls down the soft palate and has the side-effect of tongue retraction. Pulled-down facial posture also invites the gag reflex, which diminishes the interior acoustical space (pharynx) and causes loss of ring in the voice. The singer is then left with one choice—to blow too much air pressure through the larynx. Because the upper overtones are not functioning properly, the singer struggles by pushing harder on the breath pressure, resulting in a pushed, unpleasant tone.

When you see a singer with a pulled-down facial posture, you will see a singer struggling with his/her voice. Considering that hard surfaces accentuate higher overtones, this facial posture is not one that any singer should pursue, even though some professionals may be strong enough to get away with it for a period of time.

Balancing Facial Posture

The Swedish-Italian school attempts to create a balance between higher and lower overtones. Much of accomplishing this balance is the employment of both depth and lift—two opposites working together. The wide stretch of the muscles directly under the cheekbone area brings the soft palate to a high and wide position, also allowing the singer to unhinge the jaw without forcing it downward. When the facial posture is lifted (with the cheeks sunken at the back teeth area), then high overtones come into the singer's tonal production and the larynx is allowed to remain in a medium low position. The jaw can then fall down and back naturally. This stretch under the outer cheekbone area is not a "smile" technique. The muscles of the mouth should never spread, but should remain somewhat oval or rounded. (However, when a singer is in the extreme high range, the mouth position must widen somewhat to create enough space).

Case Study: Pulled-down Facial Posture

It seems that men use this pulled-down technique more often than women. I remember hearing a British baritone who was singing Mendelssohn's *Elijah* in concert in New York. He used a facial posture that was pulled downward, with the jaw forced down too far. Sadly, this was a catastrophic performance for him and for the audience. His tonal production was hooty and dark, and he was forced to push breath pressure throughout the entire performance in an attempt to fill the concert hall. I felt empathy for this singer because of his own visible discomfort and his inability to produce a healthy singing tone. As the performance progressed, he became vocally exhausted and it was obvious that he could hardly make it through to the end. Even though he was a man of approximately 60 years of age, the truth is that most people can keep their voice as long as they can keep their health. If a person is physically healthy and exercises his/her voice properly, vocal longevity can be quite easy to sustain.

Breathy Technique

I first learned of the resulting vocal fold irritation from employment of a breathy singing approach from my friend and colleague Dr. Barbara Mathis. I consider Dr. Mathis to be a great vocal technician, and she has produced some groundbreaking research on working with damaged voices.[1] As part of her research, she used a fiber optic camera to record a "vocal abuse" session, during which she screamed and yelled, belted, and finally sang with a breathy tone. Her discoveries were quite amazing—the worst damage came from singing with a breathy tone! After singing with a breathy tone, the vocal cords turned more and more red and the vocal lips swelled, proving that breathy singing was abusive to the vocal folds.

Because I grew up speaking with a breathy tone, I personally experienced this. I had always wondered why my voice became fatigued from talking. I spent a year realigning my speaking voice with a

---

1   Barbara Mathis, "Selected Vocal Exercises and Their Relationship to Specific Laryngeal Conditions." Dissertation, University of North Texas, 1990.

healthily open pharynx and a clean closure of the vocal folds. My tonal quality filled out with warmth and my tone dropped slightly as well. Now I can speak and sing all day without fatigue. Working on the speaking voice was at the foundation of the teaching of Dr. Gillis Bratt, the primary technical teacher of Kirsten Flagstad. They worked for six months on her speaking voice before she was invited to start singing in her lessons.

When I began working with Allan Lindquest in 1979 my vocal cords would not come together properly after inhalation. This was due to years of using too much breath pressure to force phonation, and from the resulting high-larynx position. The vocal cords were bowed and would not come together fully, making clear, resonant tone impossible. Lindquest gave me exercises that changed my singing dramatically: he instructed me on speaking the /e/ vowel with a slight firmness at the vocal bands; and he used some of Garcia's *coup de glotte* exercises, which brought my vocal folds to a healthy approximation, making it easier and easier to sing. Using these exercises, I was able to reverse the problems that I had acquired over about fifteen years of incorrect singing and instruction—after about two days my tone became healthy and resonant.

At a recent recital performance I attended in New York City, the singer used a lot of breathy tone for dramatic effect. She prides herself in being a "mezzo-contralto", when in fact she is most likely a soprano. The voice had little to no ring, and there was a great deal of false color in her tone.

After only about three songs, vocal fatigue began to set in, and by the end of the hour the singer was trying desperately just to get through the performance—due to the swelling of the vocal cords from the use of breathy tone. In essence, a breathy technique brings the singer more and more toward a throaty production. Unfortunately, this technique is sometimes taught as an attempt to "lighten" the voice. The result is unfortunate for the singer.

Causes of a High Larynx Position in Singing

Singing in the Wrong Vocal Category (Fach)

Singing in the wrong vocal *fach* can be extremely damaging to a young singer. I can speak from personal experience about this subject since I was trained as a tenor even though I am actually a lyric baritone. Singing in the wrong *fach* can cause the laryngeal muscles to squeeze; the singer then employs too much breath pressure, and the vocal folds become irritated from the high larynx position.

Choral Music: Singing in the Wrong Section

In my case, an additional culprit was choral singing. Most choirs have a shortage of tenors, and conductors often use lyric baritones to fill the section. This is extremely detrimental to a young singer's vocal health. I discourage any singer from falling into this trap, no matter the political ramifications. I also encourage choral conductors to please *not* use lyric baritones in the tenor section.

Lack of Information About Healthy Technique

In their early training, some instructors may not learn to hear the difference between healthy ring in the voice, and squeeze of the throat (high larynx). They may not know specific techniques or exercises to release the larynx in a healthy way because they are not afforded the opportunity of apprenticeship, auditing master teachers on how to distinguish vocal category and how to release the larynx.

Laryngeal Release

Laryngeal release is the basis of healthy singing and it must be covered in a singer's training as well as in a singing teacher's training (vocal pedagogy). Without knowledge of laryngeal release and how to achieve it, the training is incomplete, making the singer ripe for more vocal difficulties later in his/her career.

Recognizing Voice Types

Young teachers need to learn the difference between a *spinto* tenor and a large lyric tenor, a middle weight mezzo as opposed to a dramatic mezzo, a bass-baritone as opposed to a bass, a *basso profundo* as compared to a *basso cantante*. Each of these voice types sings different repertoire with differing vocal demands. A young teacher must learn all of these different voice types and the acoustical characteristics in each vocal *fach*. Singers must be committed to the process of excellent singing, but teachers must be committed to learning all of the vocal characteristics of every voice type.

Working with Young Singers

In school settings, teachers are often working with very young singers, and are afraid to address the issue of the high larynx. Their fear—and I understand that fear—is of a depressed larynx technique, which is also incorrect and can be damaging. However, it is critical that every singer learn a slightly low larynx production, without depressing the larynx with the root of the tongue. If taught in coordination with the /ŋ/ tongue position, the slightly lowered larynx makes for a healthy, warm, and balanced vocal tone that includes both higher and lower overtones.

Problems of Young, Large-Voiced Singers

While I do not believe in allowing younger singers to produce sound with a big, over-produced type of tonal production, every young, large-voiced singer must be allowed to engage the healthy fullness of his/her instrument with full body connection. The larger-voiced singer who is trying desperately to "lighten up the voice" often suffers a squeeze of the laryngeal muscles resulting from a high larynx position. Use of the Italian *appoggio* can assist in helping singers achieve a slightly lower larynx, as it controls the sub-glottic breath pressure. The laryngeal tilt is of major importance in helping the larger-voiced singer to achieve complete pharyngeal vowel space.

Vocal Fatigue: Causes and Dangers

I must say emphatically that a singer should rarely if ever experience vocal fatigue. If he/she is singing correctly, the voice should not tire easily. I often speak and sing while I teach for seven hours per day, six days per week. I do not experience vocal fatigue in my voice studio. This is because I consistently self-monitor my vocal behavior. If a singer does feel fatigued after a lesson, something may be wrong in his/her approach. Many singers have reported to me that their previous teacher told them that "the muscles had to get used to the new technique." If a singer feels an ache in the laryngeal muscles when they start to open the throat, that is fine, but a scratchy feeling at the vocal folds is a warning. Ignoring vocal fatigue can pave the way for future vocal damage. Repetitive fatigue is an indicator that the technique being used and/or studied is incorrect or unhealthy and should be avoided. Or it could be an indicator of a physical issue like acid reflux.

Checklist: Causes of Vocal Fatigue

Vocal fatigue can stem from social behaviors as well as incorrect singing behaviors. Each point is an important factor in good vocal health.

- Social behaviors: Smoking or drinking alcoholic beverages; talking in noisy environments.
- Incorrect posture: Dropped chest, hyperextended chest, or collapsed rib cage.
- Incorrect posture: Singing with a forward thrust of the head position.
- Use of mouth vowels instead of pharyngeal vowels, with an absence of sufficient acoustical space.
- Unsupported singing: Lack of connection to the resistance of the breath pressure in the lower back and abdominal muscles. This often means the singer is too loose in their body, lacking sufficient resistance to the outflow of breath.

- Singing with a flat, bunched, or retracted tongue.
- Pushing: Forcing too much breath pressure through the larynx
- Belting: Using too much chest voice pushed up too high in the scale.
- Locking the upper abdominal wall (over-compression of breath)
- Pulling in the abdominal wall, overblowing the vocal folds
- Overdoing the "heave reflex", encouraging a gag reflex at the tongue root.
- Singing in the wrong vocal *fach*.
- Using a forward jaw position that raises the larynx and separates the cords.
- Singing with a high larynx or low soft palate, or both.
- Singing with a straight tone
- Using the "smile" technique
- Singing with a pulled-down facial posture
- Singing with a breathy tone — vocal cords too far apart
- Singing with a pressed tone — vocal cords too squeezed together

CHAPTER 14

Creating a Positive Learning Environment

The information in this chapter is drawn from my experience of over 40 years of teaching, and on psychological concepts employed by Allan Lindquest and Ruth Hersh, who have been great mentors in teaching me the deep value of respecting singers throughout their developmental period.

Characteristics of the Inspired Teacher

There are many inspired teachers in the field of vocal education, and there are particular characteristics that make them exceptional. Some of the characteristics of such teachers are: a deep desire to learn more about singing, which creates an excitement about the learning process; the ability to be a good listener, which creates psychological space for the student to participate in the process of learning to sing; a positive and balanced emotional attitude, which affects the ability to relate to others in a healthy way; and an ability to bring a positive attitude into the learning environment.

Embracing these characteristics, in combination with the use of excellent teaching tools, promotes high standards in achieving technical and musical goals. The inspired teacher usually enjoys helping others, enhancing lives by sharing information in a positive way. These teachers possess a healthy ego and strong self-esteem, which gives them an advantage in becoming excellent at their job.

Keeping Vocally Fit

A healthy vocal exercise routine is an important factor for the singing teacher as well as for amateur and career-oriented singers. Allan Lindquest once recommended that I give myself a private 45-minute voice lesson every morning in order to prepare my voice for six to seven hours of teaching. When I employ careful self-supervision in my own vocal work, the result is extremely positive, and I feel that I can use my voice to its fullest potential throughout the entire day.

Psychological and Vocal Guidelines for Structuring a Successful Voice Lesson

I have developed this structure in my voice studio over the course of many years of teaching and I use it in every lesson I teach. I find that by using these guidelines, singers can make the most efficient and enjoyable progress toward their goals.

Always welcome the singer with a positive statement.

For instance, "It's nice to see you," or "Don't you look nice today," etc. Beginning a teaching hour with a positive feeling can make all the difference in how efficiently the lesson will progress. It also sets up a positive relationship between teacher and student, creating a feeling of safety and cooperation in the learning environment.

Refresh the singer on the work that was accomplished in the previous session.

I sometimes use a statement such as, "In our last lesson, you achieved a loose jaw. Today, I hope to revisit the same exercise we did last week and add some work on the tongue as well!" Such a statement again achieves a positive psychological response. It makes the singer aware that there is a process with an attainable outcome. It also invites the singer to understand that the process is moving forward toward accomplishing a higher level of singing. Explaining a concept for process in a neutral way depersonalizes it and creates a feeling of teamwork.

Move from simple to complex.

Simplicity in the beginning of the session is important. Always begin the lesson with something that the singer does well, and then move to more difficult vocal tasks, and make the transition a slow one. This will raise the level of the efficiency of the lesson. Notate the student's accomplishments in a calendar or journal—this is a great tool in planning for the following lesson.

Develop multiple ways of explaining vocal concepts and functions.

Often a teacher can hear and diagnose a vocal problem, but perhaps he/she cannot access a tool that can solve the problem immediately. Lindquest often told me, "*If you want to be in the 90% level of effectiveness in your teaching, you must find at least four or five ways to explain each vocal concept and gather four or five exercises that encourage the correct vocal function.*" During his many years as a master teacher of singing, Lindquest collected exercises that worked efficiently, designed to move the singer to a high level of vocalism; he shared many of these concepts with me during my study with him in 1979.

Depersonalize observations.

Never use a statement like, "Your tongue is tight." Depersonalize it by saying something like, "Your body seems to want to hold onto your tongue today, so let's see what we can do to help release it." The latter statement depersonalizes the observation so that the singer feels observed but not criticized. This is critically important.

Invite a response by asking a question.

Questions that invite curiosity make for an excellent tool in encouraging partnership. "Would you like to know the next step in accomplishing balance in coloratura function?" This is wonderful psychological tool, and it makes the singer feel a part of the process and curious about future achievements.

Invite the next step by using statements such as, *"Can you add more body connection at the beginning of that phrase?"* or *"I hear that we need a little more pharyngeal space. Do you feel that as well?"* Questions invite the singer to respond to a request rather than a command. Another positive psychological statement is, *"I think you would just love it if you added a little more . . ."*

Learn to avoid negative words.

Using words that have a negative connotation immediately creates a negative learning atmosphere. Words such as *"no"* create the physical response of tightening the body, setting up tension blockages that distort healthy singing. Avoid beginning any sentence with *"Why don't you . . ."* or *"You should . . ."*, or *"You shouldn't . . ."*. Instead, use a request such as the following: *"Can you release the tongue at that onset?"* Requesting, rather than commanding, is a much healthier style of communication, and it results in a shared process.

After isolating individual concepts, work toward coordination of the whole.

After isolating important concepts, encourage the singer to think in coordination. We gradually train healthy singing response in the muscles so that healthy singing becomes automatic, reflexive, and balanced. This may take some time, but the result will be more lasting and complete.

An excellent tool for this kind of work is to focus on healthy posture during vocalization. An example of this would be an exercise in which the singer speaks the vowels with the jaw slightly unhinged down and back, soft palate high and wide, larynx low, and cords closed. This can be accomplished rather simply, giving the singer the feeling that he/she can succeed in an exercise that requires coordination.

Singing is a process: Invest in the process, not the result.

Many have written books on the subject, and it might be worth it to pursue some of these books on process-oriented learning. It takes an investment of time to master singing, and both teacher and singer must learn patience in this area. Singing is a life-long study and it requires dedication, work, and excitement about the journey. We continually grow.

Train the singer to become independent.

Professional singers need autonomy as a way of building independence. Encouraging young singers to study their process of development can begin the development of independence. By making lessons a joint effort, the teacher opens the opportunity to build a higher level of vocal and psychological self-esteem for the singer. It also helps the student begin the path toward self-dialogue with his/her own instrument.

Review what was accomplished and set goals.

End the lesson by reviewing what was accomplished, and validate the singer on that accomplishment; then give constructive homework or goals for the next week. I often end a session with a statement such as, "*Okay, since you accomplished this goal this week, I would like you to work on . . . and we will continue to build on that concept next session.*"

End with success.

By giving the singer an honest and positive mirror of what has been accomplished, the instructor is also offering tools with which to practice effectively that week. Patience is the responsibility of both the teacher the student.

Always end with a positive statement.

Such as "*You accomplished a lot today*", or "*Have a good week.*"

Remember—always take every opportunity to inspire!

Additional Tools for Positive, Productive Learning
Work with the "Inspired Response"

In addition to being a brilliant vocal pedagogue, Allan Lindquest was also a master psychologist in dealing with singers. He believed strongly in the importance of positive teaching and its psychological benefits for both teacher and singer. His many years of studying positive psychological triggers elevated him to the level of master teacher. He connected psychological triggers with physical triggers in the body; he called this "the psycho-emotional response in singing," referring to the body's physical neuromuscular response to a given emotion.

Working through *inspired response* rather than *command response* was the basis of Lindquest's philosophy of teaching, and this is a philosophy that I have adopted in my own teaching career. Some psychologists believe that learning through a positively inspired response (rather than a negatively inspired one) speeds the process of learning by up to five times, making technical and musical development a much faster process. Feelings of joy and laughter have an uplifting response in the human spirit, and these kinds of emotional responses reflect a safe, positive learning environment.

The development of this kind of positive teaching environment is entirely dependent upon the instructor. If adopted, it facilitates a true, deep desire for knowledge. Teaching must inspire in order to bolster the singer's self-esteem, the foundation of success for every career-oriented singer.

Engage the Laugh Reflex

Laughter is not only reflective of a positive emotion, but it is also an exceptional teaching tool, engaging all the necessary muscles to sustain what is called support, a coordination of the entire body. Laughter, inspired from a healthy sense of humor, releases tension in the body, and this release can create a healthy emotional and physical response for singing. (*Note:* Sarcasm is not humor.)

Use of anecdotes geared toward the subject of singing can be a wonderful aid for helping the singer feel more relaxed in a lesson. Laughter as a part of the basis of healthy teaching can result in more efficient learning and faster achievement of musical goals. Many inspired teachers use laughter as a tool in connecting to the singer emotionally. Allan Lindquest once said, "Good singing is next to good laughter, and one who cannot laugh cannot sing." He means that we all need an elastic, flexibly engaged body in singing.

Several years ago, I worked with two students who were dealing with depression. It was very difficult for them to make light of life, or laugh at themselves. Finally, when they did achieve a healthy laugh reflex in the voice studio, their singing improved dramatically.

Learn to Draw Focus Without Criticism

Pointing out problems (and offering solutions) is part of the voice teacher's job. However, it is important to find positive ways to identify problem areas. I have found there are several ways of drawing a singer's attention to a problem without making it a negative experience. We as teachers should report, not criticize.

Compliment the Singer

This is one of my favorite tools. For example, "Your jaw is much more released this week! Have you been practicing this release on your own?" Asking a question regarding such a vocal issue can simply bring the singer's attention to it. It does not matter if the student released the jaw that week. But as a teacher, you have done your job by bringing their attention to the issue in a positive way. The singer feels visible and important, and the teacher has brought focus to an issue that will probably be addressed with much more fervor.

Make a positive statement. Another way of involving the singer in a positive way is to simply make a statement such as, "You have really worked on your jaw release this week! Good for you!" Such a comment brings the singer's attention to the issue without criticism. I remember that Allan Lindquest once said, "Singing well is 90 per cent psychological. Whether a singer is emotionally balanced enough to have a singing career often depends upon how they were treated in early study!" You, the teacher, are responsible for creating a positive environment.

If an issue is recurring, simply make a request. "I would really love for you to enjoy a freer jaw, so I will offer you a couple of exercises as homework for that issue, okay?"

Give the singer homework. In using this approach, you can request without commanding or demanding. It also makes the singer feel a sense of partnership through this kind of involvement.

Be honest with the singer. If a student truly does not understand a certain concept, ask the student what he/she thinks would help. Simply asking this question will help the student develop a self-dialogue with his/her own body and voice. Most likely, the student will be able to focus on that and come back with more information the next lesson.

Final Words

"There is no teacher and there is no student, only two minds that come together." Luciano Pavarotti

"Good singing is next to good laughter and one who cannot laugh, cannot sing." Allan R. Lindquest

"Can you remember an inspired moment in your life? Can you remember your feeling at that point and can you draw from that experience? Music is inspired and therefore inspiration is its fuel." James Levine

CHAPTER 15

The Importance of Psychology in Singing

Lindquest described his teaching philosophy: "*When teaching, we must treat the entire person, not just the voice! It is important to understand how critically important it is to encourage singers psychologically.*" As singers, we are our own instruments, and how well we perform depends on how well we feel emotionally, spiritually, and physically. If we are being criticized rather than instructed, then we will not sing well and we will not grow artistically.

Master teachers develop not only their pool of vocal knowledge, but they also develop positive psychological tools, partly through working on their own psychological issues. Allan Lindquest once said to me in a lesson, "*Great singing is inspired by the spirit. When the human spirit is free, the resulting singing will be free as well.*" Since I was young in my singing and teaching, I thought vocal technique could cure any problem. But over the years I began to realize how much wisdom was reflected in

Lindquest's statement. I have come to believe that psychological balance can be a determining factor in whether or not a singer can compete in the professional arena, or whether they can achieve their goals.

Finding a positive approach to vocal instruction creates forward momentum in learning. A positive approach can be achieved through simply reporting, without judgment or criticism. Our job as instructors is to mirror what the student needs, and then offer pedagogical tools to fulfill those needs. We can reflect or report, making an observation without shaming or insulting the singer or his/her talent. Singing exposes a deep part of the inner self, a part that should feel safe in any learning environment. There is no need for abusive behavior from teacher or student. Professionalism does not entail control or "put down" statements from either side. The student has an equal responsibility to behave ethically in the professional studio setting.

A singer's strength of the inner self (reflecting a healthy ego) can often be either established or broken in a voice studio. It is the teacher's responsibility to create a positive, safe environment in which to learn; an environment that does not reflect judgment or harsh criticism, and one that builds strength of character and ethics in dealing with others. If an instructor behaves unethically or unprofessionally, then the message is being sent to the student that this behavior is acceptable. In the real professional world, employers do not put up with dysfunctional egos. The days of the "demanding diva" are over. There are too many singers, and the hiring pool is too large.

Teachers have a huge influence on a student's life, and this creates a power differential, one that can be used to help the singer, or one that can be abused. For healthy learning to flourish, every instructor needs to adopt positive professional behavior in the voice studio, based on a healthy partnership between singer and teacher. This partnership can be instrumental in moving a singer toward a career level. It should never become emotionally enmeshed.

The Role of Language in Teaching

Language style can play a large role both in the development of teaching skills, and in the vocal progress of the singer. We all develop a teaching language, be it positive or negative. Allan Lindquest was a master psychologist, and knew exactly what to say in order to inspire a singer. The following lists derive from my observation of Lindquest's teaching in the summer of 1979; they offer simple examples of what is effective and what is ineffective in use of language. As a model for developing positive language in teaching style, I have found them to be tremendously helpful and powerful tools.

Checklist: Avoid the Following Behaviors

- Avoid the word 'NO' during lessons.

- Avoid saying "should", "should not", "why did you" or "why didn't you".

- Avoid starting lessons late or giving a great deal of extra time.

- Avoid singing along with students while they are singing.

- Avoid lecturing without giving the singer time to employ concepts physically themselves.

- Avoid speaking on the telephone or eating in professional lessons.

- Avoid talking about other more advanced singers glowingly in front of less advanced students.

- Avoid making unrealistic promises regarding the singer's career goals, i.e. "I can make you the next Caruso!" No one has this kind of power.

- Avoid talking about our personal life in a lesson.

- Avoid making students an integral part of the teacher's personal life, taking on the role of a mother or father figure.

- Avoid offering abusive statements like, "You will never have a career without me!"

- Avoid shouting at students.

Checklist: Incorporate These Behaviors into Your Teaching

- Start lessons on time and end on time, within reason.

- Greet the student with a positive statement like, "You look nice today!" or "It is really nice to see you today!"

- Make requests rather than commanding: requests offer the singer the opportunity to be a part of the process, which helps establish autonomy. For instance, *"Can you add a little more of x or y?"*, or *"This is not the total voice here, so let's add x or more y!"*

- Compare progress with past lessons, mirroring how to move forward and complimenting the singer for his/her accomplishments.

- Encourage realistically within the singer's talent, considering the professional market.

- Speak of study as a partnership between teacher and singer, defining the student's goals and responsibilities, and offering positive support in the learning process with ideas on how to accomplish both short-term and long-term goals.

- Keep friendship and the professional hour separate.

- Offer help without being controlling.

- Guide the students toward a healthy self-dialogue with his/her voice. This offers the opportunity for mutual discussion at the next lesson.

- Congratulate the singer on his/her accomplishments while mirroring a realistic view of these accomplishments, statements that acknowledge the singer's hard work, while offering a realistic picture of what needs to be accomplished in order to move forward toward the professional arena. For example, *"I can tell that you have done a lot of work on your tongue tension this week. There is still a little left-over tension in the tongue, but I know that with concentrated practice it will be gone completely very soon."*

Psychological Training in the Vocal Pedagogy Curriculum

I have always been curious why a positive psychological approach to teaching has not been uniformly adopted in the training of music educators. Since inspiration is the primary motivator for learning, why would positive psychological training not offer a fundamental, powerful tool in teacher training? Even though many teachers use a naturally positive approach, offering solid psychological tools to young, developing vocal teachers would be an investment in the emotional health of our next generation of singers.

Why is it that many learning environments encourage competitiveness, which usually leads to the toxic emotion of jealousy? Each singer has a special and unique voice to offer, and validating each individual singer through positive emotional support from the instructor can trigger vocal self-confidence. While a teacher's job is not to be the singer's psychologist, inspiring singers in a positive way can only reap benefits for both the teacher and the student.

Dysfunction in the Voice Studio: the Psychologically Abusive Teacher

At one time or another, most singers have been subjected to negative, unprofessional behavior in a voice studio. It is important to realize that abusive teachers are emotionally empty, usually suffering from low self-esteem. The only way these people can feel powerful or valid is to wield power or control over others. I recommend that these individuals be avoided at all cost. The limited knowledge they might have cannot be shared fully from an unhealthy mind. The vocal instructor (and student, for that matter) has a responsibility to search for and sustain emotional balance, whether through counseling or group work. Taking emotional self-responsibility establishes a basic foundation for a healthy teaching environment.

Hopefully, one day abusive teachers will be a thing of the past. I won't spend much time on the subject of the abusive teacher—it is unfortunate that that the topic even has to be mentioned. I can say that I have spent a lot of time attempting to repair the emotional and vocal damage caused by emotionally abusive teachers. We all know that there are those who take a certain amount of satisfaction in the "put down" mentality. This is an abuse of the power differential between teacher and student, and it reflects the emotional emptiness of the abuser, and an unhealthy ego.

My favorite saying on this topic is "negativity creates inefficiency". A negative studio environment destroys any hope of partnership between singer and teacher. We have all heard the excuse, "*I must toughen you for the profession!*" In truth, this is merely a frail attempt at justifying bad and/or abusive behavior. The smoke screen of abuse often disguises a lack of true wisdom and knowledge. Avoid these types of "guru" teachers at all cost. The emotional damage they cause is not worth the limited knowledge they may possess. Before choosing a school, look at the teaching faculty first.

Case Study of Abusive Instruction: Metropolitan Opera Singer

I once taught a singer who made her Met debut in *Lulu* many years ago. She had previously studied with a coach who would scream "NO!" every time he would stop playing the piano. When she first studied with me, every time I would stop playing the piano, a fear reflex would take over and she would jump. It took about six months for this fear reflex to dissipate. We accomplished a lot in our partnership, but it took an investment of kindness and time to overcome her past negative experiences.

In contrast to negative behavior, I had the opportunity to observe the students of Dr. Barbara Mathis when she was on faculty at Lamar University. She embraced a positive approach to her teaching, while keeping high standards of excellence in her studio. She vocalized her students with a consistent series of Lindquest vocal exercises, and maintained a positive attitude, and they were sounding like young professionals by their sophomore year at the University.

Words are powerful and we can spend years overcoming negative messages. My hope is that we all will find room and time to be respectful toward one another. Students must do the work in order to compete in the professional world of singing. Teachers are a guiding influence.

Support or Codependency?

There is a fine line between support and codependency, so the teacher must know that he/she is giving in order to give, not to receive. This is one of the hardest lessons to learn—that the teacher has a job to do and that is to enhance the life of another. The greatest gift a teacher can give is to help others realize or rediscover their dreams, making them independent professionals. As one who has worked on vocal realignment with many professional singers, it is important to know how to nurture those individuals who have not been treated well in the past. It may take time to build a bridge of trust, but keep a positive approach and it will pay off.

Interview with Psychologist Patty Forbes

Patty Forbes is a practicing psychologist and a great friend. We have known each other for many years, and I offer you her responses to questions dealt with in this chapter.

What are the attributes of a fine teacher?

- Creating a connection based on trust. A teacher encourages emotional exposure by creating a safe environment. When a student places him/herself in the authority of a teacher, there is an inherent vulnerability present.

- Surrendering to "I don't know."

- Helping a student to find their truth—their authentic self. We spend a lifetime building defenses around our emotional selves. Great singers are more than the sum of their technique! They are able to be emotionally honest—using their life experiences rather than projecting an impression (literally and figuratively). Barbara Cook is a good example. She was naked up there on stage, yet her power lies in her ownership of her life experiences.

- Having high expectations—it's important to always have a high standard—have students reach for the bar. This sends a message that the student is capable of better.

- Giving positive reinforcement.

- Fine teachers *enjoy* their work and their students.

What behaviors should teachers avoid?

- Negative reinforcement.

- Narcissistic behaviors – the trap of *Me—My* career, *My* experience.

- Bullying aggression, competition, and unrealized dreams cannot be imposed on the student.

- Beware the narcissistic injury. Your students do not reflect you in the world; understand that this is a process, and that you can't control the pace of progress.

What books do you recommend to teachers?

Daring Greatly[1], by Dr. Brené Brown. Dr. Brown delves into the strength that vulnerability lends, and dispels the myth that it is a weakness.

The Power of Now[2], by Eckhart Tolle.

A Return to Love[3], *b*y Marianne Williamson. The book deals with perspective change ("*Our deepest fear is not that we are inadequate. Our deepest fear is that we are powerful beyond measure*").

---

1 Brené Brown. *Daring Greatly: How the Courage to Be Vulnerable Transforms The Way We live, Love, Parent and Lead.* Avery: 2012.
2 Eckhart Tolle. *The Power of Now: A guide to Spiritual Enlightenment.* New World Library, 1999.
3 Marianne Williamson. *A Return to Love: Reflections on the Principles of "A Course in Miracles".* HarperOne: 1996.

What can a teacher do to improve his/her psychological teaching skills?

A frustrating student doesn't always make you feel like a good teacher! Your approach must be grounded, so that a student's progress, or lack of, doesn't affect your self-esteem. We all feel great about ourselves when we have a success.

How should a singer react to emotional abuse in the voice studio?

Abusive teachers can trigger a regressive response—a helpless/hopeless feeling that relates to an earlier life experience such as being bullied, or family drama. Follow your gut—it will never let you down. Psychic trauma is more difficult to heal than physical trauma. Do not try to convince yourself that you are "being too sensitive" or that the teacher just has a certain style. If you feel emotional abuse, you must leave.

How should a teacher react to an abusive student?

In the teacher-student relationship, the teacher is the authority, so if a student is behaving in a way that feels abusive to you, it is important to first assess your own feelings and why you are feeling attacked (your student doesn't know you well enough to not like you!).

If a student is acting in a hostile way, the behavior most likely stems from his/her own frustration. He/she may use the defense of *projection*, a very common defense mechanism that involves ascribing one's own unacceptable qualities or feelings to other people. In order to justify their behavior, people who are angry will often project their anger onto others. The difficult student may be frustrated with him/herself, but then blame the teacher.

CHAPTER 16

Lesson Design: Organizing a Sequence of Exercises

Every singer has a unique voice with unique needs. While instruction needs to be individualized, certain common vocal functions must be covered in order to reach a high level of results. Most singers need specific exercise sequencing in order to develop a healthy daily vocal exercise routine. Once established in the lesson, a similar sequence used on a daily basis can be the foundation of consistency in the singer's practice, and can help develop the core of self-supervision for career-level development. Disjointed, sporadic, or otherwise disorganized teaching leaves the singer's physical vocal muscles, as well as his/her mind, confused.

The big question is: "How should a voice lesson be organized, and what is the purpose of each exercise employed?" There are instructors who focus on lesson design, each with their own approach. My teacher, Allan Lindquest, whose teaching career spanned 70 years, sought to define the function of each exercise, and create a sequence of exercises that would develop the most efficient path toward vocal growth. He once said to me, "David, we are training the muscles as well as the mind's concentration in order to inspire a positive singing response! When a correct response is trained in the body and mind, then repetition can be a great teacher!"

Over a period of several years I taught a series of master classes at Lamar University, during which time I was able to observe the teaching of Dr. Barbara Mathis, a student of Allan Lindquest. She worked with her students consistently, using a sequence of exercises that were based primarily on Lindquest's concepts and exercises. The results were astounding, and by the time her students were in their second year at the university they sounded like young professionals. This proved to me what excellent and consistent vocalization can do for a young singer. The particular lesson sequence set forth in this chapter is based on exercises that have had a high-level success rate in my over 40 years teaching experience.

Finding Balanced Posture

When a singer walks into the voice studio, it provides an opportunity for the instructor to observe the singer's posture. Posture is an indicator of how the singer uses their body in daily life. It can also reflect aspects of the personality, such as social self-esteem and self-confidence levels. Is the singer proud or happy to walk into the room, or apologetic for his/her presence? Balanced posture is the foundation for a released inhalation, and body engagement (support) at the onset. It is also a major factor in helping to create the balance between healthy sub-glottic compression and controlled air flow for efficient singing.

It is important that the instructor observe which aspects of the singer's posture are correct, and which aspects would disturb healthy body/voice coordination. Are the hip sockets and knees locked, or bent? If they are locked, the singer will not be able to breathe efficiently. Is the chest too high, inviting too much upper chest breathing? Is the back ribcage open and tall for healthy inhalation, or compressed from a chest that is too high?

Look for the following basic postural characteristics:

- Open chest without upward pull or hyper-extension.
- Long, tall back ribcage to allow for more flexibility in back breathing.
- Slight relaxation at the hip sockets and knees in order for the chest to be relaxed, yet open.
- A head posture that is aligned with the ears approximately over the shoulder area. Avoid a forward thrust of the head position.
- Released neck, often a result of the tall back ribcage.
- Forward stretch of the sternum (not upward).

After observing the singer's posture, approach the subject of physical alignment very carefully. Some students may not be that comfortable in their bodies; working physically might bring up fear or anxiety. It is crucial to be slow and methodical in approaching body connection, in order to allow the singer a certain level of comfort. If a student is not comfortable with touch, the instructor needs additional tools related to body alignment, many of which can be found in Chapter 2. Evelyn Reynolds often used the "boxing" stance to help her singers avoid pulling-up too much in posture. Lindquest used the "fencing" posture concept to achieve a similar result.

Working with the Breath

Body alignment and breath management are inextricably linked. Many individuals do not breathe properly, or low enough, for excellent singing. Work with the singer to achieve good body alignment as the foundation for inspiring healthy inhalation and breath usage.

Tall, Suspended Ribcage

The back ribcage is longer than the front of the ribcage. The feeling of a suspended, tall, and flexible back ribcage can be a wonderful foundation for inhalation, and it is key in producing balanced phonation.

Many singers are disconnected from the feeling of elongation of the back ribcage; I often recommend the Alexander Technique as a tool for learning about the suspended back ribs.

Exhalation

After good alignment has been established, then work slowly on exhalation—that is, getting rid of breath in the body—which in turn inspires automatic, healthy inhalation. For example, have the singer speak a sustained vowel on a pitch, and then exhale following each phonation. This will ensure the natural response of inhalation. Work slowly and methodically with great attention toward keeping the body aligned.

Panting is also useful as a tool for releasing the diaphragm and establishing breath motion, especially if the singer's body is tense. Have the singer pant, then sing a vowel, alternating panting and phonation. (For an exercise that incorporates this concept, please refer to the lesson sequence later in the chapter.

Stretching the Voice[1]

The experience of making sound is the foundation of building a solid base for healthy technique, and it is important that the singer experience this early in the lesson. While it can be important to explain concepts, long lectures do not facilitate direct learning.

After establishing balanced physical posture, have the singer begin to make sound as soon as possible in the lesson. Lindquest would start lessons by having each singer do what he called "sirening through the registers" or stretching the voice on a slow glissando from chest voice to middle voice to head voice and back down again. He used the vowel sequence of /a/ in the low range, to /o/ in the middle range, to /u/ in the high range.

---

1   Dr. Barbara Mathis used the term "stretching the voice" in the presentation of her doctoral research to the New York Chapter of NATS.

```
          u
     o        o
  a              a
```

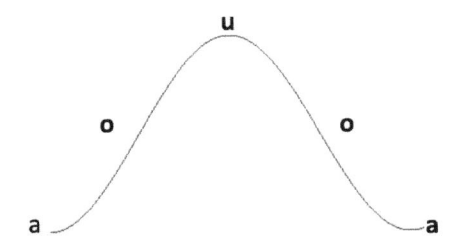

This exercise awakens phonation throughout the registers and makes the singer aware of the different sensations necessary for each individual register. (The /o/ and /u/ vowels encourage a laryngeal tilt in the middle register, lengthening the vocal tract). The physical sensations are subtle and feel slightly different from one register to another.

Laryngeal Tilt and Opening the Throat (Pharynx)

After establishing body alignment and connection, a next important step is learning the laryngeal tilt, and the open throat as the primary resonator in singing. I use two basic exercises, either of which usually works in helping the singer to realize the open throat (pharynx, the primary resonator).

Exercise 16.1

m m m m m   i e a o u
(humming with tongue
through the lips)

Exercise 16.2

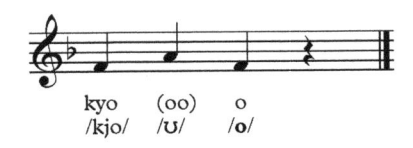

kyo   (oo)   o
/kjo/ /ʊ/   /o/

Imagery

I find two images to be helpful in working toward opening the throat. First is the "pre-vomit" feeling in the base of the larynx (the feeling that the throat widens as the soft palate widens). Second is the image of dropping the vowel back and down slightly, with a forward tongue posture. I find that both images work for the majority of singers, but each time you teach or study the images, one might work more efficiently than the other.

Establishing Ring in Tonal Production

Lindquest did not believe in telling singers to "place the voice forward." Rather, he would speak about the importance of forming pharyngeal vowels with a released tongue, which allows for residual frontal vibration to result. He also used the concept of the "little cry" or "whimper" in the sound, which draws the cords together. When a singer achieves maximum overtones, there is a special sound that cannot be achieved with a "placement" technique.

In an attempt to intensify the sensation of the voice vibrating in the "mask" or cheekbone area, singers can frequently close their throats. Closed-throated production deteriorates the voice over time, compromising vocal health. Dr. Johan Sundberg has scientifically proven that sound cannot be "placed". For example, try singing an open, dark and non-resonant "ah" vowel. Then sustain this sound and add the French nasal sound /œ̃/. What is the difference? What adjusts the sound toward the ring? The answer is the tongue moving forward and upward out of the pharyngeal space. This demonstrates that higher overtones are controlled primarily by the tongue position, *not* placement.

If the voice can't be "placed", then how is ring established in the voice, and how does one teach this in conjunction with open throat? Many use the "ng" sound as a way to establish ring and to guide the voice through a musical phrase on that ring. However, the "ng" must be taught very carefully in order not to close the throat (pharynx)—it must be produced with the middle of the tongue, not the back of the tongue and the tongue root must be allowed to relax slightly down and forward. If you analyze the shape of the tongue when speaking the word "singing", then you will observe that the tongue root is slightly downward as the front half of the tongue is arched and forward in the mouth space. This release in the tongue-root allows more acoustical space between the tongue-root and the back wall of the pharynx. *Note:* Singers who suffer from depressing the tongue and flattening the front of the tongue may have to concentrate on the arch of the tongue for a period of time until this issue is resolved.

Exercise 16.3

ang ang ang ang ang ang ang ang   a_____   (ng)
/ʌŋ/ /ʌŋ/ /ʌŋ/ /ʌŋ/ /ʌŋ/ /ʌŋ/ /ʌŋ/ /ʌŋ/ /ʌŋ/_____

Flagstad used what she called the "ahnging" exercise, starting on the /a/ vowel and then going to the "ng". The "ahng" syllable is repeated in order to establish ring and space as a partnership, both sharing equal importance. If a singer allows ring to dominate over space, then the result is a closed throat.

If the singer allows space to dominate over ring, then the result is overly darkened tone and a retracted tongue position. Space (open throat) and ring must work together in order to establish vocal balance and a polished, professional sound.

Analyzing Jaw, Larynx, and Tongue Posture

Jaw, neck, and larynx tension are factors that disturb healthy phonation. The more release one finds, the freer the quality of tone and the more balanced registration becomes. Always study a singer's jaw position as they vocalize, and when they get to the repertoire. I find that singers often either thrust the jaw downward muscularly, or lock it closed. Neither is desirable. Rather, the jaw must wrap gently back after each consonant, without tension. This is a skill that many great singers have developed over the years; you need only study videos of excellent career-level singers to observe the importance of this concept.

Jaw-Larynx Relationship

The jaw/larynx relationship is a key factor in preparation for applying technique to repertoire. Tense jaw muscles frequently lock the jaw closed and/or thrust it open abruptly at the consonants. In free, healthy vocal production, the larynx drops slightly after each consonant. If the jaw releases slightly back after each consonant (or at each vowel in text), then the larynx drops slightly, encouraging more open acoustical space. But the jaw must be free to accomplish this.

Lindquest used what he called the "gentle chew"—with the lips closed, chewing only in an up-and-down motion. I call this the "chewing hum". The slow up and down chewing motion teaches the jaw muscles a slow gentle elastic range of motion. This in turn allows gravity to drop the jaw instead of muscular force.

Lindquest also had an excellent exercise for finding the correct back-and-slightly-down jaw position. He simply raised his head, looked at the ceiling, allowed his jaw hang down and back with gravity; then he brought his head back to the standard aligned singing posture. This allows the singer to realize a fully relaxed jaw release.

Tongue Posture

The tongue needs to learn the "ng" position as home base, with an arch in the middle of the tongue and a broad, relaxed tongue-root. Note that this is only an approximate home position—the tongue is not frozen in one position during pronunciation, but moves freely for different vowel/consonant relationships in language. Using the "ng" as home base standardizes the higher overtones throughout all of the five basic vowels. Lindquest called this the acoustical alignment of the vowels. It is a wonderful tool for singers who suffer from too much vocal weight (using too much vocal cord mass too high in pitch).

Jaw-Tongue Independence

In order to stabilize the acoustical space when singing repertoire, there must be a certain amount of independence between jaw and tongue in pronunciation of text. I encourage the use of tongue-jaw isolation exercises based on Italian syllables, performed without the jaw closing—the tongue-tip must brush up onto the hard palate behind the upper teeth without the jaw closing completely. Use flipped or dentalized consonants to achieve this, such as in the following exercises:

Exercise 16.4

da me ni po tu____

Exercise 16.5

de____ nta____ le

Balancing Registration Using Vowel Sequencing

Next, it is important to consider how the individual singer moves through registration. Does the singer have breaks in the voice, and/or difficulty navigating the *passaggio* transitions? If so, work with a logical sequence of vowels that will inspire a balance in registration. In the Old Italian School, teachers worked with open vowels in the low range, moving to rounder vowels in the middle range, and toward smaller vowels in the upper *passaggio* range. This not only dropped vocal weight, or heaviness, in the voice, but it also inspired the larynx to drop lower for the higher pitches. This is because /o/ and /u/ tend to be lower-larynx vowels.

Exercise 16.6

a o u o a

Exercise 16.7

a e i o u o a e i

Exercise 16.8

al - le - lu - ia

Lindquest also recommended employing the Sieber *Vocalises* as a step between vocalization and singing repertoire. The vowel sequencing in the *Vocalises* is designed to balance registration.

Flexibility

It is important to consistently work with vocal flexibility, or the coloratura function. Quick-moving scales should be included in every lesson to encourage flexibility. In coloratura function, I use the image that the vowel is spoken quickly at the glottis or even under the cords, which inspires a small body response in the lower abdominal muscles.

Note: Coloratura exercise needs to be done with rounder vowels at first, such as /o/. Then later the singer can more toward the /a/ vowel once the vowel takes on an oval shape in the back of the throat. The use of /h/ should be avoided during this study. The Sieber *School of Velocity for Singing* (Op. 42-43) offers a wide variety of exercises to cultivate vocal flexibility.

Applying Technique to Repertoire

One of the more challenging aspects in lesson design is applying technique to repertoire. I recommend avoiding repertoire that has been studied earlier in vocal development, since these pieces probably have old and incorrect muscle memory. Instead, work on newer repertoire, which will be more available to employing newer and healthier vocal habits. That said, I have found two approaches to be helpful in transitioning from vocalises to repertoire—what I call "orchestrating the music into the voice"—the cuperto (tiny /u/), and the "ng".

Applying the Cuperto to Repertoire

One of the major concepts of the Italian and Swedish-Italian Schools is the use of the pharyngeal stretch of the deep Italian /u/ vowel. First work each phrase on the open-throated /u/ vowel. Then work the phrase, singing only on the vowels, while keeping the Italian /u/ stretch in the pharynx. Finally, add the consonants without allowing the breath to stop at the consonants and without the throat shape changing dramatically for vowel change. This encourages a legato line, elongating the vibrational time of each vowel in text. Also, revisit the concept that the jaw moves slightly back after each consonant, as this assists in sustaining a more open-throated function.

I also use the image of "brushing the consonants on the same flow of air as the vowels," which seems to work beautifully for the singer who struggles with legato line. If the singer accomplishes this and the line is still not legato, then he/she is probably thrusting the jaw forward, which raises the larynx and elongates the vibrational time of the consonants instead of the vowels. If the jaw gently wraps back after each consonant, the legato will be encouraged to function more efficiently.

Working With /ŋ/ in Repertoire

Kirsten Flagstad used the /ŋ/ as a tool for working ring into the voice, but only after the pharynx was open. Using the "ng" is a great approach to aligning the vowels and consonants on a similar resonance line, creating more consistency from vowel to vowel and throughout the consonants. The "ng" is also a great tool for assisting in development of legato line. It tells the singer when the tongue-root bunches or tenses. When using "ng", use the image of a wide soft palate and a wide tongue-root. This will begin to balance the voice more.

The Cool-Down

Always save a little time at the end of a lesson for a cool-down—an exercise such as a lip or tongue trill—just to free and release the voice after working hard during the hour. This also allows the singer to use an exercise that is reflexive and does not take a lot of thinking to accomplish. I prefer the tongue/lip trill because it releases any tongue tension that has built up during the hour.

Question/Answer Session

Leave five minutes at the end of each lesson to answer any questions that the singer might have about the lesson. This is the opportunity for the teacher to make the teacher-student relationship a partnership. I suggest the following as a way of approaching the question/answer session:

> "So [singer's name], as your homework this week, I would like you to focus on what we accomplished with the laryngeal tilt in the middle voice, because it establishes a much freer upper passaggio for you. Was my explanation clear enough today? Can you tell me what sensation you feel when you accomplish it freely? Do you have any questions in your mind about this concept and do you understand the benefit when practiced correctly?"

This scenario establishes the idea that the singer is an aware person who can think efficiently about his/her voice. It encourages the singer to self-dialogue with his/her voice during the week. By setting up clear concepts and goals, you are establishing a process of development that encourages the student's participation.

What was accomplished in the lesson?

Always write the major concept accomplished in that session in your calendar. Just a one- or two-word reminder by the singer's name will establish a positive reminder of what concepts to cover the next week. It also assists in establishing a forward movement in the singer's development.

A word about perfection . . .

When I teach I use the "80%" rule. If a sound is 80% correct, the rest will adjust over time. Perfectionism stops the process. Try not to fall into this trap as a teacher because it leads to frustration for both singer and teacher. The study of singing is a process and must be embraced as one. If we embrace the process rather than the result, then the result will come automatically. Perfectionism poisons the journey.

Sample Lesson

1. Glissando through the registers

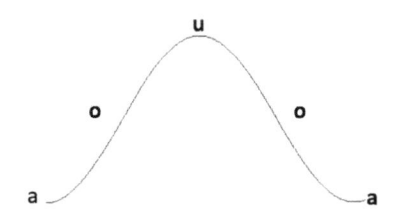

Starting low in your range, on an "ah" vowel, slowly siren up, switching to an "oh" vowel in the middle range, then to "oo" in the high range; then reverse the process coming back down.

2. Open Throat Exercise

m   m   m   m   m   i   e   a   o   u
(humming with tongue
through the lips)

The first part of this exercise is to be performed staccato with the tongue between the lips while humming. In this part of the exercise, the singer needs to imagine vibration on the sternum bone (to discourage squeezing the hum function). The singer should also imagine a stretch of space for the vowels behind the tongue-root. Then have the singer take a breath and sing the 5 vowels with the back wall of the pharynx stretched. The result will be a balance of upper and lower overtones.

3. Laryngeal Tilt

/i/_____
/y/_____

Sing this ascending major 3rd on the rounded /i/ vowel with the jaw slightly unhinged. Allow the tip of the larynx to drop "down and forward" while ascending to the upper note. This establishes a healthy head voice transition. Begin this exercise in the lower middle register.

4. Opening the Throat with the Laugh Reflex

i i i i   i i i i   i_____

The first part of the exercise is to be sung staccato, then going directly to a legato line with the lower laryngeal muscles widening. The staccato should be performed on the laugh reflex, which naturally opens the throat.

5. The Panting Exercise

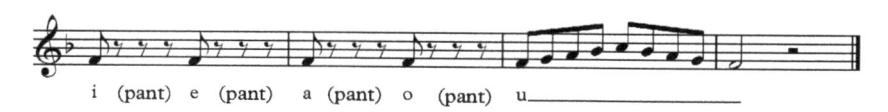

i (pant) e (pant) a (pant) o (pant) u_____

Chapter 16 | Lesson Design: Organizing a Sequence of Exercises

6. Cuperto Exercise

a— o— a— o— a   u————

This exercise is designed to assist in head voice development. Make certain that the /u/ vowel is very small, yet the jaw must be slightly released. The tongue should be in a similar position of the /i/ vowel. Also make certain that the tongue-root is wide and not bunched or narrowed.

7. Arpeggiated Cuperto (Tiny /u/)

u———————————————————

In singing the /u/, the tongue needs to assume a position similar to that of the /i/ vowel.

8. Alleluia

al - le - lu - ia
/ɔ/ /œ/

On the second note round the "ah" vowel toward "aw"; on the second note of the "le" round the /ɛ/ vowel toward /œ/ as in the French word "fleur". This elongates the vocal tract and allows for more cord closure.

9. Arpeggio on a Beneficial Vowel Sequence

a e i o   u o a e i
i e a o   u o i e a

A Modern Guide to Old World Singing | David L. Jones

Use the vowel sequence that benefits the singer the most. These vowel sequences are designed to balance registration by dropping vocal weight.

10. Cord Closure / Vowel and Pitch Change

e a e a e a e a   e a e a e a e a   e
i o i o i o i o   i o i o i o i o   i

Perform this and the following exercise with the jaw stabilized, allowing the tongue to move freely back and forth. The motion of the tongue allows it to release when ascending higher in pitch. Make certain that the embouchure or mouth shape is rounded and not spread. This exercise is designed to apply the ring of the closed vowels to the open vowels and the space of the open vowels to the closed vowels.

11. Cord Closure/Vowel and Pitch Change—Extended Version

e a e a e a e a   e a e a e a e a   e a e a e a e a   e
i o i o i o i o   i o i o i o i o   i o i o i o i o   is

This exercise is an extended version of the previous exercise, with a wider range. Because of the movement of the tongue, the singer will feel release in the upper range. Again, make certain that the embouchure is rounded and not spread. Also allow for the head to move upward in position as the jaw releases for the high range.

12. Coloratura Function

a o a o a o a o   a o a o a o a o   a

This exercise is designed to begin flexibility work. In working on this exercise, re-speak the vowel quickly at the cords. This is a concept that Lindquest used when I studied with him. You will feel a very small pulsation in the solar plexus area as a result of the intention to move the voice, but it should not be a large motion.

13. Coloratura Function—Wider Range

a o a o a o a o a o a o a o a o a o a o a o a o a

This exercise involves more range. Moving between the /a/ and the /o/ encourages faster coloratura movement. The vowel changes may later be substituted with the simple /a/ vowel.

14. Repertoire

This part of the lesson can be dedicated to working technically on repertoire, making certain that the larynx drops slightly at each vowel in text and that the jaw wraps gently back for each vowel in text. For some students, the Sieber *Vocalises* can be a helpful bridge to working on repertoire.

15. Revisit the Panting Exercise

i (pant) e (pant) a (pant) o (pant) u_____

This insures that the body has not become tense with longer vocalization.

16. Revisit the Arpeggiated Version of the Cuperto

u_____

This cools down the voice and can be used after singing repertoire to thin the cords. The /u/ vowel needs to retain (include) the ring of the /i/ vowel.

RECOMMENDED READING

- John Bradshaw: Healing the Shame that Binds You
- Nathaniel Brandon: The Six Pillars of Self-Esteem
- Janet Williams: Nail Your Next Audition (www.nailyournextaudition.com)

DAVID JONES RESOURCES

- An *Introductory Lesson with David Jones: A Resource for Teachers and Singers* (double CD vocal pedagogy course) available at www.cdbaby.com/david.
- Website: www.voiceteacher.com (contains articles on the voice and vocal training).
- David Jones Teacher Mentoring Program: Seminars for Teachers and Singers. For information: jones@voiceteacher.com.
- David Jones can be found on Facebook at *The David Jones Voice Studio*, where he posts frequently on vocal topics.

FORTHCOMING FROM DAVID JONES

- The Singer/Teacher Exercise Manual: A Guide to Logical Vocalization in Singing.
- Ten Fundamental Lessons in Singing (DVD).

ABOUT THE AUTHOR

David L. Jones has developed an international career as author, vocal pedagogue, and teacher of singers and teachers in Europe and the U.S., having worked as guest faculty at Universities and Conservatories. His website, www.voiceteacher.com, and his professional Facebook page, The David Jones Voice Studio, contain articles based on the concepts of the Swedish-Italian and Italian Singing Schools. His writing reflects common issues and concerns that answer questions for both vocal instructor and vocal student.

A graduate of Texas Christian University, Mr. Jones continued his vocal education at the University of North Texas. He has conducted research at the Groningen University Hospital (Groningen, The Netherlands) and has been guest faculty at the Laboratoire de la voix voice clinic in Paris. Through his association with the medical profession (and the vocal medical research of Dr. Barbara Mathis) he has had opportunity to learn and experience how Old World vocal concepts (frequently in conjunction with voice therapy) can be therapeutic in resolving many voice disorders. He has also worked with professional singers referred by laryngologist Dr. Benjamin Asher in New York.

In 1979, David L Jones studied the concepts of the Swedish-Italian and Italian Schools of singing with internationally known vocal pedagogue Allan R. Lindquest (1891-1984), member of the American Academy of Teachers of Singing and charter member of NATS. It was through Mr. Jones' study with Lindquest that he learned the concepts of Lindquest's teachers, who included Enrico Caruso, Mme. Haldis Ingebjard-Isene (teacher of Flagstad), Joseph Hislop, Maestro Rosati (teacher of Gigli) and Mme. Paola Novikova. Mr. Jones later studied with Virginia Botkin (student of Lindquest) and Dr. Suzanne Hickman (student of Botkin), which continued the development of Mr. Jones' teaching career. As invited guest faculty at the Operahögskolan / Stockholm, he had the opportunity to share the concepts that his teacher Allan Lindquest studied in Stockholm.

In 1982, Mr. Jones studied with Dixie Neill, instructor of Ben Hepner, and later with Evelyn Reynolds, whose instructors included Lola Fletcher (student of Herbert Witherspoon), tenor Hollis Arment, William Vennard, author of *Singing: The Mechanism and the Technic*, and Ralph Erolle, instructor of the well-known American soprano Arleen Auger.

David Jones has trained singers performing at such opera houses and festivals as the Metropolitan Opera, New York City Opera, San Francisco Opera, Chicago Lyric Opera, Berlin Staatsoper, Vienna Staatsoper, Opera North U.K., the Royal Opera House / Covent Garden, the Glyndebourne Opera Festival, Salzburg Festival, and L'Opera Bastille in Paris.

Mr. Jones' writing has appeared in both European NATS publications, and in Classical Singer Magazine. He now dedicates his energy toward sharing information with teachers, presenting seminars for teachers twice yearly in New York City as well as in Europe, writing articles, and teaching internationally. Information regarding David Jones' upcoming events may be found at his Facebook page, The David Jones Voice Studio, or at his website www.voiceteacher.com.

Lightning Source UK Ltd.
Milton Keynes UK
UKHW021259040219
336708UK00015B/952/P